"A joyride. . . . Lederer celebrates the semantic antics of our language."
—*Boston Herald*

THE WRITE WAY

"An entertaining, clearly written, concise guide to writing. . . . Ideal for anyone who wants to be a better writer."
—*The Times Record* (Brunswick, ME)

"This commonsense approach to good writing belongs on every library shelf. . . . Anyone familiar with Lederer's previous books on the use and abuse of the English language will not be surprised by the abundance of humor used on these pages to lighten what might otherwise be a very dreary topic."
—*Kliatt*

ADVENTURES OF A VERBIVORE

"*Adventures of a Verbivore* should be required reading for all students of English 101, and language lovers in general."
—Barbara Samson Mills, *Baltimore Sun*

"Lederer leads us on joyous forays. . . . He knows how to entertain while educating and is dedicated to the fascinating history of the words we use to communicate—and to the recording of our unintentional and often very funny misspeaks and miswrites."
—Judyth Rigler, *San Antonio Express News*

"[*Adventures of a Verbivore* is] for anyone who savors language, enjoys puzzles and word games, is frustrated with learning vocabulary and grammar—or is in danger of forgetting the joy or just the simple fun of language."

—*Kirkus Reviews*

THE MIRACLE OF LANGUAGE

"Richard Lederer has done it again—another delightful, witty, and hugely absorbing celebration of the English language. Is there no stopping the man?"

—Bill Bryson, author of *Made in America*

"Wise and engaging. . . . With *The Miracle of Language*, Lederer, America's foremost wag of words, has also become a sage. . . . That is not to say Lederer has abandoned humor—far from it. *Miracle* is filled with many gems."

—*The San Diego Union-Tribune*

"A veritable Cook's Tour of the wonderful English language—from its major highways to its little-known but fascinating byways and back roads."

—Don Hauptman, author of *Cruel and Unusual Plans*

"Entertaining and enlightening. . . . A delightful and edifying collection."

—*Publishers Weekly*

Books by Richard Lederer

Pun and Games
Nothing Risqué, Nothing Gained
Literary Trivia (with Michael Gilleland)
Adventures of a Verbivore
More Anguished English
The Miracle of Language
The Play of Words
Crazy English
Get Thee to a Punnery
Anguished English
Basic Verbal Skills (with Philip Burnham)
Fractured English
The Write Way
The Word Circus

CRAZY
ENGLISH

~

THE ULTIMATE
JOY RIDE
THROUGH
OUR LANGUAGE

~

(G)o 5-3476

Richard Lederer

POCKET BOOKS
New York   London   Toronto   Sydney

Pocket Books
A Division of Simon & Schuster, Inc.
1230 Avenue of the Americas
New York, NY 10020

This Pocket Books hardcover edition July 2009

POCKET and colophon are registered trademarks
of Simon & Schuster, Inc.

For information about special discounts for bulk purchases,
please contact Simon & Schuster Special Sales at 1-800-506-1949
or business@simonandschuster.com

The Simon & Schuster Speakers Bureau can bring authors to your live
event. For more information or to book an event contact the Simon &
Schuster Speakers Bureau at 866-248-3049 or visit our website at www.
simonspeakers.com.

Manufactured in the United States of America

10 9 8 7 6 5 4 3 2 1

ISBN 978-1-4391-5871-5

These titles were originally published individually by Pocket Books.

*To my family, for always encouraging me
to build castles in the air;*

*To Pete and Robin, for putting
the foundations underneath;*

To Stacy, for her lovely interior decorating.

Contents

1

THE STRANGE CASE OF THE ENGLISH LANGUAGE

2

THE NAME IS THE GAME

CONTENTS

3

FIGURATIVELY SPEAKING

4

UNMECHANICAL ENGLISH

5

THE SOUNDS OF ENGLISH

CONTENTS

6

ENGLISH AT PLAY

7

THE LAST WORD ABOUT WORDS

1

THE STRANGE CASE OF THE ENGLISH LANGUAGE

"Like the fabled Jabberwock, words have jaws that
bite and claws that catch."

—JAMES J. KILPATRICK

English Is a
Crazy Language

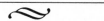

English is the most widely spoken language in the history of our planet, used in some way by at least one out of every seven human beings around the globe. Half of the world's books are written in English, and the majority of international telephone calls are made in English. Sixty percent of the world's radio programs are beamed in English, and more than seventy percent of international mail is written and addressed in English. Eighty percent of all computer texts, including all web sites, are stored in English.

English has acquired the largest vocabulary of all the world's languages, perhaps as many as two million words, and has generated one of the noblest bodies of literature in the annals of the human race. Nonetheless, it is now time to face the fact that English is a crazy language—the most loopy and wiggy of all tongues.

In what other language do people drive in a parkway and park in a driveway?

In what other language do people play at a recital and recite at a play?

Why does night fall but never break and day break but never fall?

Why is it that when we transport something by car, it's called *a shipment,* but when we transport something by ship, it's called *cargo?*

Why do we pack suits in a garment bag and garments in a suitcase?

Why do privates eat in the general mess and generals eat in the private mess?

Why do we call it *newsprint* when it contains no printing but when we put print on it, we call it a *newspaper?*

Why does a man get a *her*nia and a woman a *hys*terectomy?

Why—in our crazy language—can your nose run and your feet smell?

Language is like the air we breathe. It's invisible, inescapable, indispensable, and we take it for granted. But, when we take the time to step back and listen to the sounds that escape from the holes in people's faces and to explore the paradoxes and vagaries of English, we find that hot dogs can be cold, darkrooms can be lit, homework can be done in school, nightmares can take place in broad daylight while morning sickness and daydreaming can take place at night, tomboys are girls and midwives can be men, hours—especially happy hours and rush hours—often last longer than sixty minutes, quicksand works *very* slowly, boxing rings are square, silverware and glasses can be made of plastic and tablecloths of paper, most telephones are dialed by being punched (or pushed?), and most bathrooms don't have any baths in them. In fact, a dog can go to the bathroom under a tree—no bath, no room; it's still going to the bathroom. And doesn't it seem a little bizarre that we go to the bathroom in order to go to the bathroom?

Why is it that a woman can man a station but a man can't woman one, that a man can father a movement but a woman can't mother one, and that a king rules a kingdom but a queen doesn't rule a queendom? How did all those Renaissance men reproduce when there don't seem to have been any Renaissance women?

Sometimes you have to believe that all English speakers should be committed to an asylum for the verbally insane:

In what other language do they call the third hand on the clock the second hand?

Why do they call them *apartments* when they're all together?

Why do we call them *buildings,* when they're already built?

Why is it called a *TV set* when you get only one?

Why is *phonetic* not spelled phonetically? Why is it so hard to remember how to spell *mnemonic?* Why doesn't *onomatopoeia* sound like what it is? Why is the word *abbreviation* so long? Why is *diminutive* so undiminutive? Why does the word *monosyllabic* consist of five syllables? Why is there no synonym for *synonym* or *thesaurus?* And why is there an *s* in *lisp?*

English is crazy.

If adults commit adultery, do infants commit infantry? If olive oil is made from olives, what do they make baby oil from? If a vegetarian eats vegetables, what does a humanitarian consume? If *pro* and *con* are opposites, is *congress* the opposite of *progress?*

Why can you call a woman a mouse but not a rat—a kitten but not a cat? Why is it that a woman can be a vision, but not a sight—unless your eyes hurt? Then she can be "a sight for sore eyes."

A writer is someone who writes, and a stinger is something that stings. But fingers don't fing, grocers don't groce, hammers don't ham, humdingers don't humding, ushers don't ush, and haberdashers do not haberdash.

If the plural of *tooth* is *teeth,* shouldn't the plural of *booth* be *beeth?* One goose, two geese—so one moose, two meese? One index, two indices—one Kleenex, two Kleenices? If people ring a bell today and rang a bell yesterday, why don't we say that they flang a ball? If they wrote a letter, perhaps they also bote their tongue. If the teacher taught, why isn't it also true that the preacher praught? Why is it that the sun shone yesterday while I shined my shoes, that I treaded water and then trod on the beach, and that I flew out to see a World Series game in which my favorite player flied out?

If we conceive a conception and receive at a reception, why don't we grieve a greption and believe a beleption? If a firefighter fights fire, what does a freedom fighter fight? If a horsehair mat is made from the hair of horses, from what is a mohair coat made?

A slim chance and *a fat chance* are the same, as are *a caregiver* and *a caretaker, a bad licking* and *a good licking,* and "What's going on?" and "What's coming off?" But *a wise man* and *a wise guy* are opposites. How can *sharp speech* and *blunt speech* be the same and *quite a lot* and *quite a few* the same, while *overlook* and *oversee* are opposites? How can the weather be *hot as hell* one day and *cold as hell* the next?

If *button* and *unbutton* and *tie* and *untie* are opposites, why are *loosen* and *unloosen* and *ravel* and *unravel* the same? If *bad* is the opposite of *good, hard* the opposite of *soft,* and *up* the opposite of *down,* why are *badly* and *goodly, hardly* and *softly,* and *upright* and *downright* not opposing pairs? If harmless actions are the opposite of harmful actions, why are shameful and shameless behavior the same and pricey objects less expensive than priceless ones? If appropriate and inappropriate remarks and passable and impassable mountain trails are opposites, why are flammable and inflammable materials, heritable and inheritable property, and passive and impassive people the same? How can valuable objects be less valuable than invaluable ones? If *uplift* is the same as *lift up,* why are *upset* and *set up* opposite in meaning? Why are *pertinent* and *impertinent, canny* and *uncanny,* and *famous* and *infamous* neither opposites nor the same? How can *raise* and *raze* and *reckless* and *wreckless* be opposites when each pair contains the same sound?

Why is it that when the sun or the moon or the stars are out, they are visible, but when the lights are out, they are invisible; that when I clip a coupon from a newspaper I separate it, but when I clip a coupon to a newspaper, I fasten it; and that when I wind up my watch, I start it, but when I wind up this essay, I shall end it?

English is a crazy language.

How can expressions like "I'm mad about my flat," "No football coaches allowed," "I'll come by in the morning and knock you up," and "Keep your pecker up" convey such different messages in two countries that purport to speak the same English?

How can it be easier to assent than to dissent but harder to ascend than to descend? Why is it that a man with hair on his head has more hair than a man with hairs on his head; that if you decide to be bad forever, you choose to be bad for good; and that if you choose to wear only your left shoe, then your left one is right and your right one is left? Right?

Small wonder that we English users are constantly standing meaning on its head. Let's look at a number of familiar English words and phrases that turn out to mean the opposite of or something very different from what we think they mean:

A waiter. Why do they call those food servers *waiters,* when it's the customers who do the waiting?

I could care less. *I couldn't care less* is the clearer, more accurate version. Why do so many people delete the negative from this statement? Because they are afraid that the *n't . . . less* combination will make a double negative, which is a no-no.

I really miss not seeing you. Whenever people say this to me, I feel like responding, "All right, I'll leave!" Here speakers throw in a gratuitous negative, *not,* even though *I really miss seeing you* is what they want to say.

The movie kept me literally glued to my seat. The chances of our buttocks' being literally epoxied to a seat are about as small as the chances of our literally rolling in the aisles while watching a funny movie or literally drowning in tears while watching a sad one. We actually mean *The movie kept me figuratively glued to my seat*—but who needs *figuratively*, anyway?

A nonstop flight. Never get on one of these. You'll never get down.

A near miss. *A near miss* is, in reality, a collision. A close call is actually *a near hit*.

My idea fell between the cracks. If something *fell between the cracks,* didn't it land smack on the planks or the concrete? Shouldn't that be *my idea fell into the cracks* (or *between the boards*)?

A hot water heater. Who heats hot water? This is similar to **garbage disposal.** Actually, the stuff isn't garbage until after you dispose of it.

A hot cup of coffee. Here again the English language gets us in hot water. Who cares if the cup is hot? Surely we mean *a cup of hot coffee*.

Doughnut holes. Aren't those little treats really *doughnut balls?* The holes are what's left in the original doughnut. (And if a candy cane is shaped like a cane, why isn't a doughnut shaped like a nut?)

I want to have my cake and eat it too. Shouldn't this timeworn cliché be *I want to eat my cake and have it too?* Isn't the logical sequence that one hopes to eat the cake and then still possess it?

A one-night stand. So who's standing? Similarly, **to sleep with someone.** Who's sleeping?

I'll follow you to the ends of the earth. Let the word go out to the four corners of the earth that ever since Columbus we have known that the earth doesn't have any ends.

It's neither here nor there. Then where is it?

Extraordinary. If *extra-fine* means "even finer than fine" and *extra-large* "even larger than large," why doesn't *extraordinary* mean "even more ordinary than ordinary"?

The first century B.C. These hundred years occurred much longer ago than people imagined. What we call *the first century B.C.* was in fact *the last century B.C.*

Daylight saving time. Not a single second of daylight is saved by this ploy.

The announcement was made by a nameless official. Just about everyone has a name, even officials. Surely what is meant is "The announcement was made by an unnamed official."

Preplan, preboard, preheat, and **prerecord.** Aren't people who do this simply planning, boarding, heating, and recording? Who needs the pretentious prefix? I have even seen shows "prerecorded before a live audience," certainly preferable to prerecording before a dead audience.

Pull up a chair. We don't really pull a chair up; we pull it along the ground. We don't **pick up the phone;** we pick up the receiver. And we don't really **throw up;** we throw out.

Put on your shoes and socks. This is an exceedingly difficult maneuver. Most of us put on our socks first, then our shoes.

A hit-and-run play. If you know your baseball, you know that the sequence constitutes "a run-and-hit play."

The bus goes back and forth between the terminal and the airport. Again we find mass confusion about the order of events. You have to go forth before you can go back.

I got caught in one of the biggest traffic bottlenecks of the year. The bigger the bottleneck, the more freely the contents of the bottle flow through it. To be true to the metaphor, we should say, *I got caught in one of the smallest traffic bottlenecks of the year.*

Underwater and **underground.** Things that we claim are *underwater* and *underground* are obviously surrounded by, not under the water and ground.

I lucked out. *To luck out* sounds as if you're out of luck. Don't you mean *I lucked in?*

Because we speakers and writers of English seem to have our heads screwed on backward, we constantly misperceive our bodies, often saying just the opposite of what we mean:

Watch your head. I keep seeing this sign on low doorways, but I haven't figured out how to follow the instructions. Trying to watch your head is like trying to bite your teeth.

They're head over heels in love. That's nice, but all of us do almost everything *head over heels.* If we are trying to create an image of people doing cartwheels and somersaults, why don't we say, *They're heels over head in love?*

Put your best foot forward. Now let's see . . . We have a good foot and a better foot—but we don't have a third—and best—foot. It's our better foot we want to put forward. This grammar atrocity is akin to **May the best team win.** Usually there are only two teams in the contest. Similarly, in any list of **best-sellers,** only the most popular book is genuinely a best-seller. All the rest are better-sellers.

Keep a stiff upper lip. When we are disappointed or afraid, which lip do we try to control? The lower lip, of course, is the one we are trying to keep from quivering.

I'm speaking tongue in cheek. So how can anyone understand you?

Skinny. If *fatty* means "full of fat," shouldn't *skinny* mean "full of skin"?

They do things behind my back. You want they should do things in front of your back?

They did it ass backwards. What's wrong with that? We do *everything* ass backwards.

English is weird.

In the rigid expressions that wear tonal grooves in the record of our language, *beck* can appear only with *call, cranny* with *nook, hue* with *cry, main* with *might, fettle* only with *fine, aback* with *taken, caboodle* with *kit,* and *spick* and *span* only with each other. Why must all shrifts be short, all lucre filthy, all bystanders innocent, and all bedfellows strange? I'm convinced that some shrifts are lengthy and that some lucre is squeaky clean, and I've certainly met guilty bystanders and perfectly normal bedfellows.

Why is it that only swoops are fell? Sure, the verbivorous William Shakespeare invented the expression "one fell swoop," but why can't strokes, swings, acts, and the like also be fell? Why are we allowed to vent our spleens but never our kidneys or livers? Why must it be only our minds that are boggled and never our eyes or our hearts? Why can't eyes and jars be ajar, as well as doors? Why must aspersions always be cast and never hurled or lobbed?

Doesn't it seem just a little wifty that we can make amends but never just one amend; that no matter how carefully we comb through the annals of history, we can never discover just one annal; that we can never pull a shenanigan, be in a doldrum, eat an egg Benedict, or get just one jitter, a willy, a delirium tremen, or a heebie-jeebie. Why, sifting through the wreckage of a disaster, can we never find just one smithereen?

Indeed, this whole business of plurals that don't have matching singulars reminds me to ask this burning question, one that has puzzled scholars for decades: If you have a bunch of odds and ends and you get rid of or sell off all but one of them, what do you call that doohickey with which you're left?

What do you make of the fact that we can talk about certain things and ideas only when they are absent? Once they appear, our blessed English doesn't allow us to describe them. Have you ever seen a horseful carriage or a strapful gown? Have you ever run into someone who was combobulated, sheveled, gruntled, chalant, plussed, ruly, gainly, maculate, pecunious, or peccable? Have you ever met a sung hero or experienced requited love? I know people who are no spring chickens, but where, pray tell, are the people who *are* spring chickens? Where are the people who actually *would* hurt a fly? All the time I meet people who *are* great shakes, who *can* cut the mustard, who *can* fight City Hall, who *are* my cup of tea, who *would* lift a finger to help, *and* who *would* give me the time of day, and whom I *would* touch with a ten-foot pole, but I can't talk about them in English—and that *is* a laughing matter.

If the truth be told, all languages are a little crazy. As Walt Whitman might proclaim, they contradict themselves. That's because language is invented, not discovered, by boys and girls and men and women, not computers. As such, language reflects the creative and fearful asymmetry of the human race, which, of course, isn't really a race at all.

That's why we wear a pair of pants but, except on very cold days, not a pair of shirts. That's why men wear a bathing suit and bathing trunks at the same time. That's why *brassiere* is singular but *panties* is plural. That's why there's a team in Toronto called the *Maple Leafs* and another in Minnesota called the *Timberwolves.*

That's why *six, seven, eight,* and *nine* change to *sixty, seventy, eighty,* and *ninety,* but *two, three, four,* and *five* do not become *twoty, threety, fourty,* and *fivety.* That's why first-degree murder is more serious than third-degree murder but a third-degree burn is more serious than a first-degree burn. That's why we can open up the floor, climb the walls, raise the roof, pick up the house, and bring down the house.

In his essay "The Awful German Language," Mark Twain spoofs the confusion engendered by German gender by translating literally from a conversation in a German Sunday school book: "*Gretchen.* Wilhelm, where is the turnip? *Wilhelm.* She has gone to the kitchen. *Gretchen.* Where is the accomplished and beautiful English maiden? *Wilhelm.* It has gone to the opera." Twain continues: "A tree is male, its buds are female, its leaves are neuter; horses are sexless, dogs are male, cats are female—tomcats included."

Still, you have to marvel at the unique lunacy of the English language, in which you can turn a light on and you can turn a light off and you can turn a light out, but you can't turn a light in; in which the sun comes up and goes down, but prices go up and come down—a gloriously wiggy tongue in which your house can simultaneously burn up and burn down and your car can slow up and slow down, in which you fill in a form by filling out a form, in which your alarm clock goes off by going on, in which you are inoculated for measles by being inoculated against measles, in which you add up a column of figures by adding them down, and in which you first chop a tree down—and then you chop it up.

Good Grief!

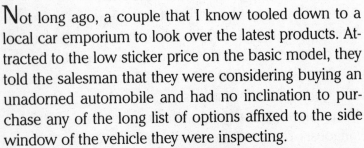

Not long ago, a couple that I know tooled down to a local car emporium to look over the latest products. Attracted to the low sticker price on the basic model, they told the salesman that they were considering buying an unadorned automobile and had no inclination to purchase any of the long list of options affixed to the side window of the vehicle they were inspecting.

"But you will have to pay $168 for the rear window wiper," the salesman explained.

"But we don't want the rear wiper," my friends protested.

And the salesman said: "We want to keep the sticker price low, but every car comes with the rear window wiper. So you have to buy it. It's a mandatory option."

Mandatory option is a telling example of the kind of pushme-pullyou doublespeak that pervades the language of business and politics these days. It is also a striking instance of an oxymoron.

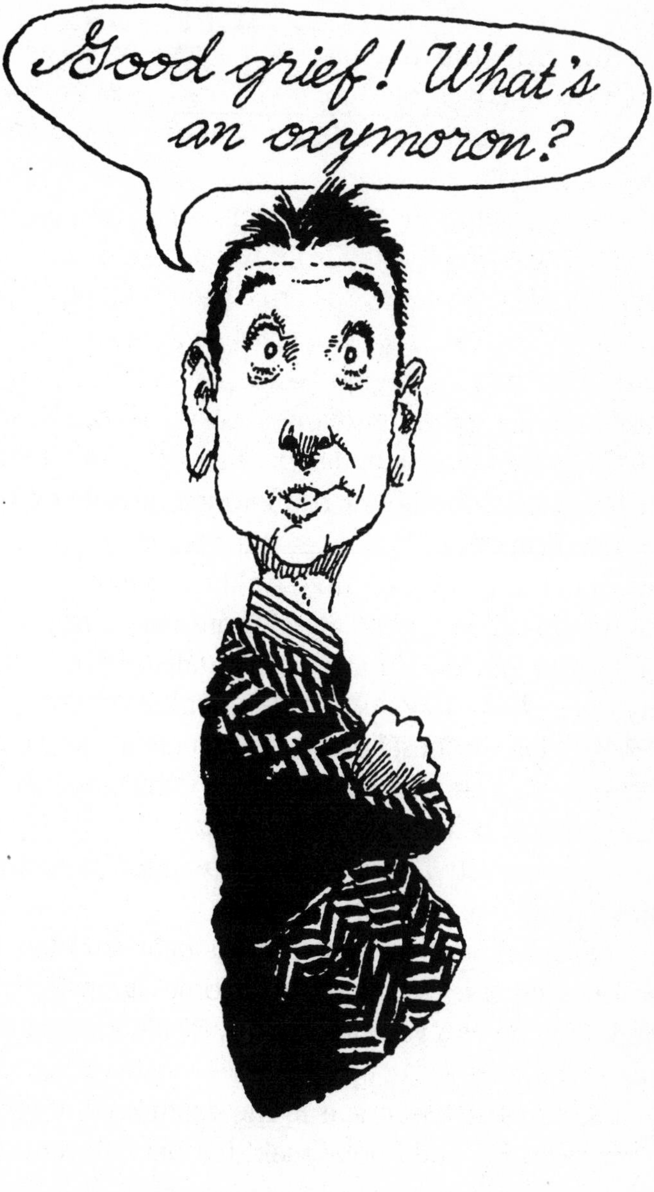
Good grief! What's an oxymoron?

"Good grief!" you exclaim. "What's an oxymoron?"

An oxymoron (I reply) is a figure of speech in which two incongruous, contradictory terms are yoked together in a small space. As a matter of fact, *good grief* is an oxymoron.

Appropriately, the word *oxymoron* is itself oxymoronic because it is formed from two Greek roots of opposite meaning—*oxys*, "sharp, keen," and *moros*, "foolish," the same root that gives us the word *moron*. Other examples of foreign word parts oxymoronically drawn to each other are *pianoforte* ("soft-loud"), *monopoly* ("one many"), and *sophomore* ("wise fool"). If you know any sophomoric sophomores, you know how apt that oxymoron is.

I have long been amused by the name of a grocery store in my town, West Street Superette, since *super* means "large" and -*ette* means "small." If you have a superette in your town, it is a "large small" store.

Perhaps the best-known oxymoron in the United States is one from comedian George Carlin's record *Toledo Window Box*, the delightful *jumbo shrimp*. Expand the expression to *fresh frozen jumbo shrimp*, and you have a double oxymoron.

Once you start collecting oxymora (just as the plural of *phenomenon* is *phenomena*, an oxymoron quickly becomes a list of oxymora), these compact two-word paradoxes start popping up everywhere you look. Among the prize specimens in my trophy case are these *minor miracles*, and I hope that they will go over better than a *lead balloon:*

old news
even odds
flat busted
pretty ugly
civil war
awful good
inside out
spendthrift
small fortune
a dull roar
growing small
same difference
dry ice (or wine or beer)
white chocolate (or gold)
voice mail
industrial park
half naked
open secret
sight unseen
baby grand
loyal opposition
working vacation
idiot savant
final draft
loose tights
student teacher
light heavyweight
original copy
recorded live

freezer burn
divorce court
criminal justice
cardinal sin
death benefit
conspicuously
absent
constructive
criticism
negative growth
build down
elevated subway
mobile home
benign neglect
plastic silverware
deliberate speed
living end
random order
flexible freeze
benevolent despot
bridegroom
tight slacks
computer jock
act naturally
press release
one-man band
Advanced BASIC
kickstand
Butthead

mobile home

Literary oxymora, created *accidentally on purpose,* include Geoffrey Chaucer's *hateful good,* Edmund Spenser's *proud humility,* John Milton's *darkness visible,* Alexander Pope's "damn with *faint praise,*" James Thomson's *expressive silence,* Lord Byron's *melancholy merriment,* Alfred, Lord Tennyson's *falsely true,* Ernest Hemingway's *scalding coolness,* and, the most quoted of all, William Shakespeare's "parting is such *sweet sorrow.*" Abraham Lincoln's political opponent, Stephen Douglas, was known as the *Little Giant,* and, more recently, Dallas Cowboys football coach Tom Landry commented before a Super Bowl that he was feeling *confidently scared.*

Now, if you are willing to stretch the oxymoronic concept and editorialize unabashedly, you will expand your oxymoronic list considerably. Thus, we can observe natural oxymora, literary oxymora, and opinion oxymora, three categories that are not always *mutually exclusive:*

nonworking mother
military intelligence
young Republican
peace offensive
Peacekeeper Missile
war games
business ethics
United Nations
athletic scholarship
safe sex
educational television

rock music
civil engineer
designer jeans
postal service
Amtrak schedule
Greater (your choice of
scapegoat city)
President (your choice
of scapegoat
president)
free love

airline food   *Microsoft Works*
legal brief   *honest politician*

Oxymora lurk even in place names, like *Little Big Horn*, *Old New York*, and *Fork Union*, and in single words, like *bittersweet, firewater, preposterous, semiboneless, spendthrift, wholesome,* and *Noyes.* If you have trouble understanding that last one, examine its first two and then its last three letters.

Good grief! Oxymora are everywhere!

The Department of Redundancy Department

On the grounds of St. Paul's School, where I taught English for almost three decades, stand two signs that announce, "Private Property: No Trespassing Without Permission." Early in my career at the school I explained to the administration that the warning was redundant, that by definition the act of trespassing is committed without permission. My suggestions that the last two words in the signs be painted out were met with polite smiles, but tradition endures and prevails in New England boarding schools. Now more than thirty-five years later, the signs still stand and so do their messages. Unauthorized visitors are still required to obtain permission before they trespass on our grounds.

I am surrounded by an army of recurrently repetitive redundancies. In fact, I am completely surrounded. Even more than that, I am completely surrounded on all sides. These repeated redundancies are in close proximity to my immediate vicinity, which is a lot worse than their being in distant proximity in a vicinity far away.

I turn on the radio or television and learn that "at 10 A.M. in the morning" a man has been found "fatally slain," "leaving no living survivors," that three convicts "have successfully escaped" (how else does one do it?), that "foreign imports" are threatening to destroy the balance of trade (by outnumbering the domestic imports, presumably), that the weather is "minus ten degrees below zero," and etc., etc.

Sports announcers inform me that a certain fullback has had his "forward progress stopped," that a promising young athlete "has a fine future ahead of him" (while my athletic future is long behind me), and that a track star has just set a "new record," a feat much more newsworthy than setting an old record.

I am adrift in a sea of American overspeak. The sea is a perfectly appropriate metaphor here, for the word *redundancy* is a combination of the Latin *undare*, "to overflow," and *re-*, "back," and literally means "to overflow again and again," which may itself be a bit redundant. It may come as an unexpected surprise (even more surprising than an expected surprise) that the ancient Greeks had a name for this rhetorical blunder— *pleonasmus.* Redundancies, or pleonasms, are the flip side of oxymorons. Instead of yoking together two opposites, we say the same thing twice.

Richard Nixon eulogized the life of statesman Adlai Stevenson with these words: "In eloquence of expression he had no peers and few equals." Peers are not superiors; they *are* equals. When asked about his vice-presidential ambitions, Mayor Robert Wagner of New York said, "I have reiterated over and over again what I have said before." Other gems of political overspeak include "I'm in favor of letting the status quo stay as it is," "I'm going to proceed ahead. Someone has to do it," and "In the 1930s we were not just a nation on our backs. We were prone on our backs." I assure you that none of these examples is a figment of my imagination, or a figment of any other part of me. They are all true facts.

The pervasive and persuasive messages of advertising are fraught with false pretenses, which are a lot more dangerous than true pretenses. The hucksters think they can treat us all like country bumpkins, even us city bumpkins. One stack of products is "100 percent pure," certainly more pristine than being fifty percent pure. Other product boxes trumpet the arrival of a "bold, new innovation," which sure beats any bold, old innovation, that is "new and improved." (Can something really be both new *and* improved?)

McDonald's hamburger emporia boast of "Billions and Billions Sold," and I wonder if billions and billions is any more than mere billions. Appliance companies keep flooding the market with hot-water heaters, even though these machines are obviously made to heat cold water. And Raid insecticide "kills bugs dead," which is just the way they should be killed.

All this linguistic overkill reminds me of Vaughn Monroe's hit song of the 1950s, "There, I've Said It Again" and stirs within me not just a sensation, but one singular sensation. "Save 40% off!" blares the typical special-sale sign. A Tucson strip joint advertises "Totally, totally nude! Live girls," much more entertaining than partially nude dead girls. Various hotels promise "a honeymoon for two"—the old-fashioned kind! Of all the adspeak that clogs my mailbox the most repetitively redundant is "free gift." Sometimes I am even offered a "complimentary free gift." I sigh with relief, grateful that I won't have to pay for that gift.

My fellow colleagues and classmates, I am here to tell you the honest truth, not to be confused with the dishonest truth, about redundancies. My past experience, which is a lot more reliable than my present or future experience, tells me that overspeak will not go away. The past history of the pleonasm gives us but a small inkling (can an inkling ever be large?) of the pleonasms that will fill our future history. Embedded in the idea of experience and history is the past, yet we persist in talking about someone's past experience and past history. Plans and warnings, in contrast, are by definition futuristic, yet every day we hear about future plans, advance warnings, and forewarnings. This chronic and chronological confusion is exemplified by the pretentious prefix *pre-*, as in *preboard, pretest, preheat, preplan,* and *prerecord.* While I concede that boarding, testing, and heating may be two-stage processes, I don't see how preplanning and prerecording differ from planning and recording. I have even seen shows "prerecorded before a live audience," certainly preferable to prerecording before a dead audience.

I do not overexaggerate, much less exaggerate, when I say that, far and away, the one and only pleonasm I most hate with a passion (rather than calmly hating it) is "at this point in time." Either "at this point" or "at this time" will do just fine, and "now" is even better. "At this point in time" is the bureaucrat's way of spelling "now" by using seventeen letters. This atrocity elicits from this old geezer (I confess that I am no longer a young geezer) an audible (louder than an inaudible) groan, exacerbates all my aches and pains, and sets me not just to ranting or to raving, but to ranting and raving. I am not just bound or just determined but bound and determined to stamp out the last vestige, rather than the first vestige, of this classic example of logorrhea and declare it not just null or just void, but null and void. May we not only cease or desist using "at this point in time," may we cease and desist.

Speaking of "aches and pains," "ranting and raving," "bound and determined," "null and void," and "cease and desist," English is riddled with the double jeopardy of these insidious pairs. Sure, some of them that look like redundancies aren't. I know that in "kith and kin" *kin* are family and relatives while *kith* are friends and neighbors, that in "scrimp and save" *scrimp* means to be frugal while *save* means to put money away, that the *beck* in "beck and call" is a beckoning gesture while the *call* is a vocal command, that in "hue and cry" *hue* is a general clamor attending a robbery while *cry* is a specific statement such as "Stop thief!", and that the *bag* in "bag and baggage" was originally the property of an individual soldier while *baggage* was the collective property of the army. I'll even concede that in "bought and paid for" one can buy something without completely paying for it and that in "fair to mid-dling," *middling* may be a notch above *fair*.

But over and above these few exceptions I do not, as I live and breathe, understand the whys and where-fores of many other various and sundry twosomes, in which the two halves (certainly not three or more halves) are for all intents and purposes one and the same and say the exact same thing. Caught betwixt and between such examples of linguistic conspicuous con-sumption, I shall not hem and haw or slip-slide. Just to pick and choose a few more examples, these hard-and-fast doublets are anything but fine and dandy, tip-top, well and good, hale and hearty, fair and just, and spick-and-span.

Redundancies are the junk food of our language. Alas and alack, when we gorge on the empty calories of pleonasms, we accumulate adipose tissue in the nooks and crannies of our linguistic waistline in dribs and drabs and bits and pieces—and I challenge you to tell me the differences between alas and alack, a nook and a cranny, a drib and a drab, and a bit and a piece. In-deed, in this day and age redundancies are multiplying by fits and starts and leaps and bounds. Rather than aid-ing and abetting these fattening snack-size doublets, let us find the ways and means to oppose them with all our vim and vigor and might and main. Lo and behold, perhaps one day they will be over and done with and we shall be free and clear of them.

The consensus of opinion is that many of these ple-onasms grow from a lack of appreciation for the root meanings of words, the source from whence (which

28

means "from from where") they come. Derived from the Latin *sensus,* meaning "opinion," and *con-,* "a collection," a consensus of opinion is a collection of opinion of opinion. Believe me, I know about these translingual redundancies. After all, I live right next door to Vermont. The citizens of that verdant patch of New England actually drive around with license plates proclaiming, "Vermont: Green Mountain State," which translates to "Green Mountain: The Green Mountain State," if you'll pardon my French. Other French misses show up on our menus—"roast beef with au jus" and "soup du jour of the day." Be sure to record these in your daily journal.

If you know your Middle English, Greek, Anglo-French, Latin, Italian, Japanese, Malay, and Chinese (doesn't everybody?), you will avoid talking about time and tide (which are simply "time and time"), Greenwich Village ("Greenvillage Village"), the La Brea Tar Pits ("the the Tar Pits Tar Pits"), an epileptic seizure ("a seizure seizure"), the hoi polloi ("the the people"), beautiful calligraphy ("beautiful beautiful writing"), correct orthography ("correct correct writing"), a bunch of grapes ("a bunch of a bunch of grapes"), a handwritten manuscript ("handwritten handwriting"), something that is very true ("truly true"), pizza pie ("pie pie"), a head honcho ("head head"), shrimp scampi ("shrimp shrimp"), rice paddy ("rice rice"), and the Gobi Desert ("the Desert Desert"). Anyone with even an elementary knowledge of Middle English and Dutch should know that *lukewarm,* from the Dutch *leuk* through the Middle

English *louke,* meaning "tepid," translates to "warm-warm." Okay, go ahead and be luke about my criticisms.

Can we ever cure ourselves of our national addiction to fatty and fattening redundancies that ooze into our parlance anywhere and everywhere, over and over, and again and again? I believe that we can. As the old adage goes, "If at first you don't succeed, try, try again." Of course, by their very nature adages are old. That is how they get to be adages.

The sum total and end result (about as final as you can get) are that we can join together (more effective than joining apart) to fight the good fight against every single one of these redundancies. We can drive them from our house and home. We can bring them, in the words of many a flight attendant and police officer, to a complete stop, and we can kill them dead. That would be so incredible it would be unbelievable.

Confusable English

I once attended a series of seminars that explored the realities of living in a nuclear age. The last of these programs included a debate about the Strategic Defense Initiative, popularly known as Star Wars, between a naval commander representing the Defense Department and a university physics professor. As one would guess, the commander stoutly defended Star Wars as being both scientifically feasible and strategically desirable. As his speech soared to its conclusion the Pentagonian exulted, "In Star Wars, America has finally come up with the penultimate defense system!"

Oops. Do you grasp the gaffe, follow the faux pas, make out the malapropism, and spot the solecism in the Commander's use of the word *penultimate?* The speaker obviously thought that *penultimate* means "the absolute ultimate." So do a lot of us, including the Tony Award winner who gushed, "I knew what my goal was when I saw Lauren Bacall touring in a play in Buffalo.

To be an actress like that—well, to me that was the penultimate!"

But *penultimate* doesn't mean the absolute ultimate. (Can anything be more than ultimate?) Derived from the Latin *paene*, "almost," and *ultimus*, "last," *penultimate* means "next to last." Thinking that *pen-* was an intensifier rather than a qualifier, our naval commander ended up saying the opposite of what he meant. The last thing we want is a penultimate defense system against nuclear weapons.

Now have a look at this message: "The Bureau of Animal Affairs will help you get those clucking, flapping pigeons off your window ledge, and will issue a summons to those who scatter food that attracts bands of the noisome birds." Oops again. The Bureau writer, like many other English users, apparently thought that *noisome* means "noisy." But *noisome* has nothing to do with noise. In truth, the word is formed from a shortening of *annoy* plus the adjectival suffix *-some*. Most frequently, *noisome* is used to describe an offensive odor, annoying to the point of being nauseating.

Similar to *noisome* is *fulsome.* A general was in the habit of extending his "most fulsome congratulations" to medal recipients. It is true that the original meaning of *fulsome* was "full, abundant," but the well-meaning general overlooked the dominant sense of the word today, "offensive to the senses or sensibility," and damned with misguided praise.

Then there's the catalog of high school English books with a cartoon on the cover showing William Shakespeare's Juliet standing on her balcony, gazing off

"O Romeo, Romeo! wherefore art thou Romeo?"

into the distance, and asking, "Wherefore art thou, teaching aids?" Lower on the page, Romeo stares up at Juliet and says, "Inside! Eighteen new publications plus many other fine materials." I would hope that most of my fellow inmates in the house of correction (of composition) caught the blooper. Quite obviously, the publisher of English materials interpreted *wherefore* as meaning "where," a mistake that has been perpetrated and perpetuated by generations of would-be Shakespearean actresses who misconstrue the famous line in *Romeo and Juliet,* "O Romeo, Romeo! wherefore art thou Romeo?" But a knowledgeable examination of Shakespeare's language—"Wherefore rejoice?/What conquest brings he home?" *(Julius Caesar);* "But wherefore could I not pronounce 'Amen'?" *(Macbeth)*—reveals that *wherefore* means "why," not "where," further proof being the redundant cliché "the whys and wherefores." Thus, those who deliver the sentence "Wherefore art thou Romeo?" should place emphasis on the word *Romeo* rather than on the word *art.* And any teaching aid that advertises itself by questioning its own existence is falling down in the marketing department.

"Bird had staggered into the All-Star Game with back-to-back stinkeroos against Indiana (7 for 19) and Milwaukee (7-24). But winning the Three-Point title always enervates him, even as taking it relatively easy for three days refreshes him," reads a news story on Celtics star forward Larry Bird. From the context of the article we can be certain that the writer succumbed to another common foot-in-mouth error and thought that *enervate* means "to energize," when it really means "to weaken."

Penultimate, noisome, fulsome, wherefore, and *enervate* are five especially deceptive, noisome, and fulsome words in sheep's clothing, words that don't mean what they look like they should mean. Here is a small quiz that presents more words that are not what they seem. Beware and be wary as you choose the correct definition for each entry. Avoid taking a simplistic (there's another one!) approach. Answers repose at the end of this book.

1. *antebellum*   *a.* against women *b.* against war *c.* after the war *d.* before the war

2. *apiary*   *a.* school for mimics *b.* place where apes are kept *c.* place where bees are kept *d.* cupboard for peas

3. *aquiline*   *a.* resembling an eagle *b.* relating to water *c.* relating to synchronized swimming *d.* resembling a porcupine

4. *cupidity*   *a.* strong desire for wealth *b.* strong desire for love *c.* strong desire for amusement parks *d.* obtuseness

5. *disinterested*   *a.* lacking a bank account *b.* unbiased *c.* bored *d.* lacking rest

6. *enormity*   *a.* great wickedness *b.* great size *c.* normal state *d.* cowardice

7. *forestress*   *a.* ancient hair style *b.* female forester *c.* dread anticipation *d.* emphasis on first part of word

8. *friable*   *a.* easily crumbled *b.* easily fried *c.* unhealthy *d.* relating to holy orders

9. *herpetology*   the study of *a.* herbs *b.* herpes *c.* female pets *d.* reptiles

10. *hippophobia*   the fear of *a.* hippopotami *b.* horses *c.* getting fat *d.* hippies

11. *infinitesimal*   *a.* very small *b.* very large *c.* relating to intestines *d.* hesitant

12. *inflammable*   *a.* calm *b.* incredulous *c.* not easily set on fire *d.* easily set on fire

13. *ingenuous*   *a.* insincere *b.* innocent *c.* clever *d.* mentally dull

14. *meretricious*   *a.* falsely attractive *b.* worthy *c.* good tasting *d.* diseased

15. *presently*   *a.* generous with gifts *b.* now *c.* soon *d.* presidentially

16. *prosody*   the study of *a.* drama *b.* music *c.* prose *d.* versification

17. *restive*   *a.* serene *b.* festive *c.* fidgety *d.* pensive

18. *risible*   *a.* disposed to laugh *b.* easily lifted *c.* fertile *d.* relating to dawn

19. *toothsome*   *a.* displaying prominent teeth *b.* missing teeth *c.* palatable *d.* serrated

20. *votary*   *a.* democratic country *b.* enthusiast *c.* electoral college *d.* revolving tool

Sesquipedalian English

～

Early in my career as a verbivore, I became fascinated with long words. I was delighted when I happened upon *inappropriateness* (seventeen letters) and *incomprehensibility* (nineteen letters), and then I was introduced to the twenty-eight-letter *antidisestablishmentarianism.* Because that word is the most famous of all polysyllabic creations, it is worth dissecting in some detail: *anti-* "against," *dis-* "reversal," *establish* (the root of the word) "to secure," *ment-* "result or agent of an action," *arian-* "believing," and *ism-* "doctrine." Stitching together these pieces, we find that *antidisestablishmentarianism* means "a doctrine against the dissolution of the establishment." In the nineteenth century, the word meant "opposition to the separation of the established church and state."

Only in my early middle age did I discover that *antidisestablishmentarianism* is a mere pygmy in the hierarchy of truly long words. Here is a sampler of giant words,

38

antidisestablishmentarianism

a mere pygmy

each of which reposes in at least one reputable dictionary. Gazing upon their length and bulk reminds us of the bizarre shapes that English words can assume.

floccinaucinihilipilification (twenty-nine letters): the categorizing of something as worthless or trivial. The word dates back to 1741 and is the longest word in the *Oxford English Dictionary.* In it the letter *i* occurs nine times and the letter *e* not at all.

hippopotomonstrosesquipedalian (thirty letters): pertaining to a very long word. How appropriate.

supercalifragilisticexpialidocious (thirty-four letters): a word invented for the film *Mary Poppins* (1964) that has become the best known word of more than twenty-eight letters. Etymologically this is not entirely a nonsense word: *super-* "above," *cali-* "beauty," *fragilistic-* "delicate," *expiali-* "to atone," and *docious-* "educable," the sum of which equals "atoning for extreme and delicate beauty [while being] highly educable."

pneumonoultramicroscopicsilicovolcanoconiosis (forty-five letters): a miners' lung disease caused by the inhalation of silicate or quartz dust. This longest of all words entered in *Webster's Third New International Dictionary* can be broken down into *pneumono-* "lung," *ultra-* "beyond," *micro-* "small," *scopic-* "to see," *silico-* "flint, quartz," *volcano-* "fiery, as from a volcano," *coni-* "dust," and *osis-* "a diseased condition," yielding "a disease of the lungs [caused by] dust from volcanic ash [so fine as to be] beyond the range of [an instrument that sees] very small [things]."

Such hippopotomonstrosesquipedalian entries have inspired me to create a polysyllabic limerick:

It's true that I have halitosis.
At least it's not
pneumonoultramicroscopicsilicovolcanoconiosis.
　　Thus, rather than floccinaucinihilipilification,
　　I feel only elation
That's supercalifragilisticexpialidocious.

Moving beyond *pneumonoultramicroscopicsilico-volcanoconiosis,* we come to *Chargoggagoggman-chauggagoggchaubunagungamaugg* (forty-five letters, fifteen of them *g*'s), a Native American name for a lake near Webster, Massachusetts. The name means "You fish on your side; I fish on my side; nobody fish in the middle."

Taumatawhakata . . . : So begins the unofficial eighty-five-letter version of the name of a hill in New Zealand, believed to be the longest place name in the world. The name means "the place where Tametea, the man with the big knee who slid, climbed, and swallowed mountains, known as Land-eater, played the flute to his loved one."

bothallchoractora . . . : the beginning of one of ten "thunderwords" in James Joyce's *Finnegans Wake,* each of which is made up of a hundred letters.

acetylseryltyrosyl . . . : These are the first of 1,185 letters that make up the protein part of the tobacco mosaic virus. Fortunately, the molecule can be reduced to the formula $C785H122ON2120248S2$.

But not done. For there is one more chemical compound whose name exceeds even the length of the above tobacco chain. Tryptophan synthetase A protein is an enzyme with 267 amino acids. When spelled in full, the word stretches to 1,913 letters: *methionyl-glutaminylarginyltyrosylglutamylserylleucylphenylalanyl-lalanylglutaminylleucyllysylglutamylarginyllysylglutamyl-glycylalanylphenylalanylvalylprolylphenylalanylyalyl-threonylleucylglycylaspartylprolylglycylisoleucylglutamyl-glutaminylserylleucyllysylisoleucylaspartylthreonylleucyli-soleucylglutamylalanylglycylalanylaspartylalanylleucyl-glutamylleucylglycylisoleucylprolylphenylalanylserylaspar-tylprolylleucelalanylaspartylglycylprolythreonylisoleucyl-glutaminylasparaginylalanylthreonylleucylarginylalanyl-phenylalanylalanylalanylglycylvalylthreonylprolylalanyl-glutaminylcysteinylphenylalanylglutamylmethionylleuc-yalanylleucylisoleucylarginylglutaminyllysylhistidylprolyl-threonylisoleucylprolylisoleucylglycylleucylleucylmethi-onyltyrosylalanylasparaginylleucylvalylphenylalanylasp-araginyllysylglycylisoleucylaspartylglutamylphenylalanyl-tyrosylalanylglutaminylcysteinylglutamyllysylvalylglycyl-valylaspartylserylvalylleucylvalylalanylaspartylvalylprol-ylvalylglutaminylglutamylserylalanylprolylphenylalanyl-arginylglutaminylalanylalanylleucylarginylhistidylaspar-aginylvalylalanylprolylisoleucylphenylalanylisoleucylcy-steinylprolylprolylaspartylalanylaspartylaspartylasparty-lleucylleucylarginylglutaminylisoleucylalanylseryltyrosyl-glycylarginylglcyltyrosylthreonyltyrosylleucylleucylserylar-ginylalanylglycylvalylthreonylglycylalanylglutamylaspa-raginylarginylalanylalanylleucylprolylleucylasparaginyl-histidylleucylvalylalanyllysylleucyllysylglutamyltyrosyla-sparaginylalanylalanylprolylprolylleucylglutaminylglycyl-phenylalanylglycylisoleucylserylalanylprolylaspartyl-glutaminylvalyllysylalanylalanylisoleucylaspartylalanyl-*

glycylalanylalanylglycylalanylisoleucylserylglycylseryl-
alanylisoleucylbalyllysylisoleucylisoleucylglutamylgluta-
minylhistidylasparaginylisoleucylglutamylprolylgluta-
myllysylmethionylleucylalanylalanylleucyllsylvalylphenyl-
alanylvalylglutaminylprolylmethionyllsylalanylalanyl-
threonylarginylserine.

So what *is* the longest word in the English language? A children's riddle says *smiles* because there is a "mile" between its first and last letters. But it is comedian Red Skelton who deserves credit for identifying the longest word of all. Skelton maintained that the longest word in the English language is the word that follows the voice that comes on your radio or television set and intones: "And now a word from our sponsors."

2

THE NAME
IS THE GAME

"To-day we have the naming of the parts."
—HENRY REED

What's in a Name?

Never pride yourself on your knowledge. Always remember that a little knowledge is a dangerous thing—especially when you discover that Alexander Pope actually wrote that famous quotation as "A little *learning* is a dangerous thing."

Let's start with your knowledge of our fellow creatures who run and crawl and creep and gallop and swim and fly and hop around our planet. The Canary Islands in the Atlantic got their name from what creature?

"Canaries, of course!" you chirp.

Wrong.

The answer is dogs. The Latin name was *Canāria Īnsula*, "Isle of the Dogs." Canaries got their name from the islands, not the other way around.

In our crazy English vocabulary, we discover that catgut is actually sheep and horse intestines and that camel's hair brushes are made from squirrel fur.

A ladybug is a beetle—and they're not all female. A

lightning bug is a beetle. And a firefly is actually a lightning bug, which, as you now know, is a beetle.

In fact, a whole menagerie of animals are not what their names indicate. Take the hedgehog. Light verse master Bob McKenty explains the truth about the spiny insectivore:

> No matter what their name alleges,
> Hedgehogs aren't hogs or hedges
> (Like kindred quadrupeds with spines
> Who aren't porks and aren't pines).

The koala bear is a marsupial, not a bear. The guinea pig is a South American rodent. It is neither a pig nor from Guinea. A prairie dog is not a dog; it too is a rodent. The horned toad is a lizard, not a toad, while a silkworm is not a worm; it's a caterpillar. Half of peacocks are actually peahens. A titmouse is neither mammal nor mammaried; it's a bird, while a crawfish is not a fish; it's a spiny lobster. A jackrabbit is a hare, not a rabbit. Blindworms are actually legless lizards, and of course they can see. A mosquito bite isn't a bite. It's a puncture.

What color is a green card? Pink, quite obviously. Which country is greener—Greenland or Iceland? Iceland, of course. By the same logic, the blackbird hen is brown, purple finches are distinctly crimson, and many greyhounds come in colors other than gray.

Where do Labrador Retrievers and Great Danes come from?

Where else but Newfoundland and Germany?

In what country did the Pennsylvania Dutch originate?

Germany. *Dutch* is actually *Deutsch* here.

French fries were invented in Belgium. *Frenching* simply describes a method of cutting vegetables into long strips.

The French phone was invented by an American, Robert Brown. Now that you are in control of that quirky fact, test your knowledge of nations and their legacies to the world. In what countries did the following items originate?:

1. Arabic numerals
2. Danish pastry
3. Turkish baths
4. Swiss steak
5. India ink
6. Panama hats
7. Dresden china
8. Russian dressing
9. Chinese gooseberries
10. the English horn
11. Jordan almonds
12. Jerusalem artichokes

Long ago, you discovered that there is no ham in a hamburger. In fact, if someone ever invented a bulky roll with a ham patty inside, we'd have a hard time coming up with a name for it.

What are the primary ingredients of each of the following delectables?:

13. buttermilk
14. litchi nuts
15. welsh rabbit
16. egg cream
17. shortbread
18. sweetbread
19. Bombay duck
20. sweetmeat

21. lemon sole
22. breadfruit
23. cold duck
24. apple butter
25. Grape-Nuts
26. plum pudding
27. Rocky Mountain oysters

How are refried beans made? Despite the name, refried beans are not fried twice. *Frijoles refritos* actually means "well fried," not "refried."

A peanut is neither a pea nor a nut; it's a legume.

Now that you're fully confident in the accuracy of the names we bestow on food, ask yourself what is:

28. a pineapple
29. a prickly pear
30. a sugarplum
31. wormwood
32. a Mexican jumping bean
33. a caraway seed

Now, how do you stack up in your knowledge of other objects and concepts in the universe?:

34. Aside from wood, what is the primary material in a lead pencil?
35. What is a briar pipe made of?
36. What kind of heavenly body is a shooting star?
37. What kind of tree is a Douglas fir?
38. What kind of tree is witch hazel?
39. What kind of tree is a banana tree?
40. What part of the body is the funny bone?
41. How many gallons of water can a ten-gallon hat hold?
42. Why do we call a pea jacket a pea jacket?

43. How do they do dry cleaning?
44. What is the primary cause of hay fever?

Finally, a brief history quiz:

45. The sides of Old Ironsides were made from what material?
46. In what month do Russians celebrate the October Revolution?
47. What was George VI's first name?
48. How was the cesarean section named?
49. How long did the Hundred Years War last?
50. How long did the Thirty Years War last?

What's Your Phobia?

According to the Mayan sacred book *Popol Vuh,* after the Creators had made the earth, carved it with mountains, valleys, and rivers, and covered it with vegetation, they formed the animals who would be guardians of the plant world and who would praise the Makers' names: " 'Speak, then, our names, praise us, your mother, your father. Invoke, then, Huracan, Chipi-Caculha, the Heart of Heaven, the Heart of Earth, the Creator, the Maker, the Forefathers. Speak, invoke us, adore us.'

"But the animals only hissed and screamed and cackled. They were unable to make words, and each screamed in a different way.

"When the Creator and the Maker saw that it was impossible for them to talk to each other, they said: 'It is impossible for them to say the names of us, their Creators and Makers. This is not well.'

"As a punishment, the birds and animals were condemned to be eaten and sacrificed by others, and the

The animals only hissed and screamed and cackled.

Creators set out to make another creature who would be able to call their names and speak their praises. This creature was man and woman."

In biblical Genesis, we read that God said, "Let us make man in our image, after our likeness," and, as in the Mayan myth of creation, God bestowed upon human beings the power of language, the power to name things: "And out of the ground the Lord God formed every beast of the field, and every fowl of the air; and brought them unto Adam to see what he would call them: and whatsoever Adam called every living creature, that was the name thereof. And Adam gave names to all cattle, and to the fowl of the air, and to every beast of the field."

The human desire and power to name everything is nowhere better demonstrated than in our ability to label our deepest fears—our phobias.

Do you have an undomesticated pet phobia? No? Think again. Does your stomach want to scream when it and you arrive at the zenith of a Ferris wheel? Does your head retract turtlelike into your body when the lightning flashes and the thunder cracks? Do you tremble at the sight of a snake or a spider, or a cat and a dog?

Such fears are called phobias. If you are afflicted with a few of these reactions, don't worry; studies show that the average person possesses three phobias. Things could be worse: Count your blessings that you are not a victim of *pantophobia*—the morbid dread of everything. Then you would be stuck with *verbaphobia,* and you wouldn't be able to enjoy this book.

Humankind is beset with a host of fears and has

managed to name practically every one of them. Phobos, "fear," was the son of Ares, the god of war, and was the nephew of Eris, goddess of discord, and brother to Deimos, "terror." The names of our deepest dreads generally include the Greek root *phobia,* meaning "fear or hatred," affixed to another root, which is also usually Greek. The two most common human phobias are *acrophobia,* a morbid fear of heights, and *claustrophobia,* a morbid fear of enclosed spaces. Look for your deepest dreads among the lists that follow. By assigning names to these terrors, you may be taking the first step in overcoming them.

Let's start with the creatures with whom we share this planet. From time immemorial, some of these organisms have inspired fear and even terror in the human breast. Each of these dreads has a label: Fear of animals is called *zoophobia,* of birds *ornithophobia,* of fish *ichthyophobia,* of reptiles *herpetophobia,* and of insects *entophobia.*

Here are the names we have contrived for the fears of more specific organisms. In each case, I leave it to you to supply the words "fear of": *acarophobia:* mites, parasites; *aelurophobia:* cats; *alektorophobia:* chickens; *apiophobia:* bees; *arachnophobia:* spiders; *bacilliphobia:* bacilli; *bacteriaphobia:* bacteria; *batarachophobia:* frogs, toads; *chidophobia:* insect stings; *cynophobia:* dogs; *eisoptrophobia:* termites; *entonophobia:* ticks; *galeophobia:* sharks; *hippophobia:* horses; *microbiophobia:* microbes; *musophobia:* mice; *myrmecophobia:* ants; *ostraconophobia:* shellfish; *parasitophobia:* parasites; *sheksophobia:* wasps; *soleciphobia:* worms; *swi-*

nophobia: swine; *taeniophobia:* tapeworms; *tauropho-bia:* bulls.

We have fewer words to express our fears of flora; evidently, plants are regarded as more docile and less threatening than other organisms: *anthophobia:* flowers, plants; *dendrophobia:* trees; *hylophobia:* forests, woods; *lachanophobia:* vegetables. Hence, if you despise eating spinach or broccoli, you are a *lachanophobe.*

For some of us, it is other people who inspire in our hearts the greatest palpitations—*anthropophobia.* If you fear men, you are afflicted with *androphobia,* if you fear women, *gynephobia,* if you fear children, *pediophobia.* If it is your relatives who won't get off your nerves, you have *syngenescophobia.* More specifically, if you are irritated by your mother-in-law, you are burdened with *pentheraphobia;* if you hate or fear your stepmother, *novercaphobia.*

If you are possessed by an irrational aversion to politicians, you have *politicophobia,* if to thieves, *kleptophobia,* if to foreigners, *xenophobia.* If these foreigners are English, you've got *Anglophobia,* if French, *Gallophobia,* if German, *Teutophobia,* if Russian, *Russophobia,* and if Chinese, *Sinophobia.* And if you break out in a cold sweat at even the thought of going to the dentist, you share with me a condition called *dentophobia.*

In addition to the various fears of people, humankind is fraught with terrors of various natural phenomena: *acousticophobia:* noise; *aerophobia:* air; *anemophobia:* cyclones, hurricanes, winds; *antlophobia:* floods; *aquaphobia:* water; *astraphobia:* lightning,

Triskaidekaphobia

thunder; *astrophobia:* stars; *auroraphobia:* northern lights; *barophobia:* gravity; *blennophobia:* slime; *brontophobia:* thunderstorms; *cheimaphobia:* cold; *chionophobia:* snow; *cometophobia:* comets; *cryophobia:* frost, ice; *cymophobia:* waves; *dinophobia:* whirlpools; *elektrophobia:* electricity; *eosophobia:* dawn; *heliophobia:* sun; *homichlophobia:* fog, humidity; *hylophobia:* wood; *koniophobia:* dust; *lilapsophobia:* tornadoes; *meteorophobia:* weather; *nephophobia:* clouds; *nyctophobia:* darkness; *ombrophobia:* rain; *phengophobia:* daylight; *photophobia:* light; *potomophobia:* rivers; *pyrophobia:* fire; *selaphobia:* flashing light; *selenophobia:* the moon; *septophobia:* decaying matter; *skiaphobia:* shadows; *thalassophobia:* the sea; *thermophobia:* heat; *xerophobia:* dry places, like deserts.

When Adam and Eve were expelled from the Garden of Eden, God said to the serpent, "I will put enmity between thee and the woman, and between thy seed and her seed." During its post-Edenic existence, humankind has acquired not only herpetophobia, but so many other fears that up to this point I have listed fewer than half of our named dreads. Naming these terrors may be a kind of magic for holding them at bay. For example, enough people fear the number thirteen that many buildings pretend not to have a thirteenth floor. Still, we assign this affliction a name—*triskaidekaphobia: tris,* "three"; *kai,* "and"; *deka,* "ten"; *phobia,* "fear."

In the pages of my local newspaper appeared a story about a woman who for thirty years was held prisoner in her apartment by *agoraphobia,* an intense fear of the outdoors and of open spaces that affects nearly two million Americans. Incredible as it may seem, there is even a label for the fear of getting peanut butter stuck to the roof of the mouth. It is called *arachibutyrophobia.*

Here are more than two hundred additional words that describe the terrors that go bump in our minds:

ablutophobia: bathing; *acousticophobia:* noise; *acrophobia:* heights; *aeronausiphobia:* airplanes; *agliophobia:* pain; *agraphobia:* sexual abuse; *aichurophobia:* being touched by pointed objects; *algophobia:* pain; *alychiphobia:* failure; *amathophobia:* dust; *amaxophobia:* riding in vehicles; *ambulophobia:* walking; *amechophobia:* being scratched; *amnesiophobia:* amnesia; *anuptaphobia:* staying single; *arithmophobia:* numbers; *asthenophobia:* weakness, fainting; *ataxiophobia:* disorder; *atelophobia:* imperfection; *automysophobia:* being dirty; *ballistrophobia:* being shot; *basophobia:* standing (for fear of falling); *bathophobia:* depth; *batophobia:* passing a tall building; *bibliophobia:* books; *blenophobia:* pins and needles; *bogyphobia:* demons and goblins; *bromidrosophobia:* body smells; *cacophobia:* ugliness; *cainophobia:* novelty; *carcinophobia:* cancer; *cardiophobia:* heart disease; *carnophobia:* meat; *cathisophobia:* sitting; *catophtrophobia:* mirrors; *centophobia:* empty spaces; *chactophobia:* hair; *cherophobia:* gaiety; *chiraptophobia:* being touched; *chorophobia:* dancing; *chrematophobia:* wealth; *chromophobia:* colors; *chronophobia:* time; *cibophobia:* food; *claustrophobia:* enclosed spaces; *climacophobia:* staircases; *clinophobia:* going to bed; *coimetrophobia:* cemeteries; *coitophobia:* sexual intercourse; *coropho-*

bia: excrement; *coprostasophobia:* constipation; *cremnophobia:* precipices; *crystallophobia:* glass; *cyberphobia:* computers; *cyprianophobia:* prostitutes; *decidophobia:* making decisions; *defecalgesiophobia:* painful defecation; *deipnophobia:* dining and dining conversation; *dementophobia:* insanity; *demophobia:* crowds; *dermatophobia:* skin disease; *didaskaleinophobia:* going to school; *dinophobia:* dizziness; *diplopiaphobia:* double vision; *diplychiphobia:* accidents; *dipsophobia:* drinking alcohol; *domatophobia:* being in a house; *doraphobia:* fur; *dromophobia:* crossing streets; *dysmorphophobia:* deformity; *dystychiphobia:* accidents; *ecclesiophobia:* churches; *ecophobia:* home; *eleutherophobia:* freedom; *emetophobia:* vomiting; *ereuthrophobia:* blushing; *ergasiophobia:* work; *erotophobia:* sexual feelings; *erythrophobia:* blushing, the color red; *eurotophobia:* female genitals; *febriphobia:* fever; *gamophobia:* marriage; *geliophobia:* laughter; *gephyrophobia:* crossing bridges; *gerascophobia:* growing old; *glossophobia:* speaking in public; *graphophobia:* writing; *gymnophobia:* nudity; *hagiophobia:* saints and holy things; *halophobia:* speaking; *hamartophobia:* error or sin; *haphephobia:* touching, being touched; *hedonophobia:* pleasure; *hematophobia:* the sight of blood; *hierophobia:* clergymen; *hodophobia:* travel; *homilophobia:* sermons; *homophobia:* homosexuals; *hoplophobia:* firearms; *hydrophophobia:* rabies; *hypnophobia:* sleep; *ideophobia:* ideas; *iophobia:* rust; *kakorrhphiophobia:* failure; *katagelophobia:* ridicule; *kenophobia:* large, empty spaces; *kinesophobia:* motion; *kopophobia:* mental or physical examination; *laliophobia:*

talking; *latrophobia:* going to the doctor; *lepraphobia:* leprosy; *linonophobia:* string; *liticaphobia:* fear of lawsuits; *lygophobia:* dark; *lyssiophobia:* becoming mad; *macrophobia:* long waits; *maieusiophobia:* childbirth; *mastigophobia:* flogging; *mechanophobia:* machinery; *megalophobia:* large objects; *menophobia:* menstruation; *merinthophobia:* being bound; *metallophobia:* metals; *metrophobia:* poetry; *misophobia:* contamination; *molysomophobia:* dirt, infection; *monophobia:* being alone; *motorphobia:* motor vehicles; *musicophobia:* music; *necrophobia:* corpses; *nosocomephobia:* hospitals; *nosophobia:* becoming ill; *nucleomitophobia:* nuclear weapons; *obesophobia:* weight gain; *ochlophobia:* crowds; *odontophobia:* teeth, especially those of animals; *odynophobia:* pain; *oenophobia:* wine; *olfactophobia:* odors; *oneirogmophobia:* wet dreams; *onomatophobia:* a certain word or name; *ophthalmophobia:* being stared at; *papaphobia:* the pope or the papacy; *paralipophobia:* responsibility; *paraphobia:* sexual perversion; *parthenophobia:* young girls; *peccatiphobia:* sinning; *pedophobia:* children; *peladophobia:* becoming bald; *peniaphobia:* poverty; *phagophobia:* eating or swallowing; *phallophobia:* male genitals; *pharmacophobia:* drugs; *phasmophobia:* ghosts; *philemaphobia:* kissing; *philophobia:* falling in love or being loved; *placophobia:* tombstones; *pnigophobia:* choking; *pogonophobia:* beards; *ponophobia:* fatigue; *proctophobia:* rectal disease; *prosophobia:* progress; *psellismophobia:* stuttering; *pteronophobia:* being tickled by feathers; *radiophobia:* X rays; *rhabdophobia:* criticism, punishment, being beaten; *rhypophobia:* filth;

rhytiphobia: getting wrinkles; *Satanophobia:* Satan; *sciophobia:* shadows; *scriptophobia:* writing; *siderodromophobia:* train travel; *sociophobia:* friendship, society; *sophophobia:* knowledge; *spectrophobia:* looking in the mirror; *stasiphobia:* standing; *staurophobia:* cross or crucifix; *stenophobia:* narrow places; *stygiophobia:* hell; *tachophobia:* speed; *taphephobia:* cemeteries, being buried alive; *tapinophobia:* small things; *technophobia:* technology; *teleophobia:* religious ceremonies; *telephonophobia:* using the telephone; *teratophobia:* monsters; *thanatophobia:* death, dying; *thassophobia:* sitting idle; *theatrophobia:* theaters; *theophobia:* God; *tomophobia:* surgical operations; *topophobia:* certain places; *toxicophobia:* poisoning; *traumatophobia:* injury; *trichophobia:* hair; *tropophobia:* changes; *tryapanophobia:* injections; *uranophobia:* heaven; *vaccinophobia:* vaccines; *venereophobia:* venereal disease; *verbaphobia:* words; *vermiophobia:* germs; *vestiophobia:* clothing; *virgivitphobia:* virgins.

When Franklin Delano Roosevelt said, in his 1933 inaugural address, "The only thing we have to fear is fear itself," he was warning us against phobophobia, the fear of being afraid. Now that you know that all your phobias have names, you may experience less fear about your fears and about fear itself.

The Secrets of "Nym"

Somebody once defined a synonym as a word you use when you can't spell the word you really want. What a synonym really is, of course, is a word with the same, or nearly the same, meaning as another word, such as *big* and *large* or *small* and *tiny*. Somebody else once quipped that a great many poems seem to have been written by a prolific Irish genius named Ann O'Nymous. Here the pun is on the word *anonymous,* and when a work is anonymous, its creator's name is not revealed.

In *synonym* and *anonymous,* the common element is *onym,* a Greek root that means "word" or "name," and many words about words themselves contain this root. Exploring the secrets of *nym* through a glossary of *nym*ble word words and name words reveals one of the brightest delights of language—its ability to talk about itself:

Acronym. Coined from two Greek roots that literally mean "high word," acronyms are words made up

Ann O'Nymous

of the initials of other words. *NASA* is formed from the key letters in National Aeronautics and Space Administration, *radar* from those in radio detecting and ranging, and *SCUBA* from self-contained underwater breathing apparatus. The years since World War II have brought a new refinement to the art of acronyming. This is the reverse acronym, or **bacronym,** in which letters are arranged to form a word that already exists in the language and cleverly underscores some quality of the words that form it. Thus, *ZIP* codes, for "zone improvement plan," reputedly add zip to our mail service, *VISTA* workers (Volunteers In Service To America) provide wider horizons (vistas) for needy Americans, members of *NOW* (National Organization for Women) are in tune with the times, and Mothers Against Drunk Driving are *MADD* about the tragedies that occur when drinking and driving are mixed.

Anatonym. A part of the body used as a verb: to *toe* the line, *foot* the bill, *face* the music.

Antonym. A word that is opposite in meaning to another word. All *happy* and *sad* takers of the Scholastic Aptitude Test are familiar with this *sweet* and *sour* concept.

Aptronym. A name that is especially suited to the profession of its owner, such as Dan Druff for a barber, Felicity Foote for a dance teacher, and James Bugg for an exterminator—all real monikers. More famously, we have Sally Ride the astronaut, Larry Speakes the White

House spokesperson, Margaret Court the tennis star, William Wordsworth the poet, Jim Kiick the football player, and Lorena Bobbitt ("bob it") the you-know-what-er.

Autonym. A word that describes itself. *Mispelled* is indeed misspelled, and *hippopotomonstrosesquipedalian* is a very long word that means "pertaining to a very long word."

Capitonym. A word that changes pronunciation and meaning when it is capitalized. Take the world of tennis, from which we can muster the Austrian star Thomas Muster, pronounced "Mooster." Hey, guy. Don't forget French tennis luminary Guy Forget, pronounced "Gee Forjay," a double capitonym. And would you like a date with Kimono Date, the recently retired Japanese tennis star?

Joining Muster, Forget, and Date are Bill Amend, who draws the comic strip *Fox Trot,* and Berkeley Breathed, creator of *Bloom County* and *Outland.*

Now sound out this list of prominent capitonyms in both their lower-case and capitalized forms:

amend	concord	levy	nice
askew	date	lima	polish
august	forget	messier	rainier
begin	guy	millet	ravel
breathed	herb	muster	reading
colon	job	natal	tangier

Job's Job

In *August,* an *august* patriarch,
  Was *reading* an ad in *Reading,* Mass.
Long-suffering *Job* secured a *job*
  To *polish* piles of *Polish* brass.

Herb's Herbs

An *herb* store owner, name of *Herb,*
  Moved to *rainier* Mt. *Rainier,*
It would have been so *nice* in *Nice,*
  And even *tangier* in *Tangier.*

Charactonym. The name of a literary character that is especially suited to his or her personality. The enormous and enduring popularity of Charles Dickens's works springs in part from the writer's skill at creating memorable charactonyms—Scrooge, the tightfisted miser; Mr. Gradgrind, the tyrannical schoolmaster; Jaggers, the rough-edged lawyer; and Miss Havesham ("have a sham"), the jilted spinster who lives in an illusion. John Bunyan's Mr. Wordly Wiseman, Susanna Centlivre's Simon Pure, and Walter Scott's Dr. Dryasdust are other famous fictional charactonyms.

Modern examples of charactonyms include Willy Loman ("low man") in Arthur Miller's *Death of a Salesman* and Jim Trueblood in Ralph Ellison's *Invisible Man.* Not many years ago, a doctor show named "Marcus Welby" ruled the television ratings. The title of the show and name of the lead character were purposely designed to make us think of "make us well be."

Consonym. Words that have the same pattern of consonants are known as consonyms; *eTHNiC* and *THeNCe, SPoNGe* and *eSPioNaGe.*

Domunym. Invented by language maven Paul Dickson, a domunym, literally "home name," is a word used to identify people from particular places: *Philadelphians, Rhode Islanders, Tacomans, Hoosiers, Liverpudlians, Oxonians,* and *Cantabridgians.*

Euonym. An especially auspicious name, such as the biblical David, "beloved," and Jesus, "savior." English language examples include Harry Truman, Martin Luther King, Jr., and Andrew Marvell.

Exonym. A place name that foreigners use instead of the name that natives use: *Cologne* for Koln, *Florence* for Firenze, *Morocco* for Maroc.

Homonym. A word spelled and pronounced like another word, but of different origin and meaning: *bat* (flying mammal) and *bat* (in baseball), *mint* (an aromatic plant) and *mint* (a place where money is made).

Malonym. A humorous homophone or sound-alike mistake: "In the middle of the field stood a toe-headed boy"; "Our menu is guaranteed to wet your appetite"; "The trouble I'm having with my prostrate gland is making me very tired."

Meronym. A term midway between two opposites, as black, *gray,* white and convex, *flat,* and concave.

Metonymy. When we use the *crown* to refer to a monarchy, *brass* to refer to military officers, and the *White House* to refer to the U.S. executive branch, we are in each case employing a metonymy, a name that stands for something else with which it is closely associated. When we call an athlete a *jock,* we make the piece of equipment stand for the person's identity. This metonymy has become so figurative that women can also be jocks.

Patronymic. Family names derived from the father's name or that of a male ancestor are patronymics. *McDonald* means "son of Donald," *O'Grady* "son of Grady," *Johnson* "son of John," and *Richards* "son of Richard."

Pseudonym. The authors of *Alice's Adventures in Wonderland, Silas Marner,* and *Nineteen Eighty-Four* have something in common besides being British. They are all better known by their pseudonyms, or pen names, than by their real names. Here are brief biographies of fifteen famous writers. From the information supplied, can you identify each pseudonym (literally "false name")? You'll find the literary identities on the answer page in the back of this book.

1. Eric Arthur Blair wrote a long fable about a society in which some animals are more equal than others.

In 1948 he published a novel about a nightmarish society of the future, one in which everybody had a Big Brother.

2. Samuel Langhorne Clemens was a steamboat pilot before he became a writer. In 1863 he took on the pen name that was a nostalgic reminder of his riverboat days.

3. In March of 1836, what has been described as the most successful writing career in history was launched with the publication of *The Pickwick Papers.* The author, of course, was Charles Dickens. In 1833, when he was only twenty-one, Dickens began contributing stories and essays to magazines and published them pseudonymously in a collection called *Sketches by* _____.

4. Charles Lutwidge Dodgson was fascinated with words, logic, and little girls. Out of these interests he fashioned a wonderland of characters—Humpty Dumptys, Jabberwocks, Mad Hatters, and White Rabbits.

5. Famous for her novels describing life in nineteenth-century England, including *Adam Bede, Silas Marner,* and *Middlemarch,* Mary Ann Evans adopted a masculine pen name, by George.

6. He meant what he said, and he said what he meant, and his books have pleased children one hundred percent. Theodor Geisel conjured up and drew creatures that now exist in the imaginations of generations of children.

7. William Sydney Porter spent almost four years in prison, where he began his career as an immensely

popular writer of short stories. Most of his tales are about life in New York and are marked by surprise endings.

8. Late in life, after a long career as a veterinary surgeon, James Alfred Wight began writing books that communicated his profound affection for animals. The titles of two of those books are taken from a hymn that begins, "All things bright and beautiful, all creatures great and small."

9. Jozef Korzeniowski was born in Poland and grew up speaking no English until he was seventeen, yet he became one of the greatest stylists ever to use the English language. A sailor as a youth, Korzeniowski is most famous for his stories and novels of the sea.

10. Hector Hugh Munro was killed in action during World War I. He left behind him the charming, often biting short stories to which he signed a pseudonym borrowed from *The Rubáiyát.*

11. An unpublished Atlanta writer named Peggy Marsh submitted an incomplete manuscript that filled a large suitcase. The title of the novel was to be *Tomorrow Is Another Day,* and its heroine was to be called Pansy. After a great number of changes, including the title and the name of the heroine, the book was published in 1936 and became an all-time best-seller, inspiring a blockbuster movie and, fifty years after that, a blockbuster sequel.

12. Russian-born Yiddish author Solomon Rabinowitz took his pen name from a Hebrew expression meaning "peace be unto you."

13. British novelist and critic John B. Wilson is

most famous for *A Clockwork Orange.* His works often combine word play and a grim view of life.

14. Baroness Karen Blixen, a Danish author who wrote primarily in English, managed a coffee plantation in British East Africa. She is best known for her tales and her autobiography, drawn from her African experience.

15. For many years, Manfred Lee and his cousin Frederic Dannay functioned as one author, an eccentric bookworm who allegedly wrote about his adventures as a detective.

Tautonym. A word composed of two identical parts, such as *tomtom, tutu,* and *goody-goody.*

In the next chapters, we'll explore in depth five especially fascinating members of the *nym* family—**eponyms, toponyms, contronyms, heteronyms,** and **retronyms.**

Brand-New Eponyms

The ancient gods snatched up the souls of those mortals who found favor in their eyes and made them into stars so that they could shine long after their deaths. Many men and women have been similarly gifted with a measure of immortality by having their names transmuted into common English words. Because of some discovery, object, deed, or quality associated with them, these chosen people—noble or petty, adored or abhorred—continue to twinkle in the heavens of the English language long after they have exited the earthly stage. The Greeks had a word for such people—*eponymos,* from which we derive the term *eponym,* meaning "after or upon a name." Stories of the origins of words made from people or places, real or imaginary, are among the richest and most entertaining about our language.

Perhaps the best-known tale of a mortal immortalized is that of John Montagu, the fourth Earl of Sandwich, from whose clever stratagem descends the word *sandwich*. Word has it that Montagu was spending a typical twenty-four-hour stretch at the gaming tables. Unwilling to forsake his cards for a meal, he ordered his servants to bring him, as his only nourishment, slices of beef slapped between slices of bread. Who would have dreamed that a compulsive gambler would go on to become history's greatest salesman of sliced bread?

King Tantalus, one of the vilest of villains in Greek mythology, is one of many literary creations that pulse just as powerfully as their flesh-and-blood counterparts. To degrade the gods and to test their omniscience, Tantalus invited them to a feast at which he planned to serve the body of his young son, Pelops. But the gods discovered the king's wicked ruse, restored the dead boy to life, and devised a punishment for Tantalus to fit his crime.

Tantalus was banished to Hades, where he was condemned to stand forevermore in a sparkling pool of water with boughs of luscious fruit overhead. He is eternally frustrated, for when he stoops to drink, the water drains away through the bottom of the pool, and when he wishes to eat, the branches of fruit sway from his reach. Ever since, when something presents itself temptingly to our view but teases us by remaining just beyond reach, we say that it *tantalizes* us.

Even cartoon and comic book characters have a place in the Eponyms Hall of Fame. In 1928, Walt Disney gave the world a Mickey—Mickey Mouse. Until the 1940s, when one said "Mickey Mouse," one meant only the all-American rodent who performed heroic deeds and squeaked his undying love for Minnie. Then came

World War II and the subsequent flooding of world markets with Mickey Mouse wristwatches. Because these watches were generally cheap affairs, subject to chronic and chronometric mainspring breakdowns, people started associating anything shoddy or trivial with *mickey mouse,* often lowercased, as in "I'm tired of having to do mickey mouse chores."

The pervasive and persuasive influence of mass marketing and advertising has dramatically speeded up the production of eponyms, and the manufacture of common nouns and verbs from brand names has become a burgeoning source of new words in the English language. When a product achieves wide popular appeal, its name may become a lowercase word for all products of its type, not just a particular brand. You might think that manufacturers would be flattered when their creations achieve such universal fame. On the contrary, companies will spend hundreds of thousands of dollars in legal fees to protect their trademarks from falling into the clutches of competitors.

Faced with such a catch-22 possibility, companies must protect and care for their trademarks, or they will be lost. Here is an alphabetical listing of fifty product names that have become somewhat generic but that have survived legal onslaughts and are still registered. If you don't believe me, look on packages containing these items, and you will still see a symbol of their registered status, such as TM or R, following each mark:

Baggies   *Beer Nuts*
Band-Aid   *Brillo Pads*

76

BVDs
Chap Stick
Coca-Cola/Coke
Cuisinart
Dictaphone
Dixie Cups
Fig Newtons
Frigidaire
Frisbee
Hi-Liter
Jeep
Jell-O
Jockey Shorts
Kitty Litter
Kleenex
Kodak
Ko-Rec-Type
Levi's
Life Savers
Liquid Paper
Mace
Magic Marker
Miltown

Novocain
NutraSweet
Ping-Pong
Plexiglas
Polaroid
Popsicle
Pop Tarts
Pyrex
Q-Tips
Rollerblade
Sanka
Scotch Tape
Sheetrock
Simoniz
Slim Jim
Styrofoam
Technicolor
TV Dinners
Vaseline
Xerox
Walkman
Wiffle Ball
X-Acto

Do you talk about xeroxing a document no matter what machine you use to do the photocopying? Beware: anyone who lowercases *xerox* runs the risk of hearing from the Xerox Corporation, which spends more than $100,000 a year to persuade the public not to say or write *xerox* when they mean "photocopy." The Johnson & Johnson Company writes admonishing letters to

The Cola Wars

any periodical that prints expressions like "band-aid diplomacy" or "band-aid economics." Although *band-aid* has come to stand for any medicinal plastic strip or merely cosmetic remedy, it is a registered trademark and, by law, should be capitalized. And, if you describe any plastic flying disk as a frisbee, you could get whammed by the Wham-O Manufacturing Company of San Gabriel, California. The idea for the plastic saucers came from the aerodynamic pie tins once manufactured by the Frisbie Bakery in Bridgeport, Connecticut, and the name *Frisbee* remains a registered asset.

For decades the Coca-Cola Company has been playing legal hardball to protect its name. While the courts have allowed other purveyors of soft drinks to use the name *Cola* because it is descriptive of the product, the Supreme Court decided in 1930 that the combination Coca-Cola and the clipped form Coke are the exclusive property of the company. In its most celebrated victory, in 1976, Coca-Cola won an injunction against Howard Johnson's restaurant chain for serving HoJo Cola in place of Coke without informing customers who asked for Coca-Cola by name.

It is ironic that the more successful a product, the more likely it is that its name will become an eponym and lose its privileged status as a result of lawsuits by competitors. The name *Zipper,* for example, was coined by the B.F. Goodrich Company in 1913 as the brand name for its slide fastener on overshoes. After numerous bouts in court, the company retained its rights to use the name on footwear, but to what avail? Zippers are everywhere, and *zipper,* now lowercased, belongs to us all. Aspirin, too, was once a brand name, but in 1921 the Bayer Company was deprived of its exclusive rights to the name. In his classic opinion, Judge Learned Hand stated that *aspirin* had become descriptive of the product itself and that consumers did not call the tablet by its chemical name, acetyl salicylic acid.

As a result of other court judgments, the sole rights to *thermos, escalator, cellophane,* and *yo-yo* slipped away from the King Seely, Otis Elevator, E. I. Du Pont, and F. Duncan companies respectively. Within the past few years the Miller Brewing Company has had to relinquish control of the word *Lite* on low-calorie beer, Parker Brothers has lost its monopoly on the name *Monopoly,* and the Nestlé Company has had to forfeit its exclusive use of the words *Toll House.*

The same fate has befallen other former brand names, such as *celluloid, corn flakes, cube steak, dry ice, formica, heroin, kerosene, lanolin, linoleum, linotype, milk of magnesia, mimeograph, pogo stick, raisin bran, shredded wheat,* and *trampoline.* These words have made such a successful journey from uppercase brand name to lowercase noun that it is difficult to believe that they were ever "owned" by a particular outfit. As more and more brand names become common descriptive terms, rather than labels that distinguish particular products, business will increasingly leave its trademark on our all-consuming English language.

Putting Words in
Their Places

Somebody once defined a hamburger as "a humble immigrant hunk of meat that came to this country from Germany and soared to fame on a bun." That somebody was perfectly right. In its native land the dish was originally called "Hamburg steak," taking its name from the West German city of Hamburg.

After the Hamburg steak arrived in the United States midway through the last century with the first great wave of German immigrants, its name began to change. Ultimately the Hamburg steak dropped its capital *H*, acquired the suffix *-er*, lost the *steak,* and moved from the platter to the plane between two slices of baked dough. Voilà: a hamburger.

The adventure in word evolution didn't stop there. Somewhere along the way, speakers of English liberally interpreted *burger* to mean "sandwich made with a bun." Once *burger* became a new word part, *cheeseburger, beefburger, baconburger, fishburger, chili-*

burger, and a trayful of other burgers entered the American scene and gullet. On a smaller scale, much the same adventure befell *frankfurter,* which takes its name from Frankfurt, Germany. *Furter* is now used to denote almost any kind of sandwich with protein slapped inside an elongated bun, as in *chickenfurter* and *fishfurter.*

Many years ago, cloth was imported into England from Silesia, then part of Germany. The material was of such poor quality that the English referred to it contemptuously as "that cloth from Silesia," or "Silesia cloth." Ultimately the phrase was shortened even further to "sleazy cloth," and that's how *sleazy* was fabricated as a popular adjective for "cheap and shoddy." Recently the word has spawned such offspring as *sleaze, sleaze-bag,* and *sleazeball.*

Place names have enriched our English language with many common words; many cities, towns, regions, and nations have become eponymously enshrined in our dictionaries, usually as uncapitalized nouns. When this happens, we call such transformations *toponyms.*

Often these words are the names of products associated with a particular location, and three of the most impressive categories of imports are alcoholic beverages, foods, and fabrics.

Among the most popular wines and liquors are amontillado (named for Montilla, Spain), asti (a town in northern Italy), beaujolais (a district in central France), bock beer (first produced in Einbeck, Germany), bordeaux (a region of southern France), bourbon (a county in Kentucky), burgundy (France), carlowitz (a town in Yugoslavia), champagne (France), chianti (a mountainous region in Italy), cognac (a commune in western France), daiquiri (a district in Cuba), gin (adapted from Geneva, Switzerland), a manhattan (New York), port (Oporto, Portugal), rum (Rome, Italy), sherry (Jerez, Spain), tequila (a Mexican district), and tokay (adapted from Tokaj in northeast Hungary).

To go with all that bubbly, on our table china (named for the country of China) may repose these foods: baloney (Bologna, Italy), brie (Brie district in France), brussels sprouts (Brussels, capital of Belgium), camembert cheese (Normandy, France), cantaloupe (papal villa of Cantalupo, Italy), cheddar cheese (Cheddar, England), cherrystone clams (Cheriton, Virginia), currants (Corinth, Greece), edam cheese (Edam, the Netherlands), java (Indonesian island of Java), lima beans (Lima, Peru), mayonnaise (from Mahon, a seaport in Minorca), parmesan cheese (Parma, an Italian commune), roquefort cheese (Roquefort, France), sardine (the Sardinian coast), swiss cheese (Switzerland), tangerine (Tangiers, Africa), vichyssoise (Vichy, France), welsh rarebit (Wales), and wiener (Wien, the German appellation for Vienna).

Among the textiles woven into the fabric of our language are calico (Calicut, India), cashmere (Kashmir, Iraq), cordovan (Cordoba, Spain), damask (Damascus, Syria), denim (de Nimes, France), duffel (Duffel, a town near Antwerp, Belgium), dungarees (Dhungaree, India), gauze (Gaza, Palestine), jeans (Genoa, Italy), madras (Madras, India), muslin (Mosul, Iraq), paisley (Paisley, Scotland), satin (Tzu-t'ing, China), suede (French for

"Sweden"), tulle (Tulle, France), and worsted (Worsted, now Worstead, England).

These product categories only begin to illustrate the place that places have in our language. Using the following descriptions, identify ten common words and put them in their places:

1. Two-piece swimsuits are named after a Pacific atoll on which hydrogen bombs were detonated—a truly explosive and figurative word.

2. The most popular of all humorous verse forms in English hails from a county in Ireland. One theory says that Irish mercenaries used to compose verses in that form about each other and then join in a chorus of "When we get back to ———— town, 'twill be a glorious morning."

3. A word for smooth-sounding flattery derives from the name of a castle in County Cork, Ireland. An inscription on the wall of the castle proclaims that anyone brave enough to scale the wall and kiss a particular stone will be rewarded with the gift of influencing others through cajolery.

4. Nearly two and a half millennia ago, a little band of ten thousand Athenians defeated a host of one hundred thousand Persians at the battle of ————. Pheidippides, a courageous runner, brought the news of the glorious victory to Athens, which lay twenty-six miles away.

5. Nineteenth-century sailors were sometimes drugged and then forced into service on ships plying the unpopular route from San Francisco to China. From the

name of that Chinese port we get the verb that means "to secure someone's services through force."

6. A contraction of "St. Mary's of Bethlehem," a sixteenth-century London hospital for the insane, has become a word for uproar or confusion.

7. Another word for disorder—in this case a wild brawl—comes down to us from the name of a fair, held in an Irish town near Dublin, infamous for its fistfights and rowdy behavior.

8. As an alternative to cumbersome tails on a formal full-dress dinner coat, a tailless dinner coat originated in an exclusive community about forty miles north of New York City. This short evening coat was an immediate sensation during the Gay Nineties; it is still obligatory at many formal functions a century later.

9. The Pilgrims found in America a wild fowl somewhat similar in appearance to a fowl they had known back in England—a bird that had acquired its name because it was first imported by way of a particular country. Because we perceive this bird as ugly in appearance and voice, we sometimes assign its name to people we don't care for.

10. The inhabitants of an ancient Greek city were noted for their ability to say a lot in a few words. During a siege of their capital, a Roman general sent a note to this city's commander warning that if the Romans captured the city, they would burn it to the ground. From within the city gates came back the terse reply: "If!" The city's name lives on in an adjective that describes spare speech.

Janus-Faced Words

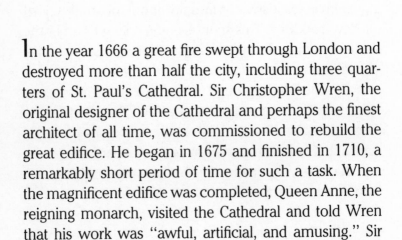

In the year 1666 a great fire swept through London and destroyed more than half the city, including three quarters of St. Paul's Cathedral. Sir Christopher Wren, the original designer of the Cathedral and perhaps the finest architect of all time, was commissioned to rebuild the great edifice. He began in 1675 and finished in 1710, a remarkably short period of time for such a task. When the magnificent edifice was completed, Queen Anne, the reigning monarch, visited the Cathedral and told Wren that his work was "awful, artificial, and amusing." Sir Christopher, so the story goes, was delighted with the royal compliment, because in those days *awful* meant "full of awe, awe-inspiring," *artificial* meant "artistic," and *amusing,* from the muses, meant "amazing."

That was three hundred years ago. Today, the older, flattering meanings of *awful, artificial,* and *amusing* have virtually disappeared from popular use. Indeed, the general rule of language is that when a single word de-

Janus

velops two polar meanings, one will become obsolete. Occasionally, though, two diametrically opposed meanings of the same English word survive, and the technical term for these contrarians is *contronym*. More popularly, they are known as Janus-faced words because the Greek god Janus had two faces that looked in opposite directions.

Here's a little finger exercise. Remember that I'm the teacher, so you must try to do what I ask. Make a circle with the fingers on your left hand by touching the tip of your index finger to the tip of your thumb. Now poke your head through that circle.

If you unsuccessfully tried to fit your head through the small digital circle, you (and almost any reader) thought that the phrase "poke your head" meant that your head was the poker. But if you raised your left hand with the circle of fingers up close to your forehead and poked your right index finger through that circle until it touched your forehead, you realized that the phrase "poke your head" has a second, and opposite, meaning: that the head is the pokee.

Here are two sentences that will solidify your understanding of how Janus-faced words work:

"The moon is VISIBLE tonight."

"The lights in the old house are always INVISIBLE."

Although the two capitalized words are opposite in meaning, both can be replaced by the same word—*out*. When the moon or sun or stars are out, they are visible. When the lights are out, they are invisible.

Here are some contronymic sentences that show

how words wander wondrously and testify to the fact that nothing in the English language is absolute:

with. alongside; against: *a.* England fought with France against Germany. *b.* England fought with France.

clip. fasten; separate: *a.* Clip the coupon to the newspaper. *b.* Clip the coupon from the newspaper.

fast. firmly in one place; rapidly from one place to another: *a.* The pegs held the tent fast. *b.* She ran fast.

bolt. to secure in place; to dart away: *a.* I'll bolt the door. *b.* Did you see the horse bolt?

trim. add things to; cut away: *a.* Let's trim the Christmas tree. *b.* Let's trim the hedge.

dust. remove material from; spread material on: *a.* Three times a week they dust the floor. *b.* Three times each season they dust the crops.

weather. withstand; wear away: *a.* Strong ships weather storms. *b.* Wind can weather rocks.

handicap. advantage, disadvantage: *a.* What's your handicap in golf? *b.* His lack of education is a handicap.

commencement. beginning; conclusion: *a.* Beautiful weather marked the commencement of spring. *b.* She won an award at her high school commencement.

hold up. support; hinder: *a.* Please hold up the sagging branch. *b.* Accidents hold up the flow of traffic.

keep up. continue to fall; continue to stay up: *a.* The farmers hope that the rain will keep up. *b.* Damocles hoped that the sword above his head would keep up.

left. departed from; remaining: *a.* Ten people left the room. *b.* Five people were left in the room.

dress. put items on; remove items from: *a.* Let's dress for the ball. *b.* Let's dress the chicken for cooking.

temper. soften; strengthen: *a.* You must temper your anger with reason. *b.* Factories temper steel with additives.

cleave. separate; adhere firmly: *a.* A strong blow will cleave a plank in two. *b.* Bits of metal cleave to a magnet.

strike. secure in place; remove: *a.* Use a firm grip to strike the nail. *b.* When the show is over, we'll strike the set.

give out. produce; stop producing: *a.* A good furnace will give out enough energy to heat the house. *b.* A broken furnace will often give out.

sanction. give approval of; censure: *a.* The NCAA plans to sanction the event. *b.* Should our country impose a new sanction on Iraq?

screen. view; hide from view: *a.* Tonight the critics will screen the film. *b.* Defensemen mustn't screen the puck.

oversight. careful supervision; neglect: *a.* The foreman was responsible for the oversight of the project. *b.* The foreman's oversight ruined the success of the project.

qualified. competent, limited: *a.* The candidate for the job was fully qualified. *b.* The dance was a qualified success.

moot. debatable, not worthy of debate: *a.* Capital punishment is a moot point. *b.* That the earth revolves around the sun is a moot point.

certain. definite, difficult to specify: *a.* I am certain about what I want in life. *b.* I have a certain feeling about the plan.

mortal. deadly, subject to death: *a.* The knight delivered a mortal blow. *b.* All humans are mortal.

a moot point

buckle. fasten together; fall apart: *a.* Safe drivers buckle their seat belts. *b.* Unsafe buildings buckle at the slightest tremor of the earth.

trip. to stumble; to move gracefully: *a.* Don't trip on the curb. *b.* Let's trip the light fantastic.

put out. generate; extinguish: *a.* The candle put out enough light for us to see. *b.* Before I went to bed, I put out the candle.

unbending. rigid; relaxing: *a.* On the job Smith is completely unbending. *b.* Relaxing on the beach is a good way of unbending.

wear. endure through use; decay through use: *a.* This suit will wear like iron. *b.* Water can cause mountains to wear.

scan. examine carefully; glance at hastily: *a.* I scan the poem. *b.* Each day, I scan the want ads.

fix. restore, remove part of: *a.* It's time to fix the fence. *b.* It's time to fix the bull.

seeded. with seeds; without seeds: *a.* The rain nourished the seeded field. *b.* Would you like some seeded raisins?

critical. opposed; essential to: *a.* Joanne is critical of our effort. *b.* Joanne is critical to our effort.

think better. admire more; be suspicious of: *a.* I think better of the first proposal than the second. *b.* If I were you, I'd think better of that proposal.

great deal. bargain; a lot of money: *a.* The cars are a great deal. *b.* The cars cost a great deal.

continue. proceed; put off proceeding: *a.* Let's continue negotiating. *b.* The judge decided to continue the case.

critical. essential; opposed: *a.* Her speech was critical to the campaign. *b.* He was critical of her speech.

stem. to emanate from; to shut off activity: *a.* The problem stems from a blown fuse. *b.* We must stem the tide of ignorance.

flush. to remove from sight; to cause to come into sight: *a.* Flush the dental floss down the drain. *b.* Flush out the quail from the bush.

below par. excellent; poor: *a.* Her below-par golf score won the tournament. *b.* I'm disappointed with your below-par performance on the spelling test.

down hill. adverse; easy: *a.* When the source of capital dried up, the fortunes of the corporation went down hill. *b.* After you switch to diet drinks, it will be all down hill for your weight-loss program.

impregnable. invulnerable to penetration; able to be impregnated: *a.* The castle was so strongly built that it was impregnable. *b.* Treatments exist for making a childless woman more impregnable.

block out. develop; conceal: *a.* The committee blocked out a plan. *b.* The smog blocked out the sun.

blow up. expand; destroy: *a.* Let's blow up the photograph of the air base. *b.* Let's blow up the air base.

take (double contronym). obtain; offer: *a.* Professional photographers take good pictures. *b.* Professional models take good pictures.

take. steal; earn: *a.* He took $100 from the dresser. *b.* He took $100 for mowing the lawn.

wind up. start; end: *a.* I have to wind up my watch. *b.* Now I have to wind up this discussion of curious and contrary contronyms.

A Hymn to Heteronyms

Here's a little poem that I've made up. As you read my ditty, note the unusual pattern of end-rhymes:

> Listen, readers, toward me bow.
> Be friendly; do not draw the bow.
> Please don't try to start a row.
> Sit peacefully, all in a row.
> Don't squeal like a big, fat sow.
> Do not the seeds of discord sow.

In the first, third, and fifth lines of this poem, *bow, row,* and *sow* all rhyme with *cow* and mean, respectively, "to bend," "argument," and "female pig." In the second, fourth, and sixth lines, *bow, row,* and *sow* all rhyme with *low* and mean, respectively, "a weapon," "a line," and "to plant."

Bow, row, and *sow* are choice examples of heteronyms—words with the same spelling as other words but with different pronunciations and meanings. Membership in the exclusive club of heteronyms is strict, and tandems such as *resume* and *résumé* and *pate* and *pâté* are not admitted because the accent constitutes a change in spelling. Pseudo-heteronymic pairs like *insult* (noun) and *insult* (verb), *refuse* (noun) and *refuse* (verb), *read* (present-tense verb) and *read* (past-tense verb), and *primer* (beginner's book) and *primer* (base coat of paint) are fairly common in the English language, but they are not true heteronyms because their etymologies are so closely related. True heteronymic pairs that are not clearly related in word formation are among the rarest of occurrences. Here's a comprehensive list of genuine, authentic, certified heteronyms. Accept no substitutes:

agape	dove	mole	rape
alum	entrance	moped	raven
axes	evening	more	reprobate
bases	fillet	nestling	resent
bass	forte	number	reside
bow	grave	object	resign
buffet	hinder	overage	resort
coax	incense	palled	route
console	lead	palsy	row
content	liver	pasty	sake
converse	lower	peaked	salve
coop	lunged	present	secretive
deserts	mare	pussy	sewer
do	minute	putting	shower
does	mobile	ragged	singer

skied	stingy	taxes	tush
slaver	sundries	tear	unionized
slough	supply	toots	wicked
sol	tarry	tower	wind
sow			wound

Rather than march along sentence by sentence, let's skip along through a poetic hymn to heteronyms:

Please go through the *entrance* of this little poem.
    I guarantee it will *entrance* you.
The *content* will certainly make you *content*,
    And the knowledge gained sure will enhance you.

A boy *moped* around when his parents refused
    For him a new *moped* to buy.
The *incense* he burned did *incense* him to go
    On a *tear* with a *tear* in his eye.

He *ragged* on his parents, felt they ran him *ragged*
    His just *deserts* they never gave.
He imagined them out on some *deserts* so dry,
    Where for water they'd search and they'd rave.

At *present* he just won't *present* or *converse*
    On the *converse* of each high-flown theory
Of circles and *axes* in math class; he has
    Many *axes* to grind, isn't cheery.

He tried to play baseball, but often *skied* out,
    So when the snows came, he just *skied*.
But he then broke a leg *putting* on his ski boots,
    And his *putting* in golf was in need.

a bass bass

He once held the *lead* in a cross country race,
    Till his legs started feeling like *lead*.
And when the pain *peaked*, he looked kind of *peaked*.
    His *liver* felt *liver*, then dead.

A *number* of times he felt *number*, all *wound*
    Up, like one with a *wound*, not a wand.
His new TV *console* just couldn't *console*
    Or *slough* off a *slough* of despond.

The *rugged* boy paced 'round his shaggy *rugged* room,
    And he spent the whole *evening* till dawn
Evening out the cross-*winds* of his hate.
    Now my anecdote *winds* on and on.

He thought: "*Does* the prancing of so many *does*
    Explain why down *dove* the white *dove*,
Or why *pussy* cat has a *pussy* old sore
    And *bass* sing in *bass* notes of their love?"

Do they always sing, "*Do* re mi" and stare, *agape*,
    At eros, *agape*, each *minute?*
Their love's not *minute;* there's an *overage* of love.
    Even *overage* fish are quite in it.

These bass fish have never been in short *supply*
    As they *supply* spawn without waiting.
With their love fluids bubbling, abundant, *secretive*,
    There's many a *secretive* mating.

Retro-Active Words

Have you noticed that a number of simple nouns have recently acquired new adjectives?

What we used to call, simply, "books," for example, we now call *hardcover books* because of the production of paperback books. What was once simply a guitar is now an *acoustic guitar* because of the popularity of electric guitars. What was once just soap is now called *bar soap* since the invention of powdered and liquid soaps.

Frank Mankiewicz, once an aide to Robert Kennedy, invented a term for these new compounds. He called them *retronyms,* using the classical word parts *retro,* "back," and *nym,* "name or word." A retronym is an adjective-noun pairing generated by a change in the meaning of the noun, usually because of advances in technology. Retronyms, like retrospectives, are backward glances.

When I grew up, there were only Coke, turf, and

mail. Nowadays, Diet Coke, new Coke, artificial turf, and e-mail have spawned the retronyms *real Coke, Classic Coke, natural turf,* and *snail mail* or *hard mail.* Once there were simply movies. Then movies began to talk, necessitating the retronym *silent movies.* Then came color movies and the contrasting term *black-and-white movies.* Once there was television. Along came color television and the retronym *black-and-white television.* Then came cable television and the retronym *on-air television.*

Even time, which used to wait for no man, now does because it can be captured on audio and videotape. As a result, we now have something called real time. Once, all we had was reality—what could be more real? Now we have virtual reality. So what are the retronyms—*unreal time* and *actual reality?*

I remember being astonished when one of my students at St. Paul's School told me that he had missed my class because he had set his alarm for A.M. rather than P.M. On our old clocks, that would have been impossible, but on digital clocks it happens all the time. So what used to be just a clock (or watch) is now an analog, versus a digital, clock.

Other retronyms we use today include:

old term (protonym)	new term	retronym
watch	wristwatch	pocket watch
telephone	Touch-Tone telephone	rotary phone

play	radio/screen television play	stage play
cigarette	filter cigarette	nonfilter cigarette
milk	skim milk	whole milk
peanut butter	crunchy peanut butter	creamy peanut butter
orange juice	frozen orange juice	fresh squeezed
pen	ballpoint pen	fountain pen
baseball	night baseball	day baseball
razor	electric/safety razor	straight razor
bicycle	mountain/ stationary bicycle	road bicycle
war	nuclear war	conventional war

Coining a retronym for an object is sometimes like waving it a nostalgic good-bye. Retronyms can signal that the thing double labeled has become outmoded and obsolete, the superseded exception rather than the rule. This is what has happened to *black-and-white TV, manual typewriters, treadle sewing machines, reel-to-reel tape recorders,* and *rotary phones.*

Given the dizzying pace of commercial innovations, retronyms are bound to keep on coming. Any day now, we'll have brand new retronyms, such as *corded tele-*

phone, phoneless car, low-definition TV, and *nonmicrowave oven.*

What with phone sex and safe sex, could we one day have the retronym *full-participation sex?* I hope not. And here are some other retronyms I pray will never come to pass—*graffitiless wall, nonelectronic book, teacher-staffed school, monogamous couple,* and *double-parent family.*

3

FIGURATIVELY SPEAKING

"Prose is a museum where all the old weapons of poetry are kept."

—T. E. HULME

A Visit to the Language Zoo

Many children's magazines feature picture puzzles in which the young readers are asked to identify a number of hidden animals. In a cloud may lurk a cow, in the leaves of a tree may be concealed a fish, and on the side of a house may be soaring an eagle. The English language is like those children's pictures. Take a gander at what follows, and you will discover almost three hundred creatures from the animal world hidden in the sentences, a veritable menagerie of zoological metaphors. (Did you catch one of them in the last sentence?)

Human beings, proclaims one dictionary, are distinguished from the other animals "by a notable development of brain with a resultant capacity for speech and abstract reasoning." Perhaps so, but how truly different is our species from our fellow organisms with whom we share the planet?

I mean holy cow, holy cats, and holy mackerel—a little bird told me that the human race is filled with congressional hawks and doves who fight like cats and dogs 'til the cows come home, Wall Street bulls and bears who make a beeline for the goose that lays the golden egg, cold fish and hotdoggers, early birds and night owls, lone wolves and social butterflies, young lions and old crows, and lame ducks, sitting ducks, and dead ducks.

Some people are horny studs on the prowl for other party animals, strutting peacocks who preen and fish for compliments, clotheshorses who put on the dog with their turtlenecks and hush puppies, young bucks and po- nytailed foxy chicks in puppy love who want to get hitched, or cool cats and kittenish lovebirds who avoid stag parties to bill and coo and pet and paw each other in their love nests.

Other people have a whale of an appetite that com- pels them to eat like pigs (not birds), drink like fish, stuff themselves to the gills, hog the lion's share, and wolf their elephantine portions until they become plump as partridges. Still others are batty, squirrelly, bug-eyed, cockeyed cuckoos who are mad as march hares and look like something the cat dragged in; crazy as coots, loons, or bedbugs; and who come at us like bats out of hell with their monkeyshines and drive us buggy with their horsing around.

As we continue to separate the sheep from the goats and to pigeonhole the "human" race, we encoun- ter catnapping, slothful sluggards; harebrained jackasses who, like fish out of water, doggedly think at a snail's pace; dumb bunnies and dumb clucks who run around like chickens with their heads cut off; birdbrained dodos who are easily gulled, buffaloed, and outfoxed; asinine

a lame duck

silly gooses who lay an egg whenever, like monkey-see-monkey-do, they parrot and ape every turkey they see; clumsy oxen who are bulls in china shops; and top dogs on their high horses, big fish in small ponds, and cocky bullies high up in the pecking order who rule the roost and never work for chicken feed.

Leapin' lizards, we can scarcely get through a day without meeting crestfallen, pussyfooting chickens who stick their heads in the sand; henpecked underdogs who get goose pimples and butterflies and turn tail; scared rabbits who play possum and cry crocodile tears before they go belly up; spineless jellyfish who clam up with a frog in the throat whenever the cat gets their tongue; mousy worms who quail and flounder and then, quiet as mice, slink off and then return to the fold with their tails between their legs; and shrimpy pipsqueaks who fawn like toadies until you want to go belly up and croak.

Let's face it. It's a dog-eat-dog world we live in. But doggone it, without beating a dead horse, I do not wish to duck or leapfrog over this subject. It's time to fish or cut bait, to take the bull by the horns, kill two birds with one stone, and, before everything goes to the dogs and we've got a tiger by the tail, to give you a bird's-eye view of the animals hiding in our language.

Dog my cats! It's a bear of a task to avoid meeting catty, shrewish, bitchy vixens with bees in their bonnets whose pet peeve and sacred cow is that all men are swine and chauvinist pigs and in their doghouse. Other brutes who get your goat and ruffle your feathers are antsy, backbiting, crabby, pigheaded old buzzards,

smelling a rat

coots, and goats who are no spring chickens, who are stubborn as mules, and who grouse, bug, badger, dog, and hound you like squawking, droning, waspish gadflies that stir up a hornets' nest and make a mountain out of a molehill.

And speaking of beastly characters that stick in your craw, watch out for the parasites, bloodsuckers, sponges, and leeches who worm their way into your consciousness and make you their scapegoats; the rat finks and stool pigeons who ferret out your deepest secrets and then squeal on you, let the cat out of the bag, and fly the coop without so much as a "Tough turkey. See you later, alligator"; the snakes-in-the-grass who come out of the woodwork, open a can of worms, and then, before you smell a rat, throw you a red herring; the serpentine quacks who make you their gullible guinea pig and cat's-paw; the lowdown curs and dirty dogs who sling the bull, give you a bum steer, and send you on a wild goose chase barking up the wrong tree on a wing and a prayer; the card sharks who hawk their fishy games, monkey with your nest egg, put the sting on you, and then fleece you; the vultures who hang like albatrosses around your neck, who live high on the hog, who feather their own nests and then—the straw that breaks the camel's back—crow about it looking like the cat that swallowed the canary; the black sheep who play cat and mouse and then cook your goose and make a monkey out of you with their shaggy dog stories before they hightail it out of there; and the lousy varmints, polecats, skunks, and eels who sell you a white elephant or a pig in a poke and, when the worm turns and you discover the fly in the ointment, weasel their way out of the deal.

It's a real jungle out there, just one unbridled rat race; in fact, it's for the birds.

But let's talk turkey and horse sense. Don't we go a tad ape and hog wild over the bright-eyed and bushy-tailed eager beavers who always go whole hog to hit the bull's-eye; the eagle-eyed tigers who are always loaded for bear; and the ducky, loosey-goosey rare birds who are wise as owls and happy as larks and clams? Lucky dogs like these are the cat's pajamas and the cat's meow, worthy of being lionized. From the time they're knee-high to a grasshopper, they're in the catbird seat and the world is their oyster.

So before you buzz off, I hope you'll agree that this exhibit of animal metaphors has been no fluke, no hog-wash, no humbug. I really give a hoot about the animals hiding in our English language, so, for my swan song, I want you to know that, straight from the horse's mouth, this has been no dog-and-pony show and no cock-and-bull story.

It really is a zoo out there.

You Said a Mouthful

Now that you have uncovered the hidden herds of animals, flocks of birds, swarms of insects, and universities of fish that metaphorically run, fly, creep, and swim through our English language, it's time to nibble on another spicy, meaty, juicy honey of a topic that I know you'll want to savor and relish. Feast your eyes now on the veritable potpourri of mushrooming food expressions that grace the table of our English language and season our tongue. As we chew the fat about the food-filled phrases that are packed like sardines and sandwiched into our everyday conversations, I'll sweeten the pot with some tidbits of food for thought guaranteed to whet your appetite.

I know what's eating you. I've heard through the grapevine that you don't give a fig because you think I'm nutty as a fruitcake; that you're fed up with me for biting off more than I can chew; that you want me to drop this subject like a hot potato because I'm a spoiled rotten weenie; and that you're giving me the raspberry for asking you to swallow a cheesy, corny, mushy, saccharine, seedy, soupy, sugarcoated, syrupy topic that just isn't your cup of tea.

I understand that you're beet red with anger that I'm feeding you a bunch of baloney, garbage, and tripe; that I've rubbed salt in your wounds by making you ruminate on a potboiler that's no more than a tempest in a teapot; that I've upset your apple cart by rehashing an old chestnut that's just pie in the sky and won't amount to a hill of beans; that you want to chew me out for putting words in your mouth; that you're boiling and simmering because you think I'm a candy-assed apple polisher who's out to egg you on.

But nuts to all that. That's the way the cookie crumbles. Eat your heart out and stop crying in your beer. I'm going to stop mincing words and start cooking with gas, take my idea off the back burner and bring home the bacon without hamming it up. No matter how you slice it, this fruitful, tasteful topic is the greatest thing since sliced bread, the icing on the cake. Rather than crying over spilt milk and leaping out of the frying pan and into the fire, I'm going to put all my eggs into one basket, take potluck, and spill the beans. I'm cool as a cucumber and confident that this crackerjack, peachy-keen, vintage feast that I've cooked up will have you eating out of the palm of my hand.

I don't wish to become embroiled in a rhubarb, but your beefing and stewing sound like sour grapes from a tough nut to crack—kind of like the pot calling the kettle black. But if you've digested the spoonfed culinary meta-

pie in the sky

phors up to this point in this meat-and-potatoes chapter, the rest will be gravy, duck soup, a piece of cake, and easy as pie—just like taking candy from a baby.

Just think of the various people we meet every day. Some have taste. Others we take with a grain of salt. Some drive us bananas and crackers. Still others are absolutely out to lunch:

- the young sprouts and broths of lads who feel their oats and are full of beans;
- the salty, crusty oldsters who are wrinkled as prunes and live to a ripe old age well beyond their salad days;
- the peppery smart cookies (no mere eggheads, they) who use their beans and noodles to cut the mustard;
- the half-baked meat heads, the flaky couch potatoes, and the pudding-headed vegetables who drive us nuts with their slow-as-molasses peabrains and who gum up the works and are always in a pickle, a jam, hot water, the soup, or a fine kettle of fish;
- the unsavory, crummy, hard-boiled, ham-fisted rotten apples with their cauliflower ears, who can cream us, beat the stuffing out of us, make us into mincemeat and hamburger, and knock us ass over teakettle and flatter than a pancake;
- the mealymouthed marshmallows, Milquetoasts, milksops, half-pints, and cream puffs who walk on eggshells and whose knees turn to jelly as they gingerly waffle and fudge on every issue to see which side their bread is buttered on;
- the carrot-topped, pizza-faced string beans and

top banana

bean poles who, with their lumpy Adam's apples, are long drinks of water;

• the top bananas, big cheeses, and big breadwinners who ride the gravy train by making a lot of lettuce and dough and who never work for peanuts or small potatoes;

• the honeys, tomatoes, dumplings, cheesecakes, and sweetie pies with their peaches-and-cream complexions, strawberry blond hair, almond eyes, and cherry lips;

• the saucy tarts who wiggle their melons and buns and fritter away their time buttering up their meal tickets and milking their sugar daddies dry;

• the salt-of-the-earth good eggs who take the cake, know their onions, make life a bowl of cherries, and become the apples of our eye and the toasts of the town.

Hot dog! I hope you're pleased as punch that this souped-up topic is a plum, not a lemon: the berries, not the pits. The proof of the pudding is in the eating, and this cream of the crop of palate-pleasing food figures is bound to sell like hotcakes. I'm no glutton for punishment for all the tea in China, but, if I'm wrong, I'll eat crow and humble pie. I don't wish to take the words right out of your mouth, but, in a nutshell, it all boils down to the fact that every day we truly eat our words.

Violent English

Everybody deplores violence these days. Many articles and books, radio and television programs, and self-help and encounter groups are designed to help us curb our tempers. And with the specters of international terrorism and nuclear warfare haunting our horizon, it may be that the future of the human race depends upon our ability to channel our violent impulses and to locate solutions based on cooperation rather than aggression.

When we *tackle, wrestle,* and *grapple* with the problem of violence, we are bound to be *struck* by a crucial idea. If our view of reality is shaped and defined by the words and phrases we use, then violence is locked deep in our thoughts, frozen in the clichés and expressions of everyday life. "I'll be *hanged!*" we are likely to exclaim as this insight *hits* us with a *vengeance.* "I believe that I've *hit* the nail right on the head!"

Let's take a *stab* at the issue of violence in our everyday parlance with a *crash* course on the words we

"I'll be hanged!"

twisting someone's arm

use to describe disagreements. First, we *rack* our brains assembling an *arsenal* of arguments. Then we attempt to *demolish* the opposition's points with a *barrage* of criticism, *attack* their positions by *nailing them dead to rights, letting them have it with both barrels,* and *shooting down* their contentions. We *break* their concentration by *puncturing* their assumptions, *cut them down to size* by *hammering* away at their weaknesses, *torpedo* their efforts with *barbed* criticism, and then, when *push* comes to *shove, assault* their integrity with character *assassination.* If all else fails, we try to *twist their arms* and *kill* them with kindness.

Now we can begin to understand the full *impact* of the expression "to have a *violent disagreement.*"

The world of business is a veritable *jungle* of *cutthroat* competition, a *rough-and-tumble* school of *hard knocks,* and a *dog-eat-dog* world of *backbiting, backstabbing,* and *hatchet* jobs. Some companies *spearhead* a trend of price *gouging.* Other firms *beat* the competition to the *punch* and gain a *stranglehold* on the market by *fighting tooth and nail* to *slash* prices in *knock-down-drag-out, no-holds-barred* price *wars.* Still other companies gain *clout* by putting the *squeeze* on their competitors with *shakeups, raids,* and *hostile takeovers.* Then the other side gets *up in arms* and *screams bloody murder* about such a *low blow.*

No wonder that business executives are often recruited by *headhunters.* No wonder that *bleeding hearts* who can't *fight their own battles* are likely to get *axed, booted, canned, discharged, dumped, fired, kicked out, sacked,* or *terminated.*

One would hope that sporting contests would provide an escape from life's daily *grind*. But once again we find mayhem and havoc embedded in the adversarial expressions of matters athletic. In fact, we can't get within *striking* distance of a big game without *running* or *bumping* into some ticket *scalper* who's out to *rip us off* and get away with *murder*. Once inside the stadium or arena, we witness two teams trying to *battle, beat, clobber, crush, dominate, maul, pulverize, rout, slaughter, steamroll, thrash, throttle, wallop, whip, wipe out, kick the pants off, make mincemeat out of, stick it to,* and *wreak havoc on* each other with *battle plans* that include *suicide squeezes, grand slams, blitzes, shotgun offenses, aerial bombs, punishing ground attacks,* and *slam dunks*. Naturally both sides hope that they won't *choke* in *sudden death* overtime.

Fleeing the battlefields of athletics at *breakneck* speed, we seek release from our violent language by taking in some entertainment. We look to *kill* some time at a *dynamite* show that's supposed to be a *smash hit blockbuster* and a *slapstick riot* that we'll get a *kick* and a *bang* out of. But the whole *shootin'* match turns out to be a *bomb* and a *dud,* rather than a *blast* and a *bash*.

The lead may be a *knockout* and *stunning bombshell,* but she *butchers* her lines and her *clashing* outfit *grates* on our nerves. Sure as *shootin',* we're *burned up* and bored to *death* with the sheer *torture* of it all. We feel like *tearing* our hair out, *eating our heart out, gnashing* our teeth, *snapping* at others, and *kicking* ourselves. So, all *bent out of shape,* we go off *half-cocked* and *beat* it home feeling like *battered, heartbroken* nervous *wrecks.* The situation is *explosive.* We've been through the *meat grinder,* and we're ready to *blow* our tops and stacks, *shoot* off our mouths, *wring* somebody's neck, *knock* his block and socks off, and go on the *warpath.* We've got a real ax to grind.

Even alcohol and drugs won't offer any releases from the prison of violence in which we English speakers are incarcerated. However *blitzed, bombed, hammered, plowed, smashed, stoned,* or *wasted* we become, we must eventually *crash.* It's like using a double-edged *sword* to *cut off* our nose to spite our face.

If language is truly a window to the world and if the words and expressions we use truly affect the way we think, can we ever really stamp out violence?

4

UNMECHANICAL
ENGLISH

"English usage is sometimes more than mere taste,
judgment, and education. Sometimes it's sheer
luck, like getting across the street."

—E. B. WHITE

Farmer Pluribus

Foxen in the Henhice

Recently I undertook an extensive study of American dialects, and a friend told me about a farmer named Eben Pluribus who spoke a most unusual kind of English. So I went to visit Farmer Pluribus, and here is a transcript of our interview:

"Mr. Pluribus, I hear that you've had some trouble on the farm."

"Well, young fella, times were hard for a spell. Almost every night them danged foxen were raiding my henhice."

"Excuse me, sir," I interjected. "Don't you mean foxes?"

"Nope, I don't," Pluribus replied. "I use oxen to plow my fields, so it's foxen that I'm trying to get rid of."

"I see. But what are henhice?" I asked.

"Easy. One mouse, two mice; one henhouse, two henhice. You must be one of them city slickers, but surely you know that henhice are what them birds live

in that, when they're little critters, they utter all them peep."

"I think I'm beginning to understand you, Mr. Pluribus. But don't you mean peeps?"

"Nope, I mean peep. More than one sheep is a flock of sheep, and more than one peep is a bunch of peep. What do you think I am, one of them old ceet?"

"I haven't meant to insult you, sir," I gulped. "But I can't quite make out what you're saying."

"Then you must be a touch slow in the head," Farmer Pluribus shot back. "One foot, two feet; one coot, two ceet. I'm just trying to easify the English language, so I make all regular plural nouns irregular. Once they're all irregular, then it's just the same like they're all regular."

"Makes perfect sense to me," I mumbled.

"Good boy," said Pluribus, and a gleam came into his eyes. "Now, as I was trying to explain, them pesky foxen made such a fuss that all the meese and lynges have gone north."

"Aha!" I shouted. "You're talking about those big antlered animals, aren't you? One goose, two geese; one moose, a herd of meese. And lynges is truly elegant— one sphinx, a row of sphinges; one lynx, a litter of lynges."

"You're a smart fella, sonny," smiled Pluribus. "You see, I used to think that my cose might scare away them foxen, but the cose were too danged busy chasing rose."

"Oh, oh. You've lost me again," I lamented. "What are cose and rose?"

"Guess you ain't so smart after all," Pluribus

sneered. "If *those* is the plural of *that,* then *cose* and *rose* got to be the plurals of *cat* and *rat.*"

"Sorry that I'm so thick, but I'm really not one of those people who talk through their hose," I apologized, picking up Pluribus's cue. "Could you please tell me what happened to the foxen in your henhice?"

"I'd be pleased to," answered Pluribus. "What happened was that my brave wife, Una, grabbed one of them frying pen and took off after them foxen."

I wondered for a moment what frying pen were and soon realized that because the plural of *man* is *men,* the plural of *pan* had to be *pen.*

"Well," Pluribus went right on talking, "the missus wasn't able to catch them foxen so she went back to the kitchen and began throwing dish and some freshly made pice at them critters."

That part of the story stumped me for a time, until I reasoned that a school of fish is made up of fish and more than one die make a roll of dice so that Una Pluribus must have grabbed a stack of dishes and pies.

Pluribus never stopped. "Them dish and pice sure scarified them foxen, and the pests have never come back. In fact, the rest of the village heard about what my wife did, and they were so proud that they sent the town band out to the farm to serenade her with tubae, harmonicae, accordia, fives, and dra."

"Hold up!" I gasped. "Give me a minute to figure out those musical instruments. The plural of *formula* is *formulae,* so the plurals of *tuba* and *harmonica* must be *tubae* and *harmonicae.* And the plurals of *phenomenon* and *criterion* are *phenomena* and *criteria,* so the plural of *accordion* must be *accordia.*"

"You must be one of them genii," Pluribus exclaimed.

"Maybe," I blushed. "One cactus, two cacti; one alumnus, an association of alumni. So one genius, a seminar of genii. But let me get back to those instruments. The plurals of *life* and *wife* are *lives* and *wives,* so the plural of *fife* must be *fives.* And the plural of *medium* is *media,* so the plural of *drum* must be *dra.* Whew! That last one was tough."

"Good boy, sonny. Well, my wife done such a good job of chasing away them foxen that the town newspaper printed up a story and ran a couple of photographim of her holding them pen, dish, and pice."

My brain was now spinning in high gear, so it took me but an instant to realize that Farmer Pluribus had regularized one of the most exotic plurals in the English language—seraph, seraphim; so photograph, photographim. I could imagine all those Pluribi bathing in their bathtubim, as in cherub, cherubim; bathtub, bathtubim.

"Well," crowed Pluribus. "I was mighty pleased that everybody was so nice to the missus, but that ain't no surprise since folks in these here parts show a lot of respect for their methren."

"Brother, brethren; mother, methren," I rejoined. "That thought makes me want to cry. Have you any boxen of Kleenices here?"

"Sure do, young fella. And I'm tickled pink that you've caught on to the way I've easified the English language. One index, two indices, and one appendix, two appendices. So one Kleenex, two Kleenices. Makes things simpler, don't it?"

I was so grateful to Farmer Pluribus for having taught me his unique dialect that I took him out to one of them local cafeteriae. Then I reported my findings to the American Dialect Society by calling from one of the telephone beeth in the place.

Yep, you've got it. One tooth, two teeth. One telephone booth, two telephone beeth. Makes things simpler, don't it?

Tense Times with Verbs

Have you heard the one about the man who went to trial for having pulled a woman down a street by the hair? When the judge asked the arresting officer, "Was she drugged?" the policeman answered, "Yes sir, a full block." Or the one about the woman who asked a Boston cab driver where she could get scrod. "I didn't know that the verb had that past tense," muttered the cabbie.

Both jokes rely on the fact that verb tenses in English are crazy, fraught with a fearful asymmetry and puzzling unpredictability. Some verbs form their past tense by adding *-d, -ed,* or *-t*—*walk, walked; bend, bent.* Others go back in time through an internal vowel change—*begin, began; sing, sang.* Another cluster adds *-d* or *-t* and undergoes an internal vowel change—*lose, lost; buy, bought.* And still others don't change at all—*set, set; put, put.* No wonder, then, that our eyes glaze and our breath quickens when we have to form

"I didn't know that the verb had that past tense."

the past tense of verbs like *dive, weave, shine, sneak,* and *baby-sit.*

The past tenses of verbs in our language cause so many of us to become tense that I've written a poem about the insanity:

The verbs in English are a fright.
How can we learn to read and write?
Today we speak, but first we spoke;
Some faucets leak, but never loke.
Today we write, but first we wrote;
We bite our tongues, but never bote.

Each day I teach, for years I taught,
And preachers preach, but never praught.
This tale I tell; this tale I told;
I smell the flowers, but never smold.

If knights still slay, as once they slew,
Then do we play, as once we plew?
If I still do as once I did,
Then do cows moo, as they once mid?

I love to win, and games I've won;
I seldom sin, and never son.
I hate to lose, and games I lost;
I didn't choose, and never chost.

I love to sing, and songs I sang;
I fling a ball, but never flang.
I strike that ball, that ball I struck;
This poem I like, but never luck.

I take a break, a break I took;
I bake a cake, but never book.
I eat that cake, that cake I ate;
I beat an egg, but never bate.

I often swim, as I once swam;
I skim some milk, but never skam.
I fly a kite that I once flew;
I tie a knot, but never tew.

I see the truth, the truth I saw;
I flee from falsehood, never flaw.
I stand for truth, as I once stood;
I land a fish, but never lood.

About these verbs I sit and think.
These verbs don't fit. They seem to wink
At me, who sat for years and thought
Of verbs that never fat or wought.

I beat an egg, but never bate.

Spellbound

In 1750, Phillip, Fourth Earl of Chesterfield, wrote, in a letter to his son, "One false spelling may fix a stigma upon a man for life." If Lord Chesterfield's chilling dictum is true, all of us are stigmatized, for who among us has not stumbled into the potholes and booby traps that dot the terrain of English orthography?

Indeed, with the possible exceptions of sports commissioners and unsuccessful presidential candidates, there is no more popular object of abuse and ridicule than our "system" of English spelling. Once, when trying to write a Presidential paper, Andrew Jackson blew his stack and cried, "It's a damn poor mind that can think of only one way to spell a word!" Linguists Otto Jespersen and Mario Pei offer more professional pronouncements: Spelling is a "pseudohistorical and antieducational abomination" that is "the world's most awesome mess."

These are strong words, but even the briefest

glance at the situation reveals that they are quite just. In what other language can one find the pairs *publicly* and *basically, four* and *forty, float* and *flotation, led* and *read* (past tense), *harass* and *embarrass, deceit* and *receipt?* In what other language can *manslaughter* and *man's laughter* be spelled with exactly the same letters? In what other language can *coffee* be misspelled *kauphy* and *usage, yowzitch*—not a single correct letter in the bunch!

Long ago T. S. Watt published a poem titled "English" in the *Manchester Guardian:*

I take it you already know
Of *tough* and *bough* and *cough* and *dough?*
Others may stumble, but not you
On *hiccough, thorough, lough,* and *through.*
Well done! And now you wish, perhaps,
To learn of less familiar traps?

Beware of *heard,* a dreadful word
That looks like *beard* and sounds like *bird.*
And *dead:* it's said like *bed,* not *bead*—
For goodness' sake don't call it "deed"!
Watch out for *meat* and *great* and *threat.*
(They rhyme with *suite* and *straight* and *debt.*)
A moth is not a moth in *mother,*
Nor *both* in *bother, broth* in *brother,*
And *here* is not a match for *there,*
Nor *dear* and *fear* for *bear* and *pear,*
And then there's *dose* and *rose* and *lose*
Just look them up—and *goose* and *choose,*

And *cork* and *work* and *card* and *ward,*
And *font* and *front* and *word* and *sword,*
And *do* and *go* and *thwart* and *cart*—
Come, come, I've hardly made a start!

A dreadful language? Man alive!
I'd mastered it when I was five.
And yet to write it, the more I tried,
I hadn't learned at fifty five.

The most prominent cause of all this whoop-de-do (also whoop-de-doo) about English orthography is the considerable distance that stretches between the sounds of our words and their spelling—a state of affairs created by the inadequacy of our Roman alphabet to represent all the sounds of English; our cheerful willingness to borrow words and, with them, unconventional sounds from other languages; and, finally, the gradual changes in the way we pronounce words, most of which have not been matched by repairs to our spelling. The result is that about eighty percent of our words are not spelled phonetically. In effect, we have two languages, one spoken and one written.

One way to explore the chasm that divides phonology from orthography is to examine how letters, alone or in combination, can represent a variety of disparate sounds. The *e*'s in *reentered,* for example, have four different pronunciations, including one silent letter. A favorite target of the scoffers is the letter string *ough,* a terror that can produce at least ten distinct sounds, as in *bough, bought, cough, dough, hiccough, lough, rough,*

thoroughbred, through, and *trough.* Further evidence that letters do not represent specific sounds comes from the story about a sign a GI saw on a post in Italy during World War II:

```
T   O   T   I
E   M   U   L
E   S   T   O
```

What did the sign spell? "TO TIE MULES TO."

What most complicates the situation is that English spelling is haunted by what William Watt calls "the little ghosts of silent letters." Indeed, it has been estimated that two thirds of our lexicon is populated with these mischievous specters, leading Thorstein Veblen to proclaim: "English orthography satisfies all the requirements of the canons of reputability under the law of conspicuous waste."

Confronted by such delicious chaos, the intrepid logophile is moved to ask: Are there contexts in which all twenty-six letters in the alphabet are mute? I believe that the answer is "yes" and offer this lineup, with multiple settings wherever possible, to demonstrate the deafening silence that rings through English orthography:

A:　algae, bread, marriage, pharaoh

B:　doubt, thumb

C:　blackguard, Connecticut, indict, science

D: edge, handkerchief, Wednesday

E: height, hope, steak, yeoman

F: halfpenny

G: gnome, reign, tight

H: bough, ghost, honor, rhyme

I: bait, business, thief, Sioux

J: rijsttafel

K: blackguard, know

L: halfpenny, Lincoln, salmon, would

M: mnemonic

N: column

O: country, laboratory, people, tortoise

P: cupboard, pneumonia, psychiatry, receipt

Q: racquet

R: forecastle, Worcester

S: aisle, debris, island, rendezvous

George Bernard Shaw

T: gourmet, listen, parfait, rapport

U: circuit, dough, gauge, guide

V: flivver, savvy

W: answer, cockswain, two, wrist

X: faux pas, grand prix, Sioux

Y: aye, crayon

Z: pince-nez, rendezvous*

Now let us reverse our field. Not only can certain letters represent a variety of sounds (and silences); we also find that a single sound can be recorded by many different letters. George Bernard Shaw, who first championed and then bequeathed a sizable (also sizeable) sum of money to the cause of spelling reform, once announced that he had discovered a new way to spell the word *fish.* His fabrication was *ghoti: gh* as in enou*gh*, *o* as in w*o*men, and *ti* as in na*ti*on. But there are many other "fish" in the sea—*phusi: ph* as in *ph*ysic, *u* as in

---

*I would welcome suggestions for improving any of the above items, especially the following: *J: rijsttafel* (pronounced *reestahfull*), an Indonesian rice dish, has other *ij* analogies, such as *nijmegan* and *rijksdaalder,* but I would prefer something that sounds more "native." *Q:* in *racquet* I am forced to contend that either the *c* or the *qu* is silent, with no basis for choosing which one. *V:* for this most elusive letter in my search, I can uncover only double-letter examples such as those listed above. This is not entirely satisfactory, as double letters can easily be found for almost every letter in the alphabet—*aardvark, babble,* etc.

busy, *si* as in pen*si*on; *ffess:* o*ff*, pre*tt*y, i*ss*ue; *ughyce:* la*ugh*, *h*ymn, o*ce*an; *Pfeechsi: Pf*eiffer, b*ee*n, fu*chs*ia; *pphiapsh:* sa*pph*ire, marr*i*age, *psh*aw; *fuise: f*at, g*ui*lt, nau*se*ous; *ftaisch:* so*ft*en, vill*ai*n, *sch*wa; *ueisci:* lieuten-ant, forf*ei*t, con*sci*ous. We stop here only because the game has become "in-*f*-able."

We can adapt Shaw's tactic to almost any word. My last name, for instance, can be represented by *Lleoddo-loyrrh,* a Frankenstein's monster sewn together from the pieces of ba*ll,* l*eo*pard, bla*dd*er, c*olo*nel, and m*yrrh.* In fact, in studying phoneme-grapheme correspondences, I have become such a Wizard of *Oh*s that I can now unveil a twenty-one-word sentence in which every word contains a long *oh* sound, yet each is spelled differently: "Although yeoman folk owe Pharaoh's Vaud bureau hoed oats, chauvinistic van Gogh, swallowing cognac oh so soulfully, sews grosgrained, picoted, brooched cha-peaux."

Now perhaps you can understand the logic behind the Rolaids commercial that asks, "How do you spell relief?" Then you see a clown or some other stooge writ-ing on a mirror or blackboard the answer: R-O-L-A-I-D-S.

Given the "awesome mess" of English spelling, the Rolaids people may have a point.

5

THE SOUNDS
OF ENGLISH

"Spanish is the language for lovers, Italian for
singers, French for diplomats, German for horses,
and English for geese."

—SPANISH PROVERB

Sound and Sense

What do these words have in common: *bash, clash, crash, dash, gash, gnash, hash, lash, mash, slash, smash, thrash,* and *trash?*

"The words all rhyme," you answer.

Right. But can you spot what it is that the thirteen words share in their content?

Faces are bashed, gashed, slashed, and smashed. Cars crash. Hopes are dashed. Enemies clash. Teeth gnash. Beef is hashed. Potatoes are mashed. Rooms are trashed. And prisoners are lashed and thrashed.

Now the pattern becomes clearer. All of these *-ash* words are verbs that express terrible actions of great violence. Why, over the more than 1500-year history of the English language, have speakers seized on the *-ash* sound cluster to create words that describe mutilation?

Listen closely to the broad *a*, and you will hear that it sounds like a drawn-out human scream. Now listen closely to the hissing sound of *sh,* and note that it too

151

takes a long time to expel. The eighteenth-century English poet Alexander Pope once wrote that "The sound must seem an echo of the sense." It appears that the agonizing, hissy, drawn-out sound of *-ash* is particularly well suited to the sense of violent actions that unfold over seconds, minutes, or even longer periods of time.

The ancient Greek philosophers Pythagoras (whose theorem of the right triangle we confront in geometry classes), Heraclitus, and Plato subscribed to what many now call the ding-dong theory of language origin. They believed that the universe is like a great bell and that every object in nature has a special "ring." Strike an object and out comes a word the sound of which is inherent in the thing itself.

"Balderdash!" you respond, uttering another mutilative *-ash* word. "Such an a priori correspondence between sound and sense can't possibly exist. Only human beings can invent words; syllables can't repose in things themselves." But, keeping an open mind (rather than a hole in the head), consider the evidence for the validity of the ding-dong theory of word formation.

Let's start with initial consonant sounds:

The word for *mother* (and *mama* and *mom*) in most languages begins with the letter *m: mater* (Latin), *mère* (French), *madre* (Spanish), *Mutter* (German), *mam* (Welsh), *mat* (Russian), and *masake* (Crow Indian). Could it be more than mere coincidence that this pervasive *m* sound for words maternal is made by the pursing of lips in the manner of the suckling babe?

Think of all the words you know that begin with *fl-*. Your list will probably include the likes of *flicker, flut-*

the ding-dong theory

ter, flurry, flip, flap, fly, flow, flash, flee, flare, fling, flush, flame, flail, and *flounce.* Could the fact that the tongue darts forward whenever we form *fl-* in our mouths account for the sense of movement, usually rapid movement, in all of these words?

Why do so many words beginning with *sn-* pertain to the nose: *snot, sneeze, snort, snore, sniff, sniffle, snuff, snuffle, snarl, snivel, snoot, snout, sneer,* and *snicker?* And why are so many other *sn-* words distasteful and unpleasant: *sneak, snide, snob, snitch, snit, snub, snafu, snoop, snipe, snake,* and *snaggletooth?* To appreciate the nasal aggression in *sn-,* form the sound and note how your nose begins to wrinkle, your nostrils flare, and your lips draw back to expose your threatening canine teeth.

Think for a moment of how forcibly the sound of an initial *b* is expelled as it flies from the lips like a watermelon seed. Then observe how many words beginning with that letter denote the expulsion of breath—*breathe, blow, blab, blather, bluster, babble, bloviate,* and *blubber*—or the application of force—*batter, blast, bang, bust, bruise, bludgeon, bump, break, butt, beat, bash, bounce,* and *bomb.*

Listen now to the sounds of vowels in the middle of words:

What happens to the pattern of internal vowels in strong, irregular verbs: *sing, sang, sung; ring, rang, rung?* Place your thumb and forefinger on your Adam's apple as you say these words aloud and you will notice that, as the verbs move backwards in time (today I sing, yesterday I sang, for years I have sung), the vowels themselves echo the process by traveling back in the throat.

Consider the short *i* vowel in words like *little, kid, slim, thin, skinny, imp, shrimp, midget, pygmy,* and *piddling.* What do these words have in common? They all denote smallness or slightness. Why? Perhaps because, when we pronounce the short *i,* we tighten our lips together and make our mouths small.

Now that you are opening your ears to sound and sense, consider these questions about a few sounds that come at the ends of words:

Why is it that many words ending with *-ng* echo with metallic resonance: *bong, boing, gong, ping, ring, clang,* and *ding-dong?*

Why is it that the final voiceless stops *p, t,* and *k* come at the end of quick-action words, like *pop, clip, snip, snap, rap, tap, slap, whip, pat, cut, slit, hit, dart, flit, crack, click, flick, smack, whack, strike,* and *peck?* Robert Browning put this pattern to sensitive use in "Meeting at Night":

A *tap* at the pane, the *quick sharp* scratch
And blue *spurt* of a lighted match

Why are almost all words that end with *-unk* unpleasant in their suggestions: *clunk, junk, punk, drunk, dunk, skunk, stunk, flunk, bunk, lunk, funk,* and *gunk?*

Why do so many words ending with *-ush* have to do with water: *flush, gush, lush, mush, rush, slush,* and *(orange) crush?*

Why does the following cluster of *-allow* words

rotund egghead

convey qualities that indicate a lack of something? A *callow* youth lacks experience, a *fallow* field lacks use, a *sallow* complexion lacks color, and a *shallow* mind lacks depth.

As a final example, why do so many words ending in *-ump* suggest a round mass: *clump, rump, lump, bump, mumps, plump, hump, stump,* and *chump* (originally a short, thick piece of wood)? No wonder the great wordsmith and creator of children's stories, Lewis Carroll, named his rotund egghead *Humpty Dumpty.* Now there's a writer who could really hear and feel the sounds of English words.

Beautiful English

Mark Twain plunked the following description into the middle of his "Double-Barreled Detective Story." Read the passage and reflect on the power of beautiful English words:

"It was a crisp and spicy morning in early October. The lilacs and laburnums, lit with the glory-fires of autumn, hung burning and flashing in the upper air, a fairy bridge provided by kind Nature for the wingless wild things that have their homes in the tree-tops and would visit together; the larch and the pomegranate flung their purple and yellow flames in brilliant broad splashes along the slanting sweep of the woodland; the sensuous fragrance of innumerable deciduous flowers rose upon the swooning atmosphere; far in the empty sky a solitary esophagus slept upon motionless wing; everywhere brooded stillness, serenity, and the peace of God."

Did the mellifluous lilting of Twain's prose beguile you into overlooking the basic meaninglessness of the passage, including the absurd sleeping esophagus?

More than fifty years ago, a poll was conducted among American writers to ascertain which English words they considered to be the "most beautiful" in the language. In replying to the question, Louis Untermeyer, the poet and critic, wrote, "The most musical words seem to be those containing the letter *l.* I think, offhand, of such words as *violet, lake, laughter, willow, lovely,* and other such *l*impid and *l*iquid syl*l*ables."

Dr. Wilfred Funk, a famous tracker of word origins, chose *tranquil, golden, hush, bobolink, thrush, lullaby, chimes, murmuring, luminous, damask, cerulean, melody, marigold, jonquil, oriole, tendril, myrrh, mignonette, gossamer, fawn, dawn, chalice, anemone, mist, oleander, amaryllis, rosemary, camellia, asphodel,* and *halcyon.*

Lowell Thomas selected *home,* Irvin S. Cobb *Chattanooga,* Charles Swain Thomas *melody,* Stephen D. Wise *nobility,* Lew Sarett *vermilion,* Bess Streeter Aldrich *gracious,* Arnold Bennett *pavement,* George Balch Nevin *lovely,* William McFee *harbors of memory,* and Elias Lieberman the one-word refrain from Edgar Allan Poe's "The Raven"—*nevermore.*

I can't resist adding my personal choices for the most luminous lines in English poetry. Try reading them aloud and listening to their magic:

Brightness falls from the air;
Queens have died young and fair;
Dust hath closed Helen's eye.

—THOMAS NASH

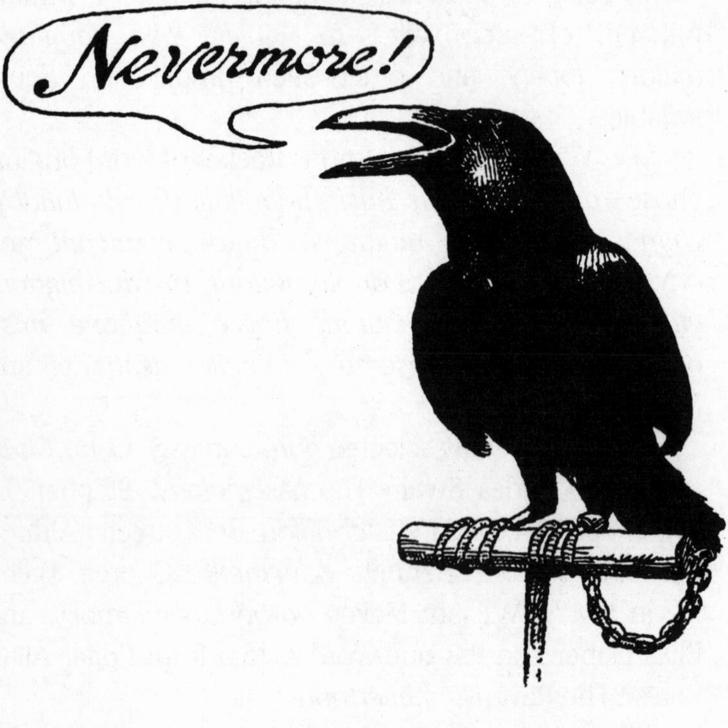
Nevermore!

In Xanadu did Kubla Khan
A stately pleasure dome decree

—SAMUEL TAYLOR COLERIDGE

She walks in beauty, like the night,
Of cloudless climes and starry skies

—LORD BYRON

Charmed magic casements, opening on the foam
Of perilous seas, in faery lands forlorn

—JOHN KEATS

The moan of doves in immemorial elms,
And murmuring of innumerable bees.

—ALFRED, LORD TENNYSON

Now that you have read several dozen words that are considered to be the most beautiful in our language, I wonder if you might answer a question. Is it possible that we find these words to be lovely just as much for their meanings and associations as for their sounds? Note, for example, that Dr. Funk's list is filled with birds and flowers. Is *bobolink* really any more attractive a word than *condor,* aside from its associations? Is *oriole* really more beautiful than *starling,* or, for that matter, are *thrush* and *hush* any more euphonious than *mush* and *crush?*

Elias Lieberman may find *nevermore* gorgeous to the ear, but H. L. Mencken once quoted a Chinese boy who was learning the English language as saying that *cellar door* was the most musical combination of sounds he had ever heard. One also thinks of the Mexican poet who picked out *cuspidor* as the most beautiful word in English.

Clearly the impact that words have upon us is baffling. Sound and meaning work their dual magic upon us in ways that ear and mind alone cannot always analyze. Consider, for example, the foreign couple who decided to name their first daughter with the most beautiful English word they had ever heard.

They named the child Diarrhea.

Alliteration Strikes
the Nation

I am an alliteration addict, a slave to the seductions of sequential syllables starting with the same sound.

Even as a baby I alliterated before I could speak a sentence. "Da-da," "ma-ma," and "bye-bye," I would gurgle gleefully. When I got a little older, I read stories and rhymes about Jack and Jill, Simple Simon, Miss Muffet, King Cole, Boy Blue, Red Riding Hood, Peter Peter Pumpkin Eater, Georgie Porgie Pudding and Pie, and Jack the Giant Killer ("fee fie foe fum . . ."), while in my comic books I followed the amusing adventures of Bugs Bunny, Porky Pig, Little Lulu, Wee Willie Winkle, Beetle Bailey, Hagar the Horrible, Donald and Daffy Duck, and Mickey, Minnie, and Mighty Mouse.

Feeding on french fries and chomping on chocolate chip cookies, munching on marshmallows and quaffing Coca-Cola, I sat watching "Romper Room," "Sesame Street," and "Captain Kangaroo" while commercials told me that M&M's melt in my mouth and that I'd better buy Birdseye and go for the gusto with a Ford in my future. Out on the street I played Kick the Can, Ring around the Rosy, and Simon Says, all the while chanting, "Eenie meenie minie moe," "Peter Piper picked a peck of pickled peppers," "How much wood would a wood-chuck chuck?", and "Sticks and stones may break my bones, but names will never hurt me."

As I grew older, I picked up other words to the wise, like "Practice makes perfect," "A miss is as good as a mile," "Look before you leap," "Where there's a will, there's a way," and "Curiosity killed the cat." And when the fickle finger of fate pointed me down the prim-rose path to great literature, I ravenously read everything from *Charlie and the Chocolate Factory* to *The Wind in the Willows, Piers Plowman* to *Pride and Prejudice,* and *Sir Gawaine and the Green Knight* to *The Great Gatsby.*

Leapin' lizards and jumpin' Jehosephat! You can bet your bottom dollar that I am an alliteration addict—a shell-shocked sad sack beating his breast and caught be-twixt and between the devil and the deep blue sea, leap-ing from the frying pan into the fire on the road to rack and ruin. In wending my way through the whys and wherefores of this alluring activity, I shall not shilly shally, dilly dally, hem and haw, beat around the bush, wear out my welcome, pull any punches, leave you in the lurch, make a mountain out of a molehill, or throw the baby out with the bathwater. After all, I'm not a prim-and-proper, dry-as-dust, dull-as-dishwater, down-in-the-dumps worrywart; a lily-livered, knock-kneed, mild-mannered, mealy-mouthed, daydreaming, tongue-tied, wishy-washy nice nelly; or a backbiting, too-big-for-

Leapin' lizards!

his-britches, birdbrained, hard-headed, bottom-of-the-barrel, party-pooping spoilsport.

Pretty please, don't raise the roof, clean my clock, throw a temper tantrum, and take me to task for being a ranting and raving crazy coot with bats in my belfry; a tattle-taling four-flusher who's out to run you ragged from stem to stern and pillar to post; or a hard-hearted, bamboozling, four-flushing flimflam man who feels free to get your goat and, to add fuel to the fire and insult to injury, or to make a monkey out of you with far-fetched tales of fiddle-faddle that contain neither rhyme nor reason, a bunch of baloney that you need like a hole in the head. My conscience is clear.

Good grief! Mind your manners, have a heart, and hold your horses. I may be fat and forty and worse for wear, but, to tell the truth, turn the tables, and lay down the law, I prefer to take the proof positive off the back burner, put the fat on the fire, bring home the bacon, and talk turkey; to come clean and bite the bullet—first and foremost and sure as shootin'—by taking a no-nonsense, down-and-dirty, daredevil, death-defying, rip-roaring, rough-and-ready, fast-and-furious, mile-a-minute, wild-and-woolly, bolt-from-the-blue approach in beating the bushes to pinpoint this hale-and-hearty, short-and-sweet, spick-and-span, safe-and-sound, ship-shape, fit-as-a-fiddle, picture-perfect, worthwhile, calm, cool, and collected tip-top topic.

In fact, throughout this entire chapter I've tried to prime the pump, come hell or high water; to bend over backward to practice what I preach; to show the method in my madness (and the madness in my method) with wit and wisdom; to give it a go with get up and go; to show the courage of my convictions with vim and vigor and derring-do; to shape up or ship out by going great guns to beat the band; to leave you pleased as punch and jumping for joy head over heels; and to lay it on the line, bag and baggage, part and parcel, and kit and caboodle to convince you that there's more here than meets the eye.

Last but not least, before I call it quits, head for the hills, burn my bridges behind me, and bid you a fond farewell, I hope you've wholeheartedly enjoyed this treasure trove of tried and true, bright-eyed and bushy-tailed, bread-and-butter, bigger-and-better, larger-than-life, cream-of-the-crop, clear-cut (not haphazard, half-hearted, or mickey mouse) alliterative expressions (the more the merrier), all of them good as gold, worth a pretty penny, a chunk of change, and big bucks, hardly a dime a dozen. Dollars to doughnuts, that's what happens when you go from rags to riches and put your money where your mouth is.

Rhyme Time

We usually think of rhyme, like alliteration, as a musical device found only in poems or commercials: "Flick your Bic," "More bounce to the ounce." But, in fact, rhyme appeals so powerfully to the human ear that, if we listen carefully, we can discover a surprising number of common everyday words and phrases that contain rhyme. Let's sneak a peek at the saga of Chicken Licken:

Once upon a rhyme time, true blue Chicken Licken got the heebie-jeebies that the sky was falling. Dashing pell-mell, helter-skelter, higgledy-piggledy, hither and thither, here, there, and everywhere, and shouting, "Yoo-hoo. May Day! May Day!", Chicken Licken came upon Henny Penny, a roly-poly, jelly-bellied old hen no longer in her heyday. Sensible as she was, Henny Penny huffed and puffed at Licken, "Tee-hee. I don't want to create ill will, but what's all this hustle bustle, hubbub, and hurly-burly about? Your tale sounds like a lot of phony baloney, folderol, razzamatazz, claptrap, and mumbo jumbo

"The sky is falling!"

to me. I don't believe in abracadabra and hocus-pocus voodoo, and I don't want to kowtow to a hodgepodge of pie in the sky. After all, haste makes waste."

"Jeepers creepers and holy moley, that's a low blow," maintained Licken, whose spirits now flew at half-staff and who was feeling left high and dry. "You forget that a stitch in time saves nine. It's no picnic trying to do my fair share by being fair and square to all those near and dear to me, and you're making such a to-do by taking potshots and calling my story a rinky-dinky hunk of junk. Well, I'm no Humpty-Dumpty crumbum, and your opinion isn't what will make or break me. I may cry, 'boo hoo,' but I'm not going to become a panhandling, rumdum hobo or commit harikari."

Backtracking, Licken ran off looking for Cocky Locky to tell him that the sky was falling. But Locky was too busy being a super-duper hotshot smoking Old Golds and Pall Malls and a hoity-toity wheeler-dealer who each day would ride downtown on the bar car and each week would pay his way on night flights with expensive airfares to wine and dine with fancy-schmancy, polo-playing bigwigs and jet-set fat cats trading on walkie-talkies for big paydays, the name of the game.

Feeling the wear and tear of walking a fine line through a stress test, off Licken scurried to Goosey Loosey, who was indeed loose as a goose and snug as a bug in a rug. "Hey, you old son of a gun," honked Goosey. "Don't be a wishy-washy namby-pamby. Let's go with the flow. I've got a crackerjack, killer-diller, no-fuss-no-muss idea that'll knock your block and socks off. Let's get down to the nitty-gritty and hustle our bustle to a spring fling wingding full of artsy-fartsy Dead Heads feeling their flower power. With the fans wearing back-packs, razzle-dazzle tie-dyed shirts, and zoot suits, it'll be a real blast from the past. It'll be better than prime time on the boob tube—a sure cure for all your gloom and doom. We'll hobnob and get palsy walsy with rich bitches with hi-fis and hotsy-totsy tootsie-wootsies who sit in the grandstand and who get sky-high and ready to do handstands on the bandstand. Then these cutesy-wutesy chicks are liable to do the hootchy-kootchy, hokey pokey, boogie-woogie, or a fantan dance and get real lovey dovey and hot to trot, ready to make hanky-panky. We'll be made in the shade and in like Flynn—in seventh heaven with all those freebies, which I promise we'll share even Stephen. But if you want to be a fuddy-duddy no-show, then it's see you later, alligator. As I always say, different strokes for different folks."

"After a while, crocodile, but not while the sky is falling," said Licken, and he ran to waylay his friend Turkey Lurkey. But plug-ugly Lurkey wasn't any help either. In fact, the redhead was more harum-scarum flibberty gibberty than Licken, acting like a Silly Billy bozo, a run-and-gun local-yokel hillbilly pogo sticking around willy-nilly and hugger mugger like a herky-jerky nitwit, a lame-brain who was drunk as a skunk with a peg leg. "What can one itsy-bitsy, teeny-weeny sky falling down matter?" gobbled Lurkey like a ding-a-ling kiwi trying to play an oboe and hurdy-gurdy at the same time.

Feeling like a Hottentot with ants in his pants, Chicken Licken decided that his court of last resort was to get back on track by consulting Foxy Loxy. Licken was sick of the humdrum responses of the ragtag hoi polloi and their honky-tonk ways, while Loxy's claim to fame was that he was a kind of guru.

"Okeydokey, Licken. Let's have a chalk talk. Your rock 'em-sock 'em story takes the cake and fills the bill, lock, stock, and barrel," said Loxy, with a tutti-frutti smile. "Yo, bro. Let's go to my den for a powwow." So off Licken and Loxy ran to Loxy's cave, where Loxy took out his handy-dandy cookbook and began to speed-read the section on slicing and dicing sweetmeat and Tex-Mex green beans and washing them down with mai tais, Tia Marias, and near beer. At this Licken sensed a double-trouble melee and yelled, "Ah ha! Oh ho! Who says that might makes right, Einstein? I'm not meals on wheels, you know. Never ever! Now it's no go, Loxy!"

"Geez Louise and hell's bells, peewee. No pain, no gain," snarled Loxy, looking less and less like a fuzzy-wuzzy Care Bear and more and more lean and mean.

"No way, Jose," shot back Licken, and he beat it lickety-split before his ass was grass. "This cave needs a sump pump and a pooper scooper, you unsanitary bowwow. I'm off to Fiji, Hong Kong, Malay, Togo, or Zululand—anyplace but here!"

Then wham-bam, thank you, ma'am, the sky fell down and killed them all. And that's what we mean by end rhyme.

6

ENGLISH
AT PLAY

"Words, words, words."
—WILLIAM SHAKESPEARE

The Play of Words

Welcome to a playground of English words. Step right through the gate and watch some of our strangest and most whimsical words as they clamber over jungle gyms, bounce up and down on seesaws, swing on rings, careen down sliding boards, and merrily whirl around on merry-go-rounds.

Most consecutive vowels. Words like *aqueous* and *sequoia* contain four consecutive vowels. *Queueing* contains five in a row, and the word *queue* has the distinction of being the only English word that retains its original pronunciation even when the last four letters are dropped. One word strings together all five major vowels: *miaoued.*

Vowels in order. At least five English words contain the five major vowels in order: *abstemious, abstentious, adventitious, facetious,* and *parecious.* At least six

contain the five vowels in reverse order: *duoliteral, quodliteral, subcontinental, uncomplimentary, unorien-tal,* and *unnoticeably.*

Most letters with one vowel. The longest com-mon word in English that contains but a single vowel is the nine-letter word *strengths.*

Repeated vowels. The longest common English words that contain one repeated vowel, and no other vowel, are *defenselessness* (fifteen letters, five *e*'s) and *strengthlessness* (sixteen letters, three *e*'s). The longest such state names are *Tennessee* (nine letters, four *e*'s) and *Mississippi* (eleven letters, four *i*'s). The sixteen-letter word *indivisibilities* contains seven *i*'s and one *e.*

Most consecutive consonants. Six consonants in a row crowd into the word *latchstring.*

Most letters with one consonant. Several five-letter words tie for the title. *Eerie* is the best example.

Alphabet words. The words *overstuffed* and *un-derstudy* contain four consecutive letters of the alpha-bet—*rstu*—in order.

Most consecutive letter pairs. The best-known example of a word containing three double letters in a row is *bookkeeper.* Perhaps a person who works for a bookkeeper should be called a subbookkeeper.

Most consecutive dots. *Beijing, Fiji,* and *hijinks* (a variant spelling of *high jinks* in some dictionaries) each contain three consecutive dotted letters.

Letter words. A number of words, when pronounced, consist entirely of letter sounds—*essay* (SA), *enemy* (NME), *excellency* (XLNC). The longest such letter string is *expediency* (XPDNC).

Pronoun word. Has there ever been another word like *ushers,* which contains five personal pronouns in succession?—*us, she, he, her, hers.*

Longest palindromic words. A palindrome is a word, sentence, or longer statement that is spelled the same when its letters are read in reverse order, as those who read on will see. The longest palindromic word entered in English dictionaries is *redivider* (nine letters), although some chemistry handbooks include the eleven-letter palindrome *detartrated.* The longest palindromic cluster embedded in an English word is composed of the first eleven letters in *sensuousness.*

Bilingual reversal. Back in March, 1866, there appeared in *Our Young Folks* magazine an extraordinary English-Latin pairing that reads forward in English and backward in Latin, retaining the same meaning in both languages and both directions:

Anger? 'Tis safe never. Bar it! Use love!
Evoles ut ira breve nefas sit; regna.

Binades. In a binade, a longer word is divided into two shorter words by taking alternate letters in order. Examples include *lounge: lug* (odd letters) and *one* (even letters) and *schooled: shoe* (odd letters) and *cold* (even letters).

Snowball words. Snowball words gain bulk as they roll along, one letter at a time. A three-layer snowball word is *damage: d am age.* A four-layer example is *fatherless: f at her less.* A crystalline five-layer snowballer is *temperamentally: t em per amen tally.*

Pyramid words. Words that contain one use of one letter, two uses of a second letter, and so on are called pyramid words. Two examples from our everyday vocabulary are *Tennessee's* (one *t,* two *n*'s, three *s*'s, and four *e*'s) and *sleeveless* (one *v,* two *l*'s, three *s*'s, and four *e*'s).

Longest isograms. An isogram is a word in which no letter of the alphabet appears more than once. The longest English isograms are *ambidextrously* (fourteen letters), *dermatoglyphics* (the science of fingerprints, fifteen letters), and *uncopyrightable* (fifteen letters).

Pair isograms. Some words consist entirely of pairs of letters, each pair occurring once. Among the best examples are *teammate* (eight letters, four pairs), *intestines* (ten letters, five pairs), and *shanghaiings* (twelve letters, six pairs).

Most meanings. The hardest-working word in English is *set,* which in some unabridged dictionaries has almost two hundred meanings. *Run* usually runs a fairly close second.

Most difficult tongue twister. Many people consider *the sixth sick sheikh's sixth sheep's sick* to be the most serpentine tongue twister in English.

Typewriter words. When we seek to find the longest English word that can be written on a single horizontal row of a standard typewriter keyboard, we naturally place our fingers on the top row of letters—*qwertyuiop*—because five of the seven vowels repose there. From that row we can type four ten-letter words: *proprietor, perpetuity, repertoire,* and, with delightful appropriateness, *typewriter.*

Shortest pangrams. Many typists know *The quick brown fox jumps over a lazy dog* as a thirty-three-letter sentence that employs every letter in the alphabet at least once. Such sentences are called pangrams. Here is a sampling of the best pangrams of even fewer letters:

- *Pack my box with five dozen liquor jugs.* (thirty-two letters)
- *Jackdaws love my big sphinx of quartz.* (thirty-one)
- *How quickly daft jumping zebras vex.* (thirty)
- *Quick wafting zephyrs vex bold Jim.* (twenty-nine)

- *Waltz, nymph, for quick jigs vex Bud.* (twenty-eight)
- *Bawds jog, flick quartz, vex nymph.* (twenty-seven)
- *Mr. Jock, TV quiz Ph.D., bags few lynx.* (twenty-six)

If you can come up with a twenty-six-letter pangram that makes easy sense and does not resort to names or initials, rush it to me and I'll make you famous.

Anagrammatical English

Can you create one word out of the letters in *new door?* The answer (ha, ha) is *one word.*

An anagram is the rearrangement of the letters in a word or phrase. For more than twenty centuries lovers of word play have found a challenging and amusing exercise of the mind in changing around the letters of anagrammatical words.

Let's start with the points of the compass—*north, south, east,* and *west.* By reshuffling all the letters in each of the four words, what new words can you create? Answers: *north* yields *thorn; south* contains *shout; east* sparks forth *seat, sate, eats,* and *teas;* and *west* gives us *stew* and *wets.*

Some words are so kaleidoscopic that they turn out to be perfect anagrams, rearranging themselves to form at least as many words as there are letters in the original word. There are many three-letter examples of perfect anagrams, such as *won, now, own* and *pat, tap, apt.* In the word *eat* we have a looping anagram: Move the first letter to the back and the past tense of the verb, *ate,* emerges; move the first letter to the back again and form the beverage we often drink after we eat, *tea.* Four-letter examples of perfect anagrams include *team, tame, meat, mate; name, mane, mean, amen; time, item, mite, emit; star, tsar, arts, rats, tars.* Have you ever noticed that the STOP you see on a stop sign yields six different four-letter words? The following little poem shows how:

> Our landlord *opts* to fill our *pots*
> Until the *tops* flow over.
> Tonight we *stop* upon this *spot,*
> Tomorrow *post* for Dover.

Perfect five-letter anagram strings exist, like *lapse, pleas, leaps, pales,* and *sepal,* as do strings of seven different words: *spare, pears, pares, spear, reaps, rapes,* and *parse.*

The joys of anagramming that most *aspire* to *praise* are found in changing a word or phrase into another word or phrase that is strikingly appropriate, as in the stunning insights that *eleven plus two* is the same as *twelve plus one,* that when we are *angered,* we are *enraged,* that when we are *wired,* we are *weird,* and that *astronomers* are *moon starers* who would be saddened if there were *no more stars.*

The *evil* thoughts that *live* in us are *vile* and may cast a *veil* over us. Even *Santa* can turn into *Satan* and the *United Nations* into *tainted unions,* and the *sainted*

Santa/Satan

become *stained instead.* Even your *teachers* can turn into *cheaters* and your *mentors* become a *monster.* It doesn't take much for a *marital* life to become a *martial* life, even in the case of a *married admirer.* Then that which was *sacred* may make you *scared,* and that which was *united* may become *untied.*

Am I getting *groans* from your *organs* with all this word play so that with *determination* you exclaim, *"I mean to rend it!"?* Good, do not remain *silent.* I *enlist* you to *listen* to an even more ingenious kind of anagram. Now the word or phrase brings forth a second word or phrase that is surprisingly apt:

Gold and silver are often *grand old evils.* They may lead to *degradedness,* which is *greed's sad end,* or to *villainousness, an evil soul's sin.* Then comes a *penitentiary: nay, I repent it; punishment: nine thumps; a sentence of death* that *faces one at the end;* and finally *desperation: a rope ends it.*

Isn't it sad that *a shoplifter* always *has to pilfer;* that *prosecutors* are often *court posers* in whose *conversation* often *voices rant on;* that a *misanthrope* is likely to say about a beggar, *"Spare him not";* and that *medical consultations* occasionally turn out to be *noted miscalculations?*

In *the nudist colony* we find *no untidy clothes,* just as in *the countryside* we find *no city dust here.* A *problem in Chinese* is usually *incomprehensible.* One blessed with *softheartedness often sheds tears* and *utters endearments: tender names. Metaphysicians* are *mystics in a heap* and *a spellbinder* is a *bland spieler. Upholsterers* try to *restore plush,* and a *waitress* may be heard to ask, "*A stew, sir?*" The *telegraph* is certainly a *great help*. And in the spirit of patriotism we may say of *the United States of America* that it *attaineth its cause—freedom!*

Turning to religion, we discover that the *serpent* in the Garden of Eden *repents* at *present*; that despite Nebuchadnezzar's *denial, Daniel nailed* and *alined* him with a curse; that one who practices *Christianity* might exclaim, "*I cry that I sin!*"; and that in its beginnings a *monastery* tolerated *no mastery* from *nasty Rome,* truly an *amen story* (as well as a quadruple anagram). One of the oldest and best-known anagrams is fashioned from a question that Pilate asked of Jesus: *Quid est veritas?* (What is truth?) The answer was already contained in the question: *Est vir qui adest.* (It is the man who is here.)

No wonder that those of us who believe in the magical potency of words have hailed *anagrams* as *ars magna,* the "great art."

Doctor Rotcod's Ailihphilia

~

Some people are destined for greatness, others for mediocrity. Otto Rotcod was born to become the palindrome made flesh. The date of Rotcod's nativity was September 3, 1939—9/3/39, an arrangement of figures that reads the same left to right and right to left—in Danbury, New Hampshire, the only area of the state with a self-reflecting ZIP code—03230. His palindromic dad, Bob, and palindromic mom, Ava, named their tot Otto.

When Rotcod was a student in junior high school, he wrote a history paper on the career of George W. Goethals, the American engineer who masterminded the building of the Panama Canal. At the end of his report, young Otto summarized Goethals's achievement by writing: *"A man! A plan! A canal! Panama!"* Rotcod surveyed his sentence with considerable pride and discovered that the statement was a palindrome, causing him to exclaim: *"A man! A plan! A canal! Panama!"* sides reversed is *"A man! A plan! A canal! Panama!"* On a

Doctor Otto Rotcod

hunch, Rotcod wrote down that exclamation and saw that it too was palindromic, yielding a mirror image of itself.

At that epiphanous moment of fearful symmetry, Rotcod became a lifelong cainamaniac—a ciloholic who spoke and wrote only in palindromes. *Ah ha!* he yelled. Years later, Rotcod became a doctor to realize the unfulfilled potential of his surname. Naturally, he married a woman named Hannah, and from their union issued five well-balanced daughters—Ada, Anna, Eve, Lil, and Nan. Having heard about this strange case of linguistic behavior, I recently visited the good doctor in his New Hampshire office and conducted an interview:

LEDERER: Dr. Rotcod, I'll begin by asking you about your preferences in life. Whom do you prefer, your father, Bob, or your mother, Ava?

—ROTCOD: *Pa's a sap.*

So you like your mother better?

—*Ma is as selfless as I am.*

What about your choice between Coke and Pepsi?

—*Pepsi is pep.*

Between Japanese and American cars?

—*Race car?*

No, sedan.

—*A Toyota.*

And your second choice?

—*Civic.*

Is golf your favorite sport?

—*Golf? No sir! Prefer prison flog.*

Which do you like better, mathematics or science?

—*I prefer pi.*

Odd or even numbers?

—*Never odd or even.*

Would you rather go to a movie or stay at home and watch television?

—*Same nice cinemas.*

I'd like to explore your political preferences. What do you do each presidential election?

—*Rise to vote, sir.*

And who do you feel has been our greatest president?

—*Name now one man.*

All right, Franklin D. Roosevelt.

—*Tut-tut. Star comedy by Democrats. Tut-tut.*

Then you are a Republican?

—*Hey, yeh.*

Let's move on to your career in medicine. What would you do first for a student who came to you with inflamed gums?

—*Draw pupil's lip upward.*

And what tranquilizer would you recommend?

—*Xanax.*

What do you tell patients who are sexually worn out?

—*Sex at noon taxes.*

Is it true that you apply straw to warts?

—*Straw? No. Too stupid a fad. I put soot on warts.*

I understand that you were recently visited by a hermit with stomach problems.

—*Recluse's ulcer?*

Yes, what kind of diet did you recommend?

—*Stressed desserts.*

You emphasized desserts in that diet?

—*I saw desserts; I'd no lemons, alas, no melon; distressed was I.*

And is it true that you encouraged the patient to consume alcoholic beverages?

—*Yo! Bottoms up—U.S. motto. Boy!*

Did you recommend lager or red rum?

—*Peels lager. Red rum did murder regal sleep.*

I understand that, when none of these ideas worked, you recommended that the patient try losing weight by fasting. What did he say?

—*"Doc, note, I dissent. A fast never prevents a fatness. I diet on cod."*

Doctor Rotcod, in addition to your fame in medical circles, you are well known for your passionate hatred of evil.

—*Evil is a name of a foeman, as I live.*

Then what is your advice to those who seek the good life?

—*Live not on evil.*

How can one do that?

—*Repel evil as a live leper.*

Do you then wish to stamp out all lies?

—*Live on evasions? No! I save no evil.*

How should one treat a liar?

—*Rail at a liar.*

Can good and evil exist together in this world?

—*No, it is opposition.*

Did evil always exist?

—*O, stone me! Not so!*

Then where did evil begin?

—*Eve.*

And Adam, too?

—*Mad Adam.*

What did Adam say when he first met Eve?

—*Madam in Eden, I'm Adam.*

And what did Eve say?

—*Eve, maiden name. Both sad in Eden? I dash to be manned. I am Eve.*

What happened when Eve saw that jewel of a forbidden fruit?

—*Eve saw diamond, erred. No maid was Eve.*

And what happened when Eve offered the fruit to Adam?

—*Won't lovers revolt now?*

So they sinned together?

—*Named under a ban—a bared nude man.*

And the result was . . . ?

—*Eve damned Eden, mad Eve.*

Can we ever escape the influence of that act?

—*Her Eve's noose we soon sever, eh?*

Well, can we?

—*No, evils live on.*

Were you ever so innocent that you did not know sin?

—*Snug, raw was I ere I saw war guns.*

And when you grew older, did you ever sin, Doctor?

—*Lived as a devil.*

How so?

—*Evil did I dwell; lewd I did live.*

And what was the result of that life?

—*Reviled did I live; evil I did deliver.*

"Madam in Eden, I'm Adam."

Apparently, you began to despair of ever overcoming evil. What were you thinking?

—*Do good's deeds live on? No, evil's deeds do, O God.*

I imagine that this state of affairs made you quite miserable.

—*Egad, a base life defiles a bad age.*

Did you ever despair that evil could be conquered?

—*No, it can—action!*

So you dedicated your life to fighting evil?

—*Now do I repay a period won.*

And you fought evil with good?

—*Did I do, O God, did I as I said I'd do? Good, I did!*

Have you finally won your battle against sin?

—*Now, sir, a war is won.*

Do you feel good about all this?

—*Revered now I live on. O did I do no evil, I wonder, ever?*

I understand that your colleagues in virtue have no doubts that they will have their reward in heaven.

—*Nor I, fool. Ah, no! We won halo—of iron!*

And what will happen to you few who have seen the light?

—*Are we not drawn onward, we few, drawn onward to new era?*

Doctor Rotcod, I thank you for this scintillating two-way interview. But how do you do it? How are you able to speak in palindromes so skillfully?

—*Because if I didn't, I'd sound something like this: "sihte kilg niht emos dnuos ditn didifie suaceb."*

194

7

THE LAST
WORD
ABOUT WORDS

"Stability in language is synonymous with
rigor mortis."

—ERNEST WEEKLEY

The Antics of Semantics

───────────
∾

Has it ever struck you how human words are? Like people, words are born, grow up, get married, have children, and even die. They may be very old, like *man* and *wife* and *grass* and *home*; they may be very young, like *moonwalk, break dancing, househusband,* and *veggies.* They may be newly born and struggling to live, as *televangelist, veejay, sound bite,* and *computer virus*; or they may repose in the tomb of history, as *leechcraft,* the Anglo-Saxon word for the practice of medicine, and *murfles,* a long defunct word for freckles or pimples.

Our lives are filled with people and words, and in both cases we are bound to be impressed with their vast numbers and infinite variety. Some words, like *OK,* are famous all over the world; others, like *foozle* (a bungling golf stroke) and *groak* (to stare at other people's food, hoping that they will offer you some), are scarcely known, even at home. There are some words that we will probably never meet, such as *schizocarps* (the pinwheels that grow on maple trees) and *vomer* (the slender bone separating the nostrils), and others that are with us practically every day of our lives, such as *I, the, and, to,* and *of,* the five most frequently used English words.

As with people, words have all sorts of shapes, sizes, backgrounds, and personalities. They may be very large, like *pneumonoultramicroscopicsilicovolcanoconiosis,* a forty-five-letter hippopotomonstrosesquipedalian word for a lung congestion contracted by language book writers who poke their noses into too many old, dusty dictionaries. They may be very small, like *a* and *I.*

Some words are multinational in their heritage, as *remacadamize,* which is Latin, Celtic, Hebrew, and Greek in parentage; some come of old English stock, as *sun* and *moon* and *grass* and *goodness;* some have a distinctly continental flavor—*kindergarten, lingerie, spaghetti;* others are unmistakably American—*stunt* and *baseball.*

Words like *remunerative, encomium,* and *perspicacious* are so dignified that they can intimidate us, while others, like *booze, burp,* and *blubber,* are markedly undignified in character. Some words, such as *ecdysiast,* H. L. Mencken's Greek-derived name for a stripteaser, love to put on fancy airs; others, like *vidiot* and *palimony,* are winkingly playful. Certain words strike us as rather beautiful, like *luminous* and *gossamer,* others as rather ugly—*guzzle* and *scrod;* some as quiet—*dawn* and *dusk;* others as noisy—*thunder* and *crash.*

Many words evolve over the centuries and reflect

A muskrat living in France . . .

the sometimes slow, sometimes instant changes in human society. A muskrat living in France is pretty much the same as one living in England, just as a twentieth-century muskrat behaves in much the same manner as its sixteenth-century ancestors. But a human being living in America today is vastly different from a person who lived during the European Renaissance. So it is with words: what they once meant is not necessarily what they mean now. Words have life after birth. Words wander wondrously.

As one example of how the meaning of a word can change very quickly, have a look at a passage from *The Octopus,* written by the American novelist Frank Norris in 1901:

> Lyman Derrick sat dictating letters to his typewriter . . .
>
> "That's all for the present," he said at length.
>
> Without reply, the typewriter rose and withdrew, thrusting her pencil into the coil of her hair, closing the door behind her, softly, discreetly. (*Book II, Chapter I*)

Norris was not fabricating a science-fiction tale featuring robot typewriters. Rather, in his day a typewriter was a person who worked on a typewriting machine, not the machine itself.

Any reader of the works of William Shakespeare knows the wayward ways that words wend over the centuries. Take *Hamlet.* When the Prince of Denmark, resolving to remember and avenge his father's murder, cries, "Yea from the table of my memory/I'll wipe away all trivial fond records," he is using *table* in its earlier sense of "a tablet" and *fond* in its earlier meaning of "foolish." When the Melancholy Dane laments, "Things rank and gross in nature possess it merely," he is using *merely* to mean "absolutely, entirely," just the opposite of today's denotation.

When Hamlet goes to see his mother in her closet, he does not visit her in a tiny room where her clothes are stored. To Shakespeare and his contemporaries, a closet was a bedchamber. In this scene, Hamlet shows the Queen two portraits, "the counterfeit presentment of two brothers." Pointing to the picture of Claudius, Hamlet cries, "Here is your husband, like a mildewed ear,/ Blasting his wholesome brother."

Queen Gertrude then sobs, "Thou turn'st my eyes into my very soul,/And there I see such black and grained spots/As will not leave their tinct." In this exchange, *counterfeit* signifies "likeness," *blasting* "poisoning," *wholesome* "healthy," *leave* "lose," and *tinct* "color."

One reason for the various revisions of the King James version of the Bible is that many of the words as they existed in the early seventeenth century are no longer in use or no longer have the same meaning. In the King James Bible, *wealth* means "well-being," *allege* means "to prove," *comprehend* "to overcome," *demand* "to ask," and *take no thought* means "be not anxious."

In Genesis, we read: "And Joseph made haste; for

his bowels did yearn upon his brother." Obviously *bowels* possessed a different meaning in Middle and early Modern English—"the center of the emotions." Most modern readers are puzzled by the word *naughty* as it appears in this passage in the Book of Jeremiah: "One basket had very good figs, even like the figs that are first ripe: and the other basket had very naughty figs, which could not be eaten, they were so bad." The puzzle is solved when we learn that *naught* and *nought* were once simply variant spellings, and *naught* meant "nought-y, or worthless."

Turning to the New Testament, we note that the Holy Ghost is not a ghost in modern terms but, rather, the Holy Spirit. And, because it has taken on new associations, the word *charity* has been changed to *love* in newer translations of Paul's ringing statement in First Corinthians: "And now abideth faith, hope, charity, these three: but the greatest of these is charity."

The archaic, inconstant meanings of words become vivid and dramatic when we see them in the contexts of long-ago literary passages:

brat: children. "O Israel, O household of the Lord,/ O Abraham's brats, O brood of blessed seed."—George Gascoigne, *A Hundred Sundry Flowers*

buxom: yielding. "And buxom to the law."—Langland, *Piers Plowman*

clown: peasant; *corn:* wheat. "The voice I hear this passing night was heard/In ancient days by emperor and clown;/Perhaps the selfsame song that found a path/ Through the sad heart of Ruth, when sick for home,/She stood in tears amid the alien corn."—John Keats, "Ode to a Nightingale"

family: household. "I was a single man . . . but I had a family of servants."—Daniel Defoe, *Journal of the Plague Year*

jaunty: noble. "See how finely bred he is, how jaunty and complaisant."—John Crowne, *The Country Wit*

rude: simple. "Each in his narrow cell forever laid/ The rude forefathers of the hamlet sleep."—Thomas Gray, "Elegy Written in a Country Churchyard"

silly: empty, useless. "The silly buckets on the deck/ That had so long remained,/I dreamt that they were filled with dew;/And when I awoke it rained."—Samuel Taylor Coleridge, "Rime of the Ancient Mariner"

Like people, words grow after they are born; once created, they seldom sit still and remain the same forever. Some words expand to take over larger territories. They begin with a precise meaning, but their boundaries widen and often grow fuzzier and less definite. A fabulous example of this expansive process is the word *fabulous.* Once *fabulous* meant "resembling or based on a fable." Later came the meaning "incredible, marvelous" because fables often contained incredible and marvelous characters and events. Nowadays the word is weakening in meaning still more, and anything can be fabulous: The latest styles of blue jeans are fabulous, as is *Paradise Lost*; the latest breakthroughs in computers are fabulous, and so is the current Picasso exhibit. A *picture* was once a painted representation of something seen; now any visual representation—photograph, pen and ink, crayon—is a picture. A *holiday* first signified "a holy day," but modern holidays include secular days off like Valentine's Day and Independence Day. Not only has the *holy* part of the compound generalized, but so has the *day* part. Thus, a holiday can now last more than twenty-four hours, as in the rather British "I'm going on holiday to the Caribbean."

Other words travel in exactly the opposite direction and narrow to acquire more specific meanings than the ones with which they started life. Once at the end of a Chinese meal, my young daughter opened a fortune cookie and read the message inside: "You are genial, clever, intellectual, and discriminating." "But," she protested, "I don't discriminate!" My perceptive child was being sensitive to the fact that *discriminate* has taken on the specialized meaning of making choices in matters of race. Much the same thing has happened to the words *segregation, colored, chauvinism, comrade, fairy, queer, queen,* and *gay.* In *Little Women* (1870), Louisa May Alcott wrote without any ambiguity whatsoever, "As Mrs. March would say, what can you do with four gay girls in the house?"

No word is born shrinkproof. The older meaning of *meat* was "food," of *liquor* "drink," and of *corn* "grain." *To starve* did not necessarily mean to lack these items. Early in its life, *starve* meant "to perish." A *hound* was originally "a dog," a *fowl* "a bird," and a *deer* "any small animal," as seen in Shakespeare's *King Lear:* "But mice and rats and such small deer/Have been Tom's food for seven long year." Originally the title *doctor* was given to anyone skilled in a learned profession. An *undertaker* once could undertake to do anything; nowadays undertakers specifically undertake to manage funerals. Incredibly, a *girl* once could be a boy, as during the Middle English period *girl* was a unisex word denoting any child or youth.

Business started out as a general term meaning literally "busy-ness; one's proper concern." After a couple of centuries of life, *business* picked up the narrower meaning of "commercial dealings." In 1925 Calvin Coolidge used the word in both its generalized and specialized senses when he stated, "The chief business of the American people is business." We today can see the word starting to generalize back to its first meaning in phrases like "I don't like this funny business one bit."

Some words are born into low station and come up in the world. With the passing of time, certain positions and ranks have acquired *prestige* (which used to mean "trickery") and *glamor* (which began life as a synonym for "grammar"); with these changes, the words describing them have risen from the humble to the exalted. Such are the histories of *knight,* which once meant "a boy," *lord* (loaf giver), *governor* (steersman), *marshal* (house servant), *squire* (shield bearer), *chamberlain* (room attendant), *constable* (stable attendant), *steward* (sty warden), *minister* (servant), and *pedagogue* (slave). In Geoffrey Chaucer's Middle English, *nice,* derived from the Latin *nescius,* "ignorant," meant "foolish, senseless," and in William Shakespeare's day, *politician* was a sinister word implying scheming, machiavellian trickery. Some would argue that the word really hasn't changed very much.

"You are the homeliest woman I have ever met!"

The reputations of other words slide downhill. Human nature being what it is, we are prone to believe the worst about people, and this cynicism is reflected in the fact that word meanings are much more likely to degrade than to upgrade. An Englishman was served a delicious meal in an American household and, afterward, complimented his hostess with "You are the homeliest woman I have ever met!" This was high praise in British English, in which *homely* means "homelike, good around the home." But because it was perceived that women who stayed home were generally unattractive, the word has taken on negative associations in American English. A similar fate has befallen *spinster*, which, as its roots indicate, meant simply "a woman who spins." The Greeks used *idiōtēs*, from the root *idios*, "private," to designate those who did not hold public office. Because such people possessed no special skill or status, the word gradually fell into disrepute.

Stink and *stench* were formerly neutral in meaning and referred to any smell, as did *reek*, which once had the innocuous meaning of "to smoke, emanate." Shakespeare wrote his great sonnet sequence just at the time that *reek* was beginning to degrade and exploited the double meaning in his whimsical Sonnet 130:

> My mistress' eyes are nothing like the sun,
> Coral is far more red than her lips' red.
> If snow be white, why then her breasts are dun,
> If hair be wires, black wires grow on her head.
> I have seen roses damasked, red and white,
> But no such roses see I on her cheeks.

And in some perfume there is more delight
Than in the breath that from my mistress reeks.

The family resemblances between words and people should come as no surprise. After all, language is not
something that cave people discovered in the woods or
turned up under a rock. Language is a human invention,
and humanness is the invention of language. The birth
of language is the dawn of humanity, and each is as old
as the other. It is people who make up words and it is
people who decide what words shall mean, people,
who are as mutable and mercurial as the muskrat is con-
stant. From a creature who is a little lower than the
angels and a little above the apes, who embraces tiger
and lamb, Apollo and Dionysus, the Oedipus Cycle and
the Three Stooges, we can expect nothing less or more
than a language in which people drive in a parkway and
park in a driveway and play at a recital and recite at a
play, a language in which a slim chance and a fat chance
are the same but a wise man and a wise guy are opposites. From such a changeful and inconstant being we
can expect nothing more or less than an outpouring of
words that are brightly rational, wonderfully serviceable,
maddeningly random, frenetically creative, and, of
course, completely crazy.

The Answers

Confusable English (page 35): 1. d 2. c 3. a 4. a 5. b 6. a 7. d 8. a 9. d 10. b 11. a 12. d 13. b 14. a 15. c 16. d 17. c 18. a 19. c 20. b.

What's in a Name? (page 49): 1. Arabic numerals are not Arabic; they were invented in India.   2. Austria   3. The Turkish bath is Roman in origin.   4. England   5. China and Egypt   6. Ecuador   7. Meissen   8. Russian dressing did not originate in Russia but is so called because one of its ingredients was caviar.   9. New Zealand   10. The English horn is an alto oboe from France.   11. Spain   12. North and South America—and they're tubers, not artichokes.

13. There is no butter in buttermilk.   14. A litchi nut is a fruit of the soapberry family.   15. Welsh rabbit, often called welsh rarebit, is a meatless dish whose primary ingredient is melted cheese.   16. An egg cream contains neither eggs nor cream. Its ingredients are milk, chocolate syrup, and a jet of seltzer water.   17. a thick cookie   18. A sweetbread is not sweet and not bread. It's from a calf's or lamb's pancreas or

thymus. 19. Bombay duck is a fish. 20. Sweetmeat isn't meat; it's a candied fruit. 21. Lemon sole is a flounder, not a sole, and it is not necessarily served with lemon. 22. Although breadfruit resembles bread in texture and color when baked, it contains no bread. 23. Cold duck is the poor man's champagne. 24. apples, sugar, and spices—but no butter 25. Grape-Nuts contains wheat and malted barley, not grapes or nuts. 26. Plum pudding usually contains raisins, currants, or other fruits, but almost never plums. 27. What appear to be oysters are actually . . . um, why don't you ask a friend?

28. The spiny fruit is neither pine nor apple. 29. A prickly pear is not a pear; it's a cactus. 30. A sugarplum is a candy, not a plum. 31. Wormwood is a European plant that yields a bitter-tasting oil but contains neither worm nor wood. 32. A Mexican jumping bean is not a bean. It's a seed with a larva inside. 33. A caraway seed is a dried fruit, not a seed.

34. Lead pencils contain no lead. They contain graphite. 35. the roots of white heather 36. a meteor 37. a pine 38. an elm 39. It's a plant, not a tree. 40. It's the ulnar nerve, not a bone at all. 41. They're big, but not big enough to hold ten gallons of liquid. The name derives from the Mexican Spanish *sombrero galón,* "hat with braids or ribbons." 42. A pea jacket isn't green, not does it resemble a pea. The name derives from the Dutch word *pijjekker,* meaning "jacket made of coarse woolen material." 43. In dry cleaning, all items are immersed in a liquid solution. 44. Hay fever is caused not by hay but by pollen.

45. wood 46. November. The Russian calendar was thirteen days behind ours. 47. Albert. When he came to the throne in 1936, he respected the wish of Queen Victoria that no future king should ever be called Albert. 48. from the Roman *caesus,* "the cut one," not from Julius Caesar. 49. One hun-

dred and sixteen years, from 1337 to 1453   50. Thirty years, of course, 1618–1648.

Pseudonyms (page 70): 1. George Orwell   2. Mark Twain   3. Boz   4. Lewis Carroll   5. George Eliot   6. Doctor Seuss   7. O. Henry   8. James Herriot   9. Joseph Conrad   10. Saki   11. Margaret Mitchell   12. Shalom Aleichem   13. Anthony Burgess   14. Isak Dinesen   15. Ellery Queen

Putting Names in Their Places (page 84): 1. bikini-Bikini   2. limerick-Limerick   3. blarney-Blarney   4. marathon-Marathon   5. to shanghai–Shanghai   6. bedlam-Bethlehem   7. donnybrook-Donnybrook   8. tuxedo–Tuxedo Park 9. turkey-Turkey   10. laconic-Laconia

ACCLAIM FOR RICHARD LEDERER
AND HIS ROLLICKING BOOKS

Adventures of a Verbivore

"*Adventures of a Verbivore* should be required reading for all students of English 101, and language lovers in general."
—Barbara Samson Mills, *Baltimore Sun*

"Lederer leads us on joyous forays. . . . He knows how to entertain while educating and is dedicated to the fascinating history of the words we use to communicate—and to the recording of our unintentional and often very funny misspeaks and miswrites. . . ."
—Judyth Rigler, *San Antonio Express-News*

"[*Adventures of a Verbivore* is] for anyone who savors language, enjoys puzzles and word games, is frustrated with learning vocabulary and grammar—or is in danger of forgetting the joy or just the simple fun of language."
—*Kirkus Reviews*

"Fascinating reading! A rollicking romp through the bountiful world of words. . . . I found *Adventures of a Verbivore* to be an eye-opener and never expect to see words in quite the same way. So I can say to word lovers, writers, speakers, and students alike, if you want to enjoy while you learn, get this book. You'll be glad you did."
—Natalie Atkin, *Minneapolis Star Tribune*

The Miracle of Language

"Richard Lederer has done it again—another delightful, witty, and hugely absorbing celebration of the English language. Is there no stopping the man?"
—Bill Bryson, author of *Made in America*

"Wise and engaging. . . . With *The Miracle of Language,* Lederer, America's foremost wag of words, has also become a sage. . . . That is not to say Lederer has abandoned humor—far from it. *Miracle* is filled with many gems."
—*San Diego Union*

"A veritable Cook's Tour of the wonderful English language—from its major highways to its little-known but fascinating by-ways and back roads."
—Don Hauptman, author of *Cruel and Unusual Puns*

"Entertaining and enlightening . . . a delightful and edifying collection."
—*Publishers Weekly*

Crazy English

"Lederer beguiles and bedazzles. . . ."

—*Los Angeles Times*

"For sheer fun, you couldn't find a nicer gift than *Crazy English* by Richard Lederer."

—James J. Kilpatrick

"*Crazy English?* Crazy like a fox, this man Lederer. Ours is a language that reveals its secrets in winks, allusions, sighs, and giggles. Richard Lederer, being a genius, has taken the giggle road. Don't be bothered that you will laugh from the first page of the book to the last—at the end you will be better equipped to convey exactly what you mean, however serious the subject may be."

—Willard Espy

"Lederer shows just how wild and wacky our language is."

—*Chicago Tribune*

"A joyride . . . Lederer celebrates the semantic antics of our language."

—*Boston Herald*

"If I had been given this book to read in high school or college . . . I would have grown up thinking of my own language as a magic moving sea of possibilities and not as a corset for my mind. The final paragraph ought to be read in every English class in the land and the book ought to be set alongside *The Elements of Style* by Strunk and White as an equal classic."

—Robert Fulghum

Books by Richard Lederer

Pun and Games
The Write Way (*with Richard Dowis*)
Nothing Risqué, Nothing Gained
Literary Trivia (*with Michael Gilleland*)
Adventures of a Verbivore
More Anguished English
The Miracle of Language
The Play of Words
Crazy English
Get Thee to a Punnery
Anguished English
Basic Verbal Skills (*with Philip Burnham*)
The Word Circus

FRACTURED
English

A PLEASURY OF
BLOOPERS AND BLUNDERS,
FLUFFS AND FLUBS,
AND GAFFES AND GOOFS

Richard Lederer
Author of *Anguished English*

POCKET BOOKS
New York   London   Toronto   Sydney   Singapore

An *Original* Publication of POCKET BOOKS

POCKET BOOKS, a division of Simon & Schuster Inc.
1230 Avenue of the Americas, New York, NY 10020

ISBN: 0-671-00036-5

First Pocket Books trade paperback printing November 1996

10   9   8   7   6

Cover design by Brigid Pearson
Front cover photo by Timothy Savard/Photoworks
Text design by Stanley S. Drate/Folio Graphics Co.

Printed in the U.S.A.

For
Al and Jan
and
Marty

ACKNOWLEDGMENTS

For the abundance of fractured fluffs and flubs in this book I am indebted to the hundreds of readers and listeners who offered up their collected goofs and gaffes for national exposure. Special thanks to the National Court Reporters Association and American Association for Medical Transcription for their continued kindness in sharing their court and medical transquips.

I am also indebted to two of my books, *Anguished English* and *More Anguished English*, from which I have drawn a small ration of bloopers. Without such a selective dusting off of some of my all-time favorites, several chapters in this book could not have been cobbled.

Contents

INTRODUCTION

*All I need now is a bit of plastic surgery
to regain the normal width of my mouth.*

Welcome to the blunderful world of bloopers, where crimes and misdemeanors against the English language go unpunished but not unpublished.

Some people are bird watchers. I watch word botchers. The result of my blooper snooping has been three anthologies of accidental assaults upon our mother tongue—*Anguished English, More Anguished English,* and now, *Fractured English.*

Between publication of the first two books, six years trooped by, during which I received about 40,000 submissions and culled the 2,000 best. Between the publication of *More Anguished English* and of this book passed three years. The span was shortened because of the growing enthusiasm of response, volume per square year, and quality of the submissions inspired by the earlier books.

I am sometimes asked if I invent any of the bloopers that appear in my collections. My answer is an emphatic "No way!" No way would I violate the code of ethics of the bloopthologist—the collector takes what he or she finds and contrives nothing. No way could I possibly manufacture the complaint composed by a student to his teacher at the end of the year: "I past all my testes. My grade should be hirer." No way could I make up the wiggy headline LEGISLATORS TAX BRAINS TO CUT DEFICIT. No way could I mangle the receptionist's voice-mail advice, "Please leave a message. The doctors are out of the office or else on the phone and me too." These uncut gems are self-evidently genuine, authentic, certified, and unpolished; they have not been manufactured by any professional humorist. And they are far funnier than anything I could fabricate from whole cloth, even with a lunatic fringe.

"Do you spend all day reading newspapers, magazines, essays, and signs?" is another question I am often asked. Again I answer, "No way." Sure, I happen to happen on some items myself, but the vast bulk are sent me by a conspiracy of super duper blooper snoopers all around our globe. Just as a certain kind of person walks through a field with eyes peeled for four-leaf clovers, blooper snoopers trek through newspapers looking for blunders.

Here's a typical submission, this one from a woman in Encino, California. I won't print her name in case she's still working for the same company:

Dear Mr. Lederer:

At my former job, a lot of us employees weren't too happy with the bosses, and there was often a lot of muttering and griping among us. One afternoon, when the bosses had gone to lunch, one of my co-workers came out of his cubicle and burst out, "There's distention among the troops!" I suggested they try some Pepto-Bismol. Then there's my current boss, not exactly what you'd call a rocket scientist. Referring to the crime of the infamous Lorena Bobbitt, she said, "She severed her husband's appendix." Try a little farther south, boss!

Why do my readers and informants so delight in bloopers and boo-boos, fluffs and flubs, and goofs and gaffes? In their article, "The Appeal of Bloopers," humorologists Donald F. and Alleen Pace Nilsen quote Thomas Fuller's dictum that "birds are entangled by their feet and men by their tongues." The Nilsens sagely add, "In both cases, we are entangled by the very things that set us free."

"Blunders and bloopers are genuinely funny," continue the Nilsens, "because they involve the reader or listener in mentally drawing together two scripts—the one that was said and the one that was intended. To qualify, the error has to be far enough away from the original to communicate some other meaning yet close enough that the listener or reader can connect it to the intended meaning."

The humor in bloopers lies, in part, in the listener's awareness of the speaker's vulnerability. It is the very artlessness of linguistic lapses that makes them so endearing and makes us feel superior. We laugh when we see and hear the verbal rugs pulled out from under somebody else. After all, we would never commit such blunders—or would we?

Aside from giving us the kick of hearing someone else screw up, bloopers are entertaining because they reveal hidden connections between words. That is one of the great joys of our English language, which possesses more than three times the number of words of any other vocabulary. We own more than 600,000 words; no one else owns even 200,000. The formula is simple: the more words in a language, the greater the likelihood that collisions will occur and (to mix a metaphor unrepentantly) that the stomach will be detonated into a rolling boil.

As I've strongly advised in my other books, bloopers are best swallowed in small doses. Don't guzzle them, or you may end up in physical and emotional distress. Listen to some people who ignored the warnings I posted in *More Anguished English:*

> Are you trying to get yourself indicted for murder? After reading *More Anguished English* cover to cover, I now better understand the expression "I died laughing." I indeed laughed so hard I lost my breath. Not that its predecessor didn't have the same effect on me, but I'd forgotten how nearly lethal your books were till I howled my way through *More Anguished English.*
> —Cynthia MacGregor, Lantana, Florida

> Here comes the reason for the lawsuit. I went into gales and fits of laughter. I ended up on the floor, supine, in catatonic spasms, split open all 432 sutures . . . and bled to death.
> —Esther Mosher, Norwell, Massachusetts

> I am, at the moment, trying to recover from reading *More Anguished English.* My GP has assured me

that the cracks in my *abominable* region will heal within a few months, and he has successfully managed to reestablish my jaw to its usual position. All I need now is a bit of plastic surgery to regain the normal width of my mouth, which at present has the likeness of a frog who has tried to swallow a dinosaur's egg.

—Hans Lemböl, Denmark

Norman Cousins, the distinguished editor who overcame a debilitating disease through laughter therapy, wrote, "Illness is not a laughing matter. Perhaps it ought to be. Laughter moves your internal organs around. It enhances respiration. It is an igniter of great expectation." Bloopers books invite you to imbibe the healthful elixirlike effects of hearty laughter:

Thanks for your belly laughs, which are worth a thousand Tylenols.

—James J. Scanlon, Providence, Rhode Island

Your books are good medicine, except for the incontinent.

—Ellen Pilgrim, Goleta, California

Even though I can only type with one hand, I feel that I must write to you about my experience with your book, *More Anguished English.* Four weeks ago, I suffered a stroke, and I have some difficulty with my speech. In order to get some practice reading aloud, I chose to read your book to my wife. The effort was a total failure for that purpose because I got to laughing so much that I couldn't pronounce any words at all. However, the effort did wonders for my weakened facial muscles. So much laughing

and smiling strengthened those muscles to the point where my smile is no longer so crooked and my drooping face is looking nearly normal again. My disposition has also improved. I highly recommend your book as essential equipment for any stroke re-habilitation facility. Thanks for your help.
—Ronald R. Lund, M.D., Casper, Wyoming

In Navajo Indian culture, there is something called the First Laugh Ceremony. Tradition dictates that each Na-vajo baby is kept on a cradle board until he or she laughs for the first time. Then the tribe throws a celebration in honor of the child's first laugh, which is considered to mark his or her birth as a social being.

May this book help you celebrate your membership in human society as *Homo guffawus,* the creature who laughs.

If you are a super duper blooper snooper and would like to contribute to my next collection of skewed and skewered sentences, please send your best howlers to richard.lederer@pobox.com, or to:

Richard Lederer
2655 South Sorrell Street
Las Vegas, NV 89102
http://www.pobox.com/~verbivore

I

SCHOOL DAZE

From the Mouths of Babes

A five-year-old girl called a daddy longlegs "a long-legged father."

After Christmas break, a teacher asked her pupils how they spent their holidays. Here is one small boy's view of retirement in a mobile-home park:

> We always spent Christmas with Grandma and Grandpa. They used to live here in a big brick house but Grandpa got retarded and they moved to Florida. They live in a place with a lot of retarded people. They live in tin huts. They ride big tricycles. They go to a big building they call a wreck hall. If it was wrecked, it is fixed now.

They play games there and do exercises but they don't do them too good. There is a swimming pool there, and they go there just to stand in the water with their hats on. I guess they don't know how to swim.

My grandma used to make cookies and stuff, but I guess she forgot how. Nobody cooks there. They all go to fast food restaurants called Early Bird. But I didn't eat any birds. I had eggs.

As you ride into the park, there is a doll house with a man sitting in it. He watches all day so they can't get out without him seeing them. They wear name badges with their names on them. I guess they don't know who they are.

My Grandma said Grandpa worked hard all his life and earned retardment. I wish they would move back home, but I guess the man in the doll house won't let them out.

Another view of senior citizenship, "What a Grandmother Is," was written by a third-grade pupil attending the West Alexandra School, in Bellflower, California:

A grandmother is a lady who has no children of her own. She likes other people's little girls. A grandfather is a man grandmother. He goes for walks with the boys and they talk about fishing and tractors and like that.

Grandmothers don't have anything to do except be there. They're old so they shouldn't play hard or run. It is enough if they drive us to the market where pretend horses are and have lots of dimes. Or if they take us for a walk, they should slow down past things like pretty leaves or caterpillars. They should never say, "Hurry up."

Usually they are fat but not too fat to tie your shoes. They wear glasses and funny underwear. They can take their teeth and gums off. When they read to us, they don't skip or mind if it is the same story again.

It is better if they don't typewrite or play cards except with us. They don't have to be smart, only answer questions like "Why do dogs hate cats?" and "How come God isn't married?"

Everybody should try to have one, especially if you don't have television, because grandmothers are the only grownups who have got time.

The pearls of wit and wisdom—and whiz and witdom—that fall from the mouths of babes are the most charming and innocent bloopers I receive from my readers. I view these "kiddisms" as bloopers-in-training and am confident that when the boys and girls grow up, many will unknowingly contribute more sophisticated and loopy goofs to my books. Here's a selection of embryonic bloopers, written and spoken by elementary-school pupils:

▶ A teacher and her kindergarten students were studying mammals. During lunch, one little boy asked, "Miss Cindy, are we considered mammals?"

"Why yes, Johnny, we are mammals."

One little girl added, "But aren't some of us fe-mammals?"

▶ A woman approached a new student at an elementary school and introduced herself, saying, "Hello, I'm the principal here."

"No, you're not," replied the little girl. "You're the princessipal!"

▶ At Disney World, a four-year-old told his mother, "Goofy is the coldest planet in the solar system." Naturally, he meant Pluto.

▶ At an airport, a 10-year-old boy asked his mother, "Why aren't helicopters called heavencopters? After all, they do rise upward."

▶ A five-year-old girl called a daddy-longlegs "a long-legged father."

▶ Conversation overheard between two little boys:
"Are you in adultsense now?"
"No, I think I'm still in Pooh-Bear-ty."

▶ A fifth-grade teacher told her students that members of her profession in the 1800s dressed in ankle-length skirts and long-sleeved blouses, even in summertime. She went on to explain that such garb was necessary because teachers were not allowed to expose their arms or legs.

A boy piped up from the back of the room: "Oh no, that can't be true. The Constitution gave everyone the right to bare arms."

▶ A little boy accompanied his parents to church for the first time one Sunday morning. After the service, the parents asked their son if he had enjoyed it. "The music was great," said the boy, "but they really should make the commercials shorter."

During an especially trying time in the classroom, a teacher shrugged her shoulders and sighed, "C'est la vie." The pupils all shouted, "La vie!"

▶ A woman asked a little boy how old he was. "I'm four," said the boy.
"And when will you be five?"
"When I'm done being four."

▶ Conversation overheard between another pair of boys:
  "Look at all the penises on the cow!"
  "Those aren't penises. Those are gutters!"

▶ A six-year-old told his baby-sitter, "We're watching the story of E.T., the Extra Cholesterol."

▶ A sixth-grade boy identified the six New England states as "Maine, Vermont, New Hampshire, Rhode Island, and Massatushy."

▶ An eight-year-old boy, on seeing a beautiful neighbor dressed in a scanty bathing suit, exclaimed, "Mom, come see Linda. She's in a new zucchini!"

▶ To teacher's question, "What is the golden rule?," a little boy responded, "When someone hits you, you hit him back."

▶ "My sister got married, and I was the ringmaster. I got to go to the wedding, but not the conception."

▶ "Auntie, the gray in your hair makes you look very extinguished."

▶ After a mother washed, conditioned, and blow-dried her three-year-old daughter's hair, the little girl thanked her for "air-conditioning my hair."

▶ A four-year-old boy answered the telephone this way: "My sister can't come to the phone. She's upstairs writing in her diarrhea."

▶ After a teacher described the symptoms that had kept her out of school for a week, one of her students suggested, "Gee, maybe you should get an autopsy."

"The child is father of the man," wrote the poet William Wordsworth. Children grow up and become junior-high and high-school students and, ultimately adults and adultresses. To find out what escapes from their mouths, their pens, and their computer keyboards, read on.

Losing the Human Race

Rosetta Stone was the first queen of Egypt.

A student once proclaimed in a history essay, "History is a never-ending thing."

Another student wrote, "We have plenty of history today because the presidents keep adding to it."

The tricks that students through the ages have played on the chronicles of history is a never-ending source of laughter:

▶ The Egyptians worshiped the god Onassis. They raped mummies in bandages. Rosetta Stone was the first queen of Egypt.

▸ The Greeks didn't like flappy or fat bodies.

▸ After the second invasion of Greece, the Athenians took refuse on their ships.

▸ The Norman invasion was when King Harold owned England, but Norm wanted it.

▸ Life during the Middle Ages was especially difficult for the pheasants.

▸ The orders of brothers were the Franciscans, the Dominicans, and the Cisterns.

▸ The Spanish Inquisition tortured people with tongs and red hot brassieres.

▸ The chief clause of the Magna Carta was that no free man should be put to death or imprisoned without his own consent.

▸ The term *Renaissance* refers to the after-birth of learning. During the Renaissance, people began to think for the first time.

▸ Michelangelo illustrated the Sixteenth Chapter of the book *The Agony and the Ecstasy*. We don't know who did the other fifteen, but they say it was one of the Teenage Mutant Ninja Turtles.

▸ My favorite character in English history is Henry VIII because he had eight wives and killed them all. Henry VIII lived in a two Door castle. During his reign, the head of the church fell into the hands of the King. Henry VIII thought so much of Wolsey that he made him a cardigan.

▸ A popular form of entertainment in the 15th century was traveling menstrals.

▸ Martin Luther is famous for nailing 95 Feces to the

door of the church in Wittenburg. He ate a diet of worms and died.

▶ Unfortunately, Marie Ann Twinette was beheaded. After she died, she had very little chance to continue her career. During the French Revolution, many French nobles requested giblets rather than the guillotine.

▶ Mexico was conquered by Kotex.

▶ "I think, therefore I am" was said by the philosopher Day Cart.

▶ Karl Marx declared that religion was the opinion of the people.

▶ Then there was the Victorian Age, when nice ladies were considered virgins. In that day in time, when people conversated, they conversated proper and with good grammer. In yesteryear, sex was considered sacred and only attempted after marriage. Women wore a lot of accessories in the Victorian age, such as griddles.

Surely, our budding scholars must have a firmer grasp of American history. Surely:

▶ The *Mayflower Compact* was a small ship that brought Columbus to America. Columbus knelt down, thanked God, and put the American flag in the ground. Tarzan is a short name for the American flag. Its full name is Tarzan Stripes.

▶ The French settlement in North America consisted of a series of military fornication up and down the Ohio River.

▶ America was founded by four fathers. The Declaration of Independence says all men are cremated equal and are well-endowed by their creator. The Constitution of the United States was adopted to secure domestic hostility. The first amendment to the Constitution gives me the right to bare arms.

▶ Benjamin Franklin got married and discovered electricity. When he went to the French court, he did not dress. They respected him.

▶ George Washington was a very social man. He had big balls and everyone enjoyed them.

▶ General Burgundy surrendered to Sara's Toga.

▶ Two hardships of the Civil War were the *Monitor* and the *Merrimack*.

▶ Abraham Lincoln lived at the Gettysburg Address. He wrote the exclamation proclamation. His pictures make him look thin and emancipated. Lincoln debated Kennedy on TV in 1960. Kennedy won because he looked good. Lincoln had pallor due to his assassination.

▶ During the early part of World War I, President Wilson urged people to stay in neutral. In the War, the unfortunate soldiers spent day after day up to their wastes in filth.

▶ The New Deal tried to make sure that the stock market will never happen again.

▶ One of the major events of the twentieth Century was World War I, which made people so sad that it brought on something called the Great Depression. World War II happened when Hitler and the Knotsies had erotic dreams of conquest all over Europe, but Franklin Roosevelt went over there and put a stop to him. Hitler committed suicide in his bunk. World War II ended on VD Day.

▶ Martin Luther was born in Germany and had a dream. He went to Washington and told his Sermon on the Monument. Later, he nailed 96 Protestants in the Watergate scandal, which made a new religious and rasial morality in the United States.

Science Friction

Dinosaurs became extinct after the flood because they were too big to get into the ark.

A student in science class wrote, "The universe is a giant orgasm." At the end of the student's essay, the teacher riposted, "Your answer gives new meaning to the Big Bang Theory."

"Scientists are hypothetical people," wrote a student of chemistry. The following student comments about science were gleaned from essays, examinations, and classroom discussions. These beguiling theories are in no way hypothetical. They are all real and attest to the high level of scientific literacy in our nation:

▶ The three types of rocks are ignacious, metaphoric, and sedentary.

▶ In some rocks we find the fossil footprints of fishes.

▶ Many dead animals of the past changed to fossils while other preferred to be oil.

▶ All animals were here before mankind. The animals lived peacefully until mankind came along and made roads, houses, hotels, and condoms.

▶ Sir Isaac Newton invented gravity.

▶ The law of gravity says no fair jumping up without coming back down.

▶ While the earth seems to be knowingly keeping its distance from the sun, it is really only centrificating.

▶ Galileo showed that the earth was round and not vice versa. He dropped his balls to prove gravity.

▶ Marie and Perrier Curie shared the Noble Prize.

▶ Marie Curie did her research at the Sore Buns Institute in France.

▶ Next week we will experience the venereal equinox.

▶ Proteins are composed of a mean old acid.

▶ The largest mammals are to be found in the sea because there is nowhere else to put them.

▶ Involuntary muscles are not as willing as voluntary ones.

▶ Methane, a greenhouse gas, comes from the burning of trees and cows.

▶ Paraffin is the next order of angels above serrafin.

► The ozone level is breaking down more rapidly today because of all our aresoles.

► Water is melted steam.

► Mushrooms always grow in damp places and so they look like umbrellas.

► A monkey has a reprehensible tail.

► Some people say we condescended from apes.

► The leopard has black spots which look like round soars on its body. Those who catch soars get leprosy.

► A cuckoo does not lay its own eggs.

► Dinosaurs became extinct after the flood because they were too big to get into the ark.

► In spring the salmon swim upstream to spoon.

► CO_2 is lighter than air because leaves absorb it, and they are on top of trees.

► To remove air from a flask, fill the flask with water, tip the water out, and put the cork in, quick.

► The three cavities of the body are the head cavity, the tooth cavity, and the abominable cavity.

► The spinal column is a long bunch of bones. The head sits on the top and you sit on the bottom.

► Most books say the sun is a star. But it still knows how to change back into the sun in the daytime.

► Cadavers are dead bodies that have donated themselves to science. This procedure is called gross anatomy.

► The cause of dew is through the earth revolving on its own axis and perspiring freely.

▶ Hot lather comes from volcanoes, and when it cools, it turns into rocks.

▶ A liter is a nest of young baby animals.

▶ The earth makes a resolution every 24 hours.

▶ Parallel lines never meet unless you bend one or both of them.

▶ Algebra was the wife of Euclid.

▶ A circle is a figure with no corners and only one side.

▶ A right angle is 90 degrees Farenhight.

▶ Genetics explains why you look like your father and if you don't, why you should.

▶ A supersaturated solution is one that holds more than it can hold.

▶ In making water, it takes everything from H to O.

▶ Respiration is composed of two acts, first inspiration, and then expectoration.

▶ An example of animal breeding is the farmer who mated a bull that gave a great deal of milk with a bull with good meat.

▶ The hydra gets its food by descending upon its prey and pushing it into its mouth with its testacles.

▶ If conditions are not favorable, bacteria go into a period of adolescence.

▶ The formula for sea water is CH_2O.

▶ Water is composed of two gins, Oxygin and Hydrogin. Oxygin is pure gin. Hydrogin is gin and water.

▶ When oxygen combines with anything, heat is given off. This is known as constipation.

▶ The hookworm larva enters the body through the soul.

▶ As the rain forests in the Amazon are shrinking, so are the Indians.

▶ A major discovery was made by Mary Leaky, who found a circle of rocks that broke wind.

▶ The skeleton is what is left after the insides have been taken out and the outsides have been taken off. The purpose of the skeleton is something to hitch meat to.

▶ You can listen to thunder after lightning and tell how close you came to getting hit. If you don't hear it, you got hit, so never mind.

▶ The Dutch people used windmills to keep the plants from sweating.

▶ Most of the houses in France are made of plaster of Paris.

A class of eighth-graders was asked to write about the pros and cons of marijuana. One student responded: "The pros are the people who sell it. The cons are the people who get caught and land in jail."

Wrote another middle-schooler: "One way to contact AIDS is through annual intercourse. To avoid getting AIDS, men should wear condoms at all times."

Other classics from hygiene classes include:

▶ The union of the egg and sperm is called deception.

▶ Human beings share a need for food, shelter, and sex with lower animals.

▶ People who squeeze their spinster muscles too tight will get constipation.

▶ It is in the virginia that the period of gesticulation is passed.

▶ Women are reproducing too fast for mankind to keep up.

▶ How is a child's sex determined? The male carries it in his jeans.

▶ The safest sex is absence.

▶ On a date, a boy tries to show how masculine he is. On this point, a girl can help greatly.

▶ Teenage suicide is a problem because approximately 400,000 teenagers attempt to commit suicide and only 7,000 succeed.

▶ In medical studies, some subjects receive medicine while the rest are given placentas.

▶ After somebody dies, their body becomes rigorous.

Finally, here are some science daffynitions concocted by our students, who are well on their way to becoming the scientists of tomorrow:

▶ *Aorta:* a man who makes long speeches.

▶ *Asexual:* reproductions through a disinterested party.

▶ *Canal:* a small stream of water made by man.

▶ *Circle:* a line which meets its other end without ending.

▶ *Cloud:* a high flying fog.

▶ *Equator:* a managerie lion running around the Earth through Africa.

▶ *Germinate:* to become a naturalized German.

▶ *Geyser:* a piece of floating ice that sometimes reaches a boiling point.

▶ *Magnet:* something you find crawling all over a dead cat.

▶ *Migration:* the headache birds get when flying south.

▶ *Momentum:* what you give a person when they are going away.

▶ *One horsepower:* the amount of energy it takes to drag a horse 500 feet in one second.

▶ *Planet:* a body of earth surrounded by sky.

▶ *Quartz:* the name for two pints.

▶ *Rabies:* Jewish priests; must be treated with respect.

▶ *Rhubarb:* a kind of celery gone bloodshot.

▶ *Sound:* a rapid series of osculations.

▶ *Thermometer:* an instrument for raising temperance.

▶ *Vacuum:* a large, empty space where the Pope lives.

▶ *Volcano:* a hole in the ground that gives off molt and lava.

Stop the Music!

The main trouble with a French horn is it's too tangled up.

▶ In the last scene of *Pagliacci,* Canio stabs Neda, who is the one he really loves. Pretty soon, Silvio gets stabbed also and they all live happily ever after.

▶ Caruso was the first Italian. Then someone heard his voice and said he would go a long way. And so he came to America.

▶ Stradivarius sold his violins on the open market with no strings attached.

▶ The principle singer of the 19th-century opera was called pre-Madonna.

► At one time, singers had to use musicians to accompany them. Since synthesizers came along, singers can now play with themselves.

► All female parts were sung by castrati. We don't know exactly what they sounded like because there are no known descendants.

When it comes to writing about classical music, students across our nation show themselves to be fit as fiddles. They pull out all the stops and never soft-pedal the facts about our musical heritage. Without blowing their own horns, chiming in, or harping on the subject, they strike a responsive chord.

Young scholars have expressed their rapture for the *Bronze Lullaby*, the *Taco Bell Cannon*, Beethoven's *Erotica*, Tchaikovsky's *Cracknutter Suite*, and Gershwin's *Rap City in Blue*. In defining musical terms, they also demonstrate that they know their brass from their oboe:

► Music sung by two people at the same time is called a duel. If they sing without music, it is called Acapulco.

► A virtuoso is a musician with real high morals.

► Contralto is a low sort of music that only ladies sing.

► Diatonic is a low-calorie Schwepps.

► Probably the most marvelous fugue was the one between the Hatfields and the McCoys.

► A harp is a nude piano.

► An oboe is an American tramp. (written by a British student)

► A Stradivarius is a prehistoric animal.

► My favorite instrument is the bassoon. It is so hard to

play, people seldom play it. That is why I like the bassoon best.

▶ The main trouble with a French horn is it's too tangled up.

▶ An opera is a song of bigly size.

▶ An interval in music is the distance from one piano to the next.

▶ The correct way to find the key to a piece of music is to use a pitchfork.

▶ *Agitato* is a state of mind when one's finger slips in the middle of playing a piece.

▶ *Refrain* means don't do it. A refrain in music is the part you'd better not try to sing.

▶ I know what a sextet is, but I'd rather not say.

Students sing a different tune and play it by ear when they write about the famous composers, even those who never existed:

▶ Most authorities agree that music of antiquity was written long ago. My favorite composer was opus. Agnus Dei was a woman composer famous for her church music.

▶ Henry Purcell was a well-known composer few people have ever heard of.

▶ Johann Sebastian Bach wrote a great many musical compositions and had a large number of children. In between, he practiced on an old spinster which he kept up in his attic. Bach died from 1750 to the present.

▶ Bach was the most famous composer in the world and so was Handel. Handel was half German, half Italian, and half English. He was very large.

▶ Beethoven wrote three symphonies: the Third, the Fifth, and the Ninth. He wrote music even though he was deaf. Beethoven was so deaf he wrote loud music. He took long walks in the forest even when everyone was calling him. I guess he could not hear so good. Beethoven expired in 1827 and later died for this. Do you know that if Beethoven were alive today, he would be celebrating the 165th anniversary of his death?

▶ Rock Mananoff was a famous post-Romantic composer of piano concerti.

▶ Aaron Copland is one of our most famous contemporary composers. It is unusual to be contemporary. Most composers do not live until they are dead.

The Revised
Nonstandard Bible

The Virg 'n' Mary

A Sunday-school teacher was talking about Christmas and the coming of Christ and she asked, "And what was Jesus' mother's name?"

"Mary," all said.

"Now what was his father's name?"

One little fellow raised his hand. "Virg."

"Virg? Where did you get that idea?"

"Well," answered the boy, "they always talk about the Virg 'n' Mary!"

Another religion teacher was telling her class the story of Lot. "Lot was warned to take his wife and flee out of the city, but his wife looked back and she was turned to salt." She looked around the class, and one little girl tentatively raised her hand. "Yes?" said the teacher.

"I was wondering," said the girl, "what happened to the flea?"

When a Hebrew school teacher intoned, "The Lord Our God is one," little Benjamin asked, "When will he be two?"

An art teacher in a Maine elementary school also taught Sunday school, where she had the little ones draw pictures of the Bible stories. Little Emma proudly presented her picture of the journey to Bethlehem. The drawing showed an airplane flying over the desert. In the passenger area were seated Joseph and Mary and little Jesus.

"The drawing is fine," said the teacher, "but who's that up front flying the plane?"

Answered Emma, "Why, that's Pontius the Pilot."

Another religion teacher told her first-graders to draw a big picture of the story of Adam and Eve and the garden of Eden. One little boy drew a big car with God at the wheel, driving Adam and Eve out of Paradise.

When yet another teacher asked her student why there was a dog in the nativity drawing, the fledging artist explained that it was a German shepherd. That dog has been joined in the gallery of Sunday-school portraiture by a grinning bear with crossed eyes—Gladly, the Cross-Eyed Bear, of course.

Sunday-school boys and girls not only produce graphic misinterpretations of the Bible in their drawings, they also rewrite biblical history with amazing grace. It is truly astonishing what happens to Bible stories when they are retold by young scholars around the world:

The Bible is full of many interesting caricatures. Michael Angelo painted them on the Sixteen Chapels.

The first five books of the Bible are Genesis, Exodus, Laxatives, Deuteronomy, and Numbers. In the first book of the Bible, Guinessis, God got tired of creating the world, so he took the Sabbath off. Adam and Eve were created from an apple tree. One of their children, Cain, asked, "Am I my brother's son? My punishment is greater than I can bare."

Noah's wife was called Joan of Ark. He built an ark, which the animals came on to in pears. Lot's wife was a pillar of salt by day but a ball of fire by night. Saddam and Gomorrah were twins.

Abraham begat Isaac and Isaac begat Jacob and Jacob begat 12 partridges. God asked Abraham to sacrifice Isaac on Mount Montezuma. Abraham took Isaac up the mountain to be circumcised. Jacob, son of Isaac, stole his brother Esau's birthmark. Esau was a man who wrote fables and sold his copyright for a mess of potash. Jacob was a patriarch who brought up his 12 sons to be patriarchs, but they did not take to it. One of Jacob's sons, Joseph, gave refuse to the Israelites.

The Jews were a proud people and throughout history they had trouble with the unsympathetic Genitals. Samson was a strongman who let himself be led astray by a Jezebel like Delilah. Samson slayed the Philistines with the axe of the apostles. He slayed them by pulling down the pillows of the temple.

Pharaoh forced the Hebrew slaves to make beds without straw. Moses was an Egyptian who lived in a hark made of bullrushes. Moses led the Hebrews to the Red Sea, where they made unleavened bread, which is bread made without any ingredients. The Egyptians were all drowned in the dessert.

Afterwards, Moses went up on Mount Cyanide to get the Ten Amendments. The First Commandment was when Eve told Adam to eat the apple. The Fifth Commandment is humor thy father and mother. The Seventh Commandment is thou shalt not admit adultery. The Ninth Commandment is thou salt not bare faults witness.

Moses ate nothing but whales and manner for 40 years. He died before he ever reached Canada. Then, Joshua led the Hebrews in the battle of Geritol. The greatest miracle in the Bible is when Joshua told his son to stand still and he obeyed him.

David was a Hebrew king skilled at playing the liar. He wrote psalms. They are called psalms because he sang them while playing the harmonica. David also fought with the Finkelsteins, a race of people who lived in Biblical times. Solomon, one of David's sons, had 300 wives and 700 porcupines.

Later came Job, who had one trouble after another. Eventually, he lost all his cattle and all his children and had to go live alone with his wife in the desert. Then came Shadrach, Meshach, and To Bed We Go, and then Salome, who was a wicked woman who wore very few clothes and took them off when she danced before Harrods.

When Mary heard that she was the Mother of Jesus, she sang the Magna Carta. When the three wise guys from the East Side arrived, they found Jesus in the manager wrapped in waddling clothes. In the Gospel of Luke they named him Enamel. Jesus was born because Mary had an immaculate contraption. St. John, the Blacksmith, dumped water on his head.

Jesus wrote the "B" Attitudes and enunciated the Golden Rule, which says to do one to others before they do one to you. He also explained, "Man doth not live by sweat alone." Jesus was crucified on his way to Calgary. It was a miracle when he rose from the dead and managed to get the tomb stone off the entrance.

The people who followed the Lord were called the 12 decibels. The epistles were the wives of the apostles. One of the opossums was St. Matthew, who was by profession a taximan.

St. Paul cavorted to Christianity. He preached holy acrimony, which is another name for marriage. A Christian should have only one wife. This is called monotony. The natives of Macedonia did not believe in Paul, so he got stoned.

Other Christians were condemned to death in large groups. They entered the arena to face wild lions, singing hymns of praise in the name of the Father, the Son, and In-the-Hole-He-Goes. The Romans went to the coliseum to watch the Christians die for the fun of it. But, as Mel Brooks says, "The meek shall inherit the earth."

Pullet Surprising Literature

His father was Mr. Shakespeare and his mother was Mrs. Shakespeare.

On a test, an English teacher in Chickasha, Oklahoma, asked her students, "What distinguished writing award did Harper Lee win for her novel, *To Kill a Mockingbird?*" One student wrote, "Harper Lee won a Pullet Surprise."

Each of the following student bloopers is indeed worthy of a pullet surprise. Only in the classroom can you discover that Victor Hugo wrote *Lame Is Rob* and that another famous French writer, Emily Zola, penned a famous letter entitled *J'acuzzi*.

Leave it to our young scholars to inform us that Albert

Campus authored *The Plaque* and that Robert Browning shows his lighter side in "The Pied Piper of Hamlet." American lit is relit with the facts that Ernest Hemingway crafted *For Whom the Belt Holds,* that John Steinbeck created *Of My Cement,* that Harper Lee's masterpiece is *Tequilla Mockingbird,* and that J. D. Salinger gave the world *Catch Her in the Rye.* Did you know that Anonymous is the man who writes all the poems that are not signed?

Mount Olympus might erupt with laughter on hearing the way students describe the gods and goddesses. Hera had only one way to control Zeus and viewed sex as a means of coming to an end. The Greek goddess of love was Alpodite. Aphrodite lives on today as a kind of haircut—the Aphro.

Vesta was a goddess who kept the home fries burning. Dionysius was the god of rivalry. Bacchus first taught the Greeks to get drunk. The messenger god was named Herpes, while the god of metalworking was Hepatitus. Persephone was a girl who had an on-and-off relationship with Pluto.

Students render—and rend—classical mythology with unintended, classic humor. Many a young scholar has defined a myth as "a female moth." One myth says that the mother of Achilles dipped him in the River Stynx until he became intolerable. Achilles appears in *The Iliad,* by Homer. Homer also wrote *The Oddity,* in which Penelope is the last hardship that Odysseus endures on his journey.

Odysseus is one of many heroes in ancient iniquity. While Odysseus is off sleeping with goddesses, Penelope has to stay at home and beat off all those suitors. When Odysseus comes home in disguise, his old nurse recognizes him by his scared thigh, which he gets from a wild bore. Odysseus has to sail between Scylla and Charybdis. Being between Scylla and Charybdis means that whichever way you go, you are going to get got.

Sophocles wrote the famous Greek play *Oedipus Wrecks*. Oedipus screws up very badly when he marries his own mother who was really his wife, which the Erkel knew it all along. Oedipus forces out his eyes and condoms himself. Oedipus and Hamlet really had a lot in common, even if Freud had not yet been invented.

The creator of Hamlet was, of course, William Shakespeare. Through their bloopers, many generations of students have gone from bard to verse:

The greatest writer of the Renaissance was William J. Shakespeare. Shakespeare was born in the year 1564, supposedly on his birthday. His father was Mr. Shakespeare, and his mother was Mrs. Shakespeare. He wrote during the era in which he lived. Actually, Shakespeare wasn't written by Shakespeare but by another man named Shakespeare.

Shakespeare never made much money and is famous only because of his plays and sonics. He lived at Windsor with his merry wives, writing hysterectomies, tragedies, comedies, and errors. I don't see why he is so popular when his writing skills are so low. He wrote in Islamic pentameter, and you can't hardly understand what he is saying.

In one of Shakespeare's famous plays, Hamlet rations out his situation by relieving himself in a long soliloquy. A soliloquy is a conversation between one person. Hamlet has an edible complex, and his mind is filled with the filth of incestuous sheets which he pours over every time he sees his mother. Hamlet decides to act madly so he gets in an antic position. In Act Five, Hamlet talks to Horatio about a skull that has been thrown up. Act Five comes right after Act Four.

In another play, Macbeth was from his mother's womb untamely ripped. He is a brave and strong man who turns bad and gradually gets worse.

King Duncan wires Macbeth that he will be spending the night at his castle. Then Lady Macbeth tries to convince Macbeth to kill King Duncan by attacking his manhood. All Macbeth does is follow his wife's odors. He kills the king on page 14. Macbeth and Lady Macbeth then suffer from quilt. In fact, they have so much quilt, they can't sleep at night.

During the banquet scene, Lady Macbeth is afraid her husband will expose himself in front of his guests. Then Lady Macbeth gets kilt. The proof that the witches in *Macbeth* were supernatural is that no one could eat what they cooked.

Romeo and Juliet are an example of a heroic couplet. This story presents a one on one situation between a man and a woman. Romeo and Juliet belonged to the families of the Montages and Copulates. They tell each other how much they are in love in the baloney scene. After much fighting in the pubic square, Romeo's last wish is to be laid by Juliet.

In *Julius Caesar*, Brutus is a tragic hero despite dying at the end. Caesar is murdered by the Ides of March because they think he is going to be made king. Dying, he gasps out the words "Tee hee, Brutus." Then he dies with these immortal words: "Veni, vedi, vici."

In *The Merchant of Venice*, the Rialto is the business part of Venus. Bassanio loved Portia, but he had no money to press his suit. *Taming of the Screw* is a play about Petruchio, who takes Kate from a bitter screw to an obedient wife. The clown in *As You Like It* is named Touch-down. In that play, Shakespeare wrote, "All the world's a stage, and everyone is just acting."

In *Anthony and Cleopatra,* Cleopatra reclined to become Mark Anthony's mistress. She took the Roman Empire one man at a time. The barge she shat on, like a burnished throne, glowed on the water. The poop was beaten gold.

Writing at the same time as Shakespeare was Miguel Cervantes. He wrote *Donkey Hote.* The next great author was John Milton. Milton wrote *Paradise Lost.* Then his wife died and he wrote *Paradise Regained.*

From its earliest beginnings to the present day, the canon of English and American literature gets reamed in the classroom:

► Caedmon composed simple hymns in praise of God, using his Germanic tool.

► Several of Herrick's poems use the tradition of *crape diem.* In "To the Virgins, to Make Much of Time," Herrick warns that if they do not loosen up, they will not have any friends. Being a virgin is OK for people who are old, like teachers and parents, and who do not want to be popular. But this poem is telling us to have some fun now so that we can die with a smile on our face.

► Many of the poems in this selection have a basic theme of death, which was quite common in the times of Romantic literature. Not even the dust of Ozymandias' remains remains.

► Edgar Allan Poe was a very curdling writer. He had several additions. One of his additions was alcohol.

Poe was a very sad man. Because he was such a sad man, he wrote very sad stories. The reason he was so sad is that he was impudent. Because he was impudent, he could never love a woman. He could only love little girls. He married a little girl, but he was impudent, so they never had any children.

▶ Mr. Murdstone treated David Copperfield's Mother like a very terranical mail shovenist.

▶ When Arthur Dimmesdale felt guilt about his sin in *The Scarlet Letter*, he felt better when he went on the scaffold and relieved himself.

▶ Henry Wadsworth Longfellow was born in Portland, Maine, while his parents were traveling abroad.

▶ Emily Dickinson was a wreck loose in society.

▶ In *The Mayor of Casterbridge*, when Henchard sold his wife to another man, their marital relationship was not healthy.

▶ Anton Chekhov was the son of Russian pheasants.

▶ In *Of Human Bondage*, Philip stays up all night studding with Mildred.

▶ Suicide was a way of life for Hemingway.

▶ Willie Loman was never more than an average salesman, and people didn't remember him for miles around. Willy Loman's suicide at the end of *Death of a Salesman*, by Author Miller, leads him to think there is a better way of life.

▶ In *A Streetcar Named Desire*, the climax is when Blanche goes to bed with Stella's husband. At the end,

Blanche goes to a mental institution, where she discovers what life is really like.

▶ *Lord of the Flies* is a story about a bunch of boys on an uninhibited desert island.

II

IT'S A
BLUNDERFUL LIFE

Poly-Tickle Speeches

"I don't want to cast asparagus at my opponent!"

During the 1968 Democratic convention in Chicago, crowds of protestors picketed the proceedings and rioted outside the convention center. Longtime Chicago mayor Richard J. Daley ordered police to quell the disruptions and explained to the press, "The police are not here to create disorder. They are here to preserve disorder!"

Mr. Daley was known for beheading the English language with such mutilations as:

▶ I resent your insinuendoes.

▶ No man is an Ireland.

▶ Today the real problem is the future.

▶ We shall reach greater and greater platitudes of achievement.

▶ Don't forget to get out early and vote often.

The mayor's creative word choices must have been contagious, because another Chicago politician was heard to shout, "I don't want to cast asparagus at my opponent!"

Life may get complicated and confused, but leave it to politicians to clear everything up. Or, as a Wisconsin state legislator proclaimed, "Good communication is essential—even if it isn't clear."

"Being in the legislature is no bed of gravy," one of these giants of political thought observed. That was the same Minnesota state senator who said, "Let's dispense with all the discussion and get to the crotch of the matter."

Poet Percy Bysshe Shelley once wrote that "poets are the unacknowledged legislators of the world." Equally true is that politicians are the unacknowledged poets of the world. They can certainly turn a phrase—inside out.

In political debate, the level of language soars to the absolute pinnacle of platitude. When confronted with a charge that the Democrats had "put New York State in a pickle," the Democratic state assembly leader thundered, "We find ourselves in this pickle because you bought that jar and filled it not with pickles but with water, and now you're trying to jam it in the public's face!"

In a nationally televised debate, Walter Mondale stated, "George Bush doesn't have the manhood to apologize."

Bush fired back: "Well, on the manhood thing, I'll put mine up against his any time."

In discussing a local flood, former California Governor Pat Brown observed, "This is the worst disaster in California since I was elected." Here are more executive and legislative platitudes that fill the anals of political science:

▶ Announced President Bill Clinton, "I believe that this country's policies should be heavily biased in favor of nondiscrimination."

▶ "We will not close any base that is not needed," proclaimed former Secretary of Defense Les Aspen, more revealingly than he may have known.

▶ "If we don't make some changes, the status quo will remain the same," said another member of Clinton's staff.

▶ "We're going to have the best-educated American people in the world," promised former Vice President Dan Quayle, who also proclaimed, "I support efforts to limit the terms of members of Congress, especially members of the House and members of the Senate."

▶ "If Lincoln were alive today, he'd roll over in his grave," said former President Gerald Ford, at a Lincoln's birthday dinner. Ford also said, "Things are more like they are now than they have ever been."

▶ Responding to a question on whether she had expected murder convictions for the Branch Davidians on trial, Attorney General Janet Reno said: "I always wait until a jury has spoken before I anticipate what they will do."

▶ Former Michigan Governor George Romney offered

clarification: "I didn't say that I didn't say it. I said that I didn't say that I said it. I want to make that very clear."

▶ Answering accusations that he failed to pay his taxes, former New York City Mayor David Dinkins reasoned, "I haven't committed a crime. What I did was fail to comply with the law."

▶ We have two incredibly credible witnesses here," announced U.S. Senator Joe Biden at the U.S. Supreme Court confirmation hearings for Clarence Thomas. One of those unbelievably believable witnesses was Thomas, now a justice on the court, who repeatedly denied "*un*categorically" Anita Hill's allegations of sexual harassment.

▶ Argued law-and-order Philadelphia mayor Frank Rizzo, who had also been chief of police, "The streets are safe in Philadelphia. It's only the people who make them unsafe."

▶ When he heard that the indicted Spiro Agnew was asking to have his corruption case tried by the House instead of in a regular court, Rep. Charles Vanik of Ohio exclaimed, "He's trying to take the decision out of the hands of 12 honest men and give it to 435 Congressmen!"

▶ Sen. Wally Horn of Iowa commented on the issue of what size basketball girls should use: "Girls shouldn't play with men's balls. Their hands are too small."

▶ "Sure, it's going to kill a lot of people, but they may be dying of something else anyway," reasoned a member of the Texas pesticide review board, on chlordane.

▶ "The exports include thumbscrews and cattle prods, just routine items for the police," stated a Commerce Department spokesman on a regulation allowing the export of various products abroad.

▶ Lawrence Summers, chief economist of the World Bank, explained why we should export toxic wastes to Third World countries: "I've always thought that the underpopulated countries in Africa are vastly underpolluted."

▶ "That lowdown scoundrel deserves to be kicked to death by a jackass—and I'm just the one to do it!" shouted a congressional candidate in Texas.

▶ A Louisiana lawmaker, loudly opposing a bill for the benefit of dependent children, shouted, "To hell with posterity. What's posterity ever done for us?" A state representative from Jackson, Louisiana, complained (when opposing an apparently popular measure), "I can't believe that we are going to let a majority of the people decide what's best for this state." Other Louisiana legislators have been recorded as saying, "I don't want to beat a dead horse to death" and "This mortality rate is killing us" and "I am not sure I understand the question, but I agree with you."

▶ A political candidate confronted by questions from a Philadelphia reporter begged off, saying, "Candidly, I cannot answer that. The question is too suppository."

▶ "Topless dancing is at the bottom of our problem!" squawked a San Francisco mayor.

▶ A West Virginia legislator with a pro-life stance, advocating tough anti-abortion legislation, stated that he was opposed to abortion except when necessary to save the life of the mother or the child.

▶ A New Hampshire congressman declared, "What the people of this state deserve is clean, fresh, wholesome pasteurized milk. And I'm going to the State House and take the bull by the horns until we get it."

▶ Explaining why he would never return to Washington, former Defense Secretary Bobby Ray Inman concocted this metaphor: "I came to a fork in the road and I took it."

▶ Reacting to the NFL's pulling the Super Bowl out of Arizona, U.S. Senator Dennis DeConcini riposted, "Those who throw rocks in glass houses had better look at yourself."

▶ Leave it to Washington, D.C. Mayor Marion Barry to say, "Outside of the killings, we have one of the lowest crime rates in the nation."

▶ U.S. Senator Barbara Boxer announced, "Those who survived the San Francisco earthquake said, 'Thank God I'm still alive.' But, of course, those who died, their lives will never be the same again."

▶ When he was governor of New Hampshire, John Sununu mangled a metaphor thusly: "The bankers' pockets are bulging with the sweat of the honest working man."

▶ Former Secretary of the Treasury John Connally explained, "In the early sixties, we were strong, we were virulent."

▶ A New Mexico state senator told the governor, "The ball is in your camp now."

▶ A newly elected justice of the peace in New Mexico, asked to enforce a law prohibiting cohabitation without benefit of marriage, said, "That would be like looking through a needle for a haystack."

▶ "Let's jump off that bridge when we come to it," said a three-time mayor with a 36-year career in politics.

The word *politics* derives from *poly*, "many," and *ticks*, "blood-sucking parasites." Here are more classics of poly-tickle science:

▶ There comes a time when you have to put principle aside and do what's right.

▶ It doesn't pay to fiddle while Rome is burning and the tigers are nipping at our heels. From time to time, you must divorce yourself from the heat of battle, drop back 10, and count your marbles.

▶ Clamping down on illegal aliens is a giant leap down a very dangerous road.

▶ Some of our friends wanted it in the bill, some wanted it out, and Jerry and I are sticking with our friends.

▶ I came out of that session smiling like a rose.

▶ Anyone working for the town should be above and beyond approach.

▶ The worm has turned and the shoe is on the other foot.

▶ We don't want to skim the cream off the crop here.

▶ To be demeanered like that is an exercise in fertility.

▶ I deny the allegations, and I defy the allegators.

- If somebody's gonna stab me in the back, I want to be there.

- When you're talking to me, keep your mouth shut.

- If you forget the complications, it's all very simple.

- It's the sediment of the house that we adjourn.

- Let's do this in one foul swoop.

- In the 1930s, we were not just on our backs. We were prone on our backs.

- I want to thank each and every one of you for having extinguished yourselves in this session.

- We'll run it up the flagpole and see who salutes that booger.

- People planning on having serious accidents should have their seat belts on.

- The poor are wallowing in the midst of the asphalt jungle.

- That bill, if passed, will derail the ship of state.

- This session has been hit by an avalanche of creeping paralysis.

- I would like to take this time to reirritate my remarks.

- The average age of a 7-year-old in this state is 13.

- In 1994, Americans stand on the horns of an enema.

- I hate to confuse myself with the facts.

- We have a permanent plan for the time being.

- Family planning has many misconceptions.

▶ It's time to grab the bull by the tail and look it squarely in the eye.

▶ The people in my district do not want this highway bypass, no matter if it goes through or around the city.

▶ I think I misquoted myself.

▶ My knowledge is no match for his ignorance.

▶ As long as I am in the Senate, there will be a nuclear suppository in our state.

▶ I don't necessarily believe what I think.

▶ I know what I believe is different from what I think.

▶ This body is becoming entirely too laxative about some matters.

▶ These numbers are not my own; they are from someone who knows what he's talking about.

▶ Panama belongs to us. We stole it fair and square.

▶ This year's grant application represents a 360-degree turn from last year.

▶ Do you realize that DNR wants to buy up millions of acres of land in northern Wisconsin that have been untouched by nature?

▶ This bill will help rural Wisconsin and sparsely populated large cities.

▶ This is a good health bill. Take it from one who has survived a terminal heart attack.

▶ My colleague is listening with a forked ear.

▶ Don't rock the trough.

A member of the Michigan House of Representatives noted, "The House will not allow you to circumvent the rules unless you do it right." I don't mean to cast asparagus, but when politicians circumvent the rules of the English language, they certainly do it right.

A Guide to Sportspeak

He threw 100 pitches in six innings, and that's a mouthful.

The Philadelphia Eagles are playing the Miami Dolphins in a televised game. The play-by-play commentator explains that Philadelphia is beginning to contain Miami's explosive offense, but a muscle-brained metaphor bursts through his line: "It appears as though the Achilles' heel of the Eagles' defense is about to rear its ugly head."

Welcome to the wonderful world of sportspeak, where modifiers are mangled, participles dangled, and metaphors mixed with abandon. The broadcast booth is an unremitting font of anguished English. Take (please!) these classic pieces of play-by-play commentary from

Jerry Coleman, for many years the radioman for the San Diego Padres:

▶ There's a long drive! Winfield is going back, back, back! He hits his head against the wall! It's rolling to second base!

▶ Next up is Fernando Gonzales, who is not playing tonight.

▶ The Padres took a three-game series from the Giants, three games to two.

▶ The pitcher has a blister on the index hand of his pitching finger.

The English language and the game of baseball would be immeasurably the poorer without the fractured diction and unruly grammar of St. Louis Cardinals pitcher and broadcaster Dizzy Dean. Dean peppered his commentaries with *ain't*s and double negatives, and when he thought a verb too colorless, he invented his own, as in "He slud into third base" or "The pitcher flang the ball." When an indignant listener complained, "Mr. Dean, don't you know the king's English?" Dizzy reflected for a moment, then replied, "Sure I do—and so's the Queen."

Ever since Dizzy Dean's verbal vagaries, broadcasters have been slaughtering the king's English:

▶ Arnie Palmer, usually a great putter, seems to be having trouble with his long putts. However, he has no trouble dropping his shorts.

▶ He's already got two championship rings under his belt.

▶ Folks, this is perfect weather for today's game. Not a breath of air.

▶ We'll be back with the recap, right after this message.

▶ That long drive actually sailed into the second balcony and hit a fan on the fly.

▶ Wrigley Field—it sort of reminds you of some of the old ballparks.

▶ We're coming up on the rubber game of a four-game series.

▶ Magic Johnson's three field goals have taken the sails out of the crowd.

▶ He threw a hundred pitches in six innings, and that's a mouthful.

▶ Listen to that! Eighty thousand football fans, and not one of them is making a sound!

▶ He ran the punt return back.

▶ They really miss the absence of Louis Lipps.

▶ Just don't think that Boston is going to blow up and dry away.

▶ The playoff picture is very complicated at this point. Let's call on Chris Berman to unweave the tapestry.

"Are you any relation to your brother Marv?" New Jersey Nets guard Leon Wood asked Steve Albert, Nets TV commentator. "I've never had major knee surgery on any other part of my body," observed Winston Bennett, University of Kentucky basketball forward. "You won't find a single four-letter word in my autobiography. I don't go for that bullshit," stated Hall of Fame pitcher Bob Feller.

Not so surprisingly, coaches and managers throw more screwballs than their players. After a close loss to St. Louis in the 1982 World Series, Milwaukee Brewers manager Harvey Kuenn revealed, "I told my players that they had nothing to be ashamed of. They could hang their heads high."

Observed New York Yankees and Mets manager Casey Stengel, "Good pitching always stops good hitting, and vice versa." Go figure.

In an award presentation to Joe DiMaggio, Yogi Berra, a Stengel protégé, gushed, "Joe, I want to thank you for teaching me that the only way to do something correctly is to do it right."

Detroit Tigers manager Sparky Anderson confided, "I've got my faults, but living in the past isn't one of them. There's no future in it." Chicago White Sox skipper Al Lopez fungoed an inadvertent pun when he said to a reporter, "Sievers will be a great insurance policy to us. He can spell Ted Kluszewski at first base." Shortly after being fired, Atlanta Braves manager Russ Nixon sighed, "I feel I did everything I could do, and probably more."

Let's not pick on the national pastime. "Football is an incredible game," proclaimed long-time Dallas Cowboys coach Tom Landry. "Sometimes it's so incredible, it's unbelievable."

Some pigskin pronouncements are so incredible, they're unbelievable. When he said, "We keep beating ourselves, but we're getting better at it," former Buffalo Bills coach Hank Bullough showed that football coaches can keep up with their counterparts in baseball. Cleveland Browns coach Sam Rutigliano blocked a metaphor as he explained why his team lost: "If you can't make the putts and can't get the man in from second in the bottom of the ninth, you're not going to win enough football games in this league."

The late Bill Peterson, who helped develop some of the nation's outstanding football coaches while building Florida State University into a national football power, was as famous for his loopy language as for his coaching abilities:

▶ I'm the football coach around here and don't you remember it.

▶ The greatest thing just happened to me. I got indicted into the Florida Sports Hall of Fame. They gave me a standing observation.

▶ You guys have to run a little more than full speed out there.

▶ You guys line up alphabetically by height.

▶ You guys pair off in groups of threes, then line up in a circle.

▶ We're not going to be a three-clouds-and-a-yard-of-dust kind of team.

Other coaches and managers manage the English language incorrectly to the point of doing it wrong. Toronto Maple Leafs coach Frank Smith announced, "I have nothing to say, and I'm going to say it just once." An unidentified NBA coach malapropped, "At some point, the team has to be held to account if there are too many fragrant fouls."

A college football coach commented on the prospects for next season: "Well, I'd say our greatest weakness is our lack of strength. Of course, I think you'll see some improvement as we get better."

Noted another coach: "We've got a lot of talent here, but we obviously need a lot of shoring up in several positions depthwise. This year we have to do a lot of weeding out and see what cream comes to the top."

Added a third: "If they ever take the emotion out of football, the stadiums will be full of no-shows."

"I blew it the way I saw it," confessed Ralph DeLeonardis, a minor-league baseball umpire, on a disputed call. That's how sportspeak works. You blow it the way you say it—and the cream comes to the top.

Blessed Bloopers

ST. JOHN OF THE MULTIPLE FEATURES

Kerry Bengston is a 10-ear member of the church.

A minister was scheduled to address a luncheon club. During the meal, the frustrated program chairperson bustled up to advise, "Something's gone wrong with the sound system. You'll have to speak up, preacher. The agnostics in this room are just terrible."

Even in the sanctuary of the church, ministers and priests can make some unholy mistakes in their sermons. Thundered one minister, "We should be as much concerned about those in spiritual danger as those in physical danger. If I were driving through town and saw that Mrs. Smith here had fallen into a canal, I wouldn't drive on and leave her there. I would stop the car, jump into the water, pull her out, and immediately begin giving her artificial insemination."

Another preacher informed his congregation, "One person who especially needs our prayers is Mrs. Jones. It appears that amputation will be necessary. In fact, gonorrhea has already set in."

Yet another minister explained: "This is my second sermon on sin. Last week's point sermon emphasized six points and went overtime, so today's sermon on sin will be pointless."

A pastor in Alabama reminded his flock, "Please don't let anything prevent you from missing this wonderful picnic."

Reading the morning scripture, a priest intoned, "Greater love hath no man than this, that he lay down his wife for his friend."

Another cleric offered this final benediction: "May all your desires be fulfilled, especially your deep desire for onion with God."

Here are some more sanctimonious slips, these from the pages of church bulletins, signs, and orders of service. I offer these, in the words of Sarah, in the book of Genesis, "so that all that hear will laugh with me." As Job said, they "fill my mouth with laughing, and thy lips with rejoicing":

▶ Support our church rummage sale: a good opportunity to get rid of anything not worth keeping but too good to throw away. Bring your husband.

▶ Please bring nonparishable foods to the church tonight.

▶ A bean supper will be held Saturday evening in the church basement. Music will follow.

▶ The choir of the Church of the Enunciation will perform in the upcoming choir festival.

▶ The rosebud on the altar this morning is to announce the birth of David Alan Beiser, the sin of Rev. and Mrs. Julius Beiser.

▶ Low self-esteem support group. 7–8:30 P.M. Eastview Baptist Church. Please use the back door.

▶ Today will be a Called Council Meeting fight after the church service. Come and vote!

▶ In November, Mr. Larkin passed out and explained the Finance Committee's budget forms for the 1994–95 church year.

▶ Monday, 11:30 A.M. to 8:30 P.M. Rain or shine. Pancake luncheon and supper under the auspices of the Sisterhood. All the pancakes you can eat!

Thursday, 7:45 P.M. Choir rehearsal. There will be no meeting of the Sisterhood this month on account of the Pancake luncheon and supper.

▶ Women in Harmony makes its debut at the Immanuel Baptist Church in Portland next week. The chorus's repertoire is clearly woman-centered, but doesn't lack broad-based appeal.

▶ Among the topics to be discussed by the church women's group will be abortion, family life, and youth in Asia.

▶ A massage by the Rev. Mr. Stuart, of the Pilgrim Holiness Church, will follow the singing.

▶ Fall Apple Pie Sale—Made from the ladies of the church.

▶ Sunday Evening Summer Program

Begins June 11, 6:00–7:30

Family Whorship Service

▶ The choir will sing "I Am But a Small Vice."

▶ We are happy to announce that we have secured the services of Rev. Struthers as our organist and choirmaster. He will also help with the youth club. We could not get a better man.

▶ Sermon: Come Onto Me

▶ The hymen for today is . . .

▶ A new worship service especially for the community. Don't dress up and come to the gym! 10:20–11:30 A.M. Sundays.

▶ In a church parking lot:
CHURCH PARKING ONLY
VIOLATORS TO WED
AT THEIR OWN EXPENSE

▶ Signs on a church:
TRUST IN GOD/HAVE FAITH IN THE LORD
SECURITY BY FRANKLIN BURGLAR ALARM, INC.

▶ Kerry Bengston is a 10-ear member of the church.

▶ Please join us for our Christmas concert and sin-along.

▶ One of our series of Lenten studies will be a sex-week study of *The Screwtape Letters*.

▶ Newburg Church tries to assist in serving a luncheon for the families of church members who have died immediately following the funeral.

▶ We invite everyone to our church, no matter what their demonination.

▶ God provided mammon, a wonderful food to take care of all the nutritional needs of the people.

▶ The outreach committee has enlisted 25 visitors to make calls on people who are not afflicted with any church.

Gavel to Gabble

DEFENSE ATTORNEY: *If the hand were on the other foot . . .*

"Well, now, Mrs. Bagley," says the lawyer to his client, who has taken the stand. "Tell the court all about it. Do you have a grudge?"

"Oh no," replies Mrs. Bagley. "But we do have a car port."

The lawyer tries again. "Well, does your husband beat you up?"

"No, I'm always the first one out of bed each morning."

"Do you still have relations?"

"Certainly. Two of my aunts, one uncle, and four cousins are still alive."

Growing desperate, the lawyer explains, "What I'm trying to find out is what grounds you have."

"Why, bless you, sir. We live in an apartment, and we don't even have a window box, let alone grounds."

"Mrs. Bagley," shrills the lawyer, now completely out of patience. "What exactly is your reason for seeking a divorce?"

"I'll tell you. It's because my husband and I can't hold an intelligent conversation!"

That swatch of testimony is made up, but exchanges that are just as loopy echo through our halls of justice.

One of the special appeals of courtroom blunders is their unique combination of high drama and low comedy. It is astonishing the regularity with which laughter invades the legal inner sanctum. All lawyers have those days when they think their brains belong to Daniel Webster and Clarence Darrow but their tongues belong to Daffy Duck and Elmer Fudd. Many a witness runs the mouth before engaging the brain and ends up tripping over the tongue while sitting in a stand.

Fortunately, America's army of court reporters are there to snare and then share all the resulting gavel-to-gabble laughter. Here's a full docket of disorder in the court, all on public record, word for word:

> **Q:** Just so I understand: it doesn't hurt when you have sex?
> **A:** No, it doesn't hurt.
> **Q:** Since that time—well, let me put it this way. Nowadays, do you ever have trouble getting an erection?

A: It's harder than before.

Q: What happened next?
A: I woke up unconscious in the hospital.

Q: What is your date of birth?
A: July fifteenth.
Q: What year?
A: Every year.

Q: What gear were you in at the moment of impact?
A: Gucci sweats and Reeboks.

Q: What was the first thing your husband said to you when he woke up that morning?
A: He said, "Where am I, Cathy?"
Q: And why did that upset you?
A: My name is Susan.

Q: Are you sexually active?
A: No, I just lie there.

Defense Attorney: If the hand were on the other foot . . .

Q: Let me get this straight, Mrs. Clarkson. Despite the fact that you had hired detectives to watch your husband's every move, you yourself stood on that corner every night, in all kinds of weather, watching your husband and a woman enter the house, seeing the lights go on downstairs, and then shortly after that in an upstairs bedroom, and then some minutes later turned out entirely. Why in the world did you do it?

A: I just wanted to be near my husband.

A woman charged with adultery was grilled by the opposing attorney:

Q: Young lady, just how do you justify your course of conduct?

A: Well, Judge, I gave him all he wanted. I kept him happy. I don't see why he should be concerned about what I did with my leftovers.

Q: What did you see when the accused took down his pants?

A: Well, it looked like a penis, only smaller.

Q: Well, you're a pretty big man, aren't you?

A: Yes, sir.

Q: How big would you say?

A: Oh, about eight inches.

Q: You don't know what it was, and you don't know what it looked like, but can you describe it?

A: No.

Q: Have you taken any trips out of the state since the accident?

A: Yes.

Q: Where did you go?

A: Georgia.

Q: For what purpose?

A: To funeralize my aunt.

Q: What was your speed at the time of the impact?

A: I don't know how fast I was going because I wasn't looking at the speed thermometer.

Q: How did your accident happen?

A: I was walking across the room and I slipped and fell on a wet spot on my back.

Q: Did the defendant have an erection?

The Defense: Objection. Calls for expert medical opinion.

The Court: I don't think so.

Q: Looking at People's Exhibit 5, a photograph, can you tell me who is in the picture?

A: That's me and Officer Geiger.

Q: Were you there when the picture was taken?

Q: But the anesthesiologist did not assist you in the operation?

A: No.

Q: But merely monitored her unconscious condition and passed gas. That sort of thing, right?

Attorney: Your Honor, I don't want to mislead you down a primrose path.

Q: This myasthenia gravis—does it affect your memory at all?

A: Yes.

Q: And in what ways does it affect your memory?

A: I forget.

Q: You forget. Can you give us an example of something that you've forgotten?

Q: Mr. Smith, I believe your prior testimony before lunch was that you were not arguing with Sam Stevens outside the bar.

A: No.

Q: Is that correct?

A: No, I wasn't.

Q: You were not arguing?

A: No.

Q: No, you were not arguing?

A: No, I wasn't.

Q: You were not arguing.

A: No.

Q: Is it correct that you were not arguing with Mr. Stevens?

A: Yes.
Q: Yes?

Q: How old is your son—the one living with you?
A: Thirty-eight or 35, I can't remember which.
Q: How long has he lived with you?
A: 45 years.

Q: And where was the location of the accident?
A: Approximately milepost 499.
Q: And where is milepost 499?
A: Probably between milepost 498 and 500.

Federal Judge: (from the bench) This seems like a fairly simple problem. Let's not make a federal case out of it.

The Court: Do you have a motion to make at this time?
Attorney: Yes. At this time, Your Honor, we would move that the jury be discharged and the jury be hung because of inability to reach a verdict.

Attorney: (in the middle of a long cross-examination) Your Honor, one of the jurors is asleep.
The Court: Well, you put him to sleep. Now wake him up.

Attorney: And can you show us a copy of that oral agreement?

Q: Sir, what is your IQ?
A: Well, I can see pretty well, I think.

Q: Where did you go next?
A: Over by the hill where all the people conjugate.

Q: Do you have copies of those estimates?
A: I don't know.
Q: Do you have copies of the purchase orders?
A: I don't know.
Q: Do you know who would know?
A: Do I know who would know? Yes.
Q: Who?
A: Me, if I knew.

The Court: Sir, I'm going to have to ask you to answer yes or no because my reporter does not have "uh-huh" and "huh-uh" buttons in her machine. And when you answer "uh-huh" and "huh-uh," she won't have a way to write it. Plus, the jury needs to hear "yes" or "no," not "uh-huh's," and "huh-uh's," okay?
Witness: Uh-huh.

Premedicated Humor

*The patient was bitten by a bat as he walked
down the street on his thumb.*

An Austin, Texas, emergency medical technician answered a call at the home of an elderly woman whose sister had collapsed. As they were placing her into the ambulance, the lady wailed, "Oh, lawdy, lawdy. I know what's the matter with her. She done got the same thing what killed her brother. It's a heretical disease."

The EMT asked what that would be, and the lady said, "The Smiling Mighty Jesus!"

When the EMT got the sister to the county hospital, she looked up the brother's medical records to find he had died of spinal meningitis.

A woman rushed into the lobby of a hospital and exclaimed, "Where's the fraternity ward?" The receptionist calmly replied, "You must mean the maternity ward."

The woman went on, "But I have to see the upturn." Patiently, the receptionist answered, "You must mean the intern."

Exasperated, the woman continued, "Fraternity, maternity, upturn, intern—I don't care wherever or whoever. Even though I use an IOU, and my husband has had a bisectomy, I haven't demonstrated for two months and I think I may be fragrant!"

That same woman later became three centimeters diluted and, narrowly avoiding a mess carriage, she ultimately went into contraptions. Her baby was born with its biblical cord wrapped around its arm, and she asked if she could have the child circumscribed before leaving the hospital.

It is ironic that the humor in hospitals, emergency rooms, and doctors' offices—usually some of the scariest places—can be exceedingly hilarious. The giddy ghost of Mrs. Malaprop haunts medical halls and application forms, where we discover all manner of strange conditions, such as swollen asteroids (adenoids), an erection (anorexia) nervosa, shudders (shingles!), and migrating headaches. All the malappropriate terms in this chapter were miscreated by anxious patients or hassled doctors and nurses.

A man went to his eye doctor, who told him he had a case of myopera and would have to wear contract lenses. That was a lot better than his friend, who had had a cadillac removed from his eye. Still, when he worked at his computer, he would have to watch out for harbor tunnel syndrome. He worried that his authoritis of the joints might be a signal of Old Timer's disease and fretted that a genital heart defect was causing a myocardial infraction and trouble with his duodemon.

Another man was in the hospital passing gull stones from his bladder while the doctor was treating a cracked dish in his spine. After the operation, his glands were completely prostrated. A hyannis hernia, hanging hammeroids, inflammation of the strocum, and a blockage of his large intesticle could have rendered him impudent.

We're not talking about just a deviant septum here. These symptoms were enough to give a body heart populations, high pretension, a peppery ulcer, and postmortem depression—even a cerebral hemorrhoid. But at least that's better than a case of headlights (head lice), sea roses of the liver, cereal palsy, or sick as hell anemia. Any of these could cause one to slip into a comma.

A woman experienced itching of the virginia during administration, which led to pulps all up her virginal area, and they had to void her reproductions. This was followed by a tubular litigation and, ultimately, mental pause. Mental pause can cause one to become a maniac depressive and act like a cyclopath.

She didn't worry about her very close veins, but she thought that a mammy-o-gram and Pabst smear might show if she had swollen nymph glands and fireballs of the eucharist. That's "fibroids of the uterus," and it's something you can't cure with simple acnepuncture, Heineken maneuver, or a bare minimum (barium) enema. Apparently, evasive surgery would be required. Afterward, she would recuperate in expensive care.

In her introduction to [sic] Humor, a collection of bloopers from medical transcription, editor Diane S. Heath writes: "Nobody appreciates a good chuckle more than the medical transcriptionist who recognizes humor in the words and situations depicted in daily dictation, perhaps because it relieves the tension or dispels the gloom associated with the content." Jest for the health of it, here is the lighter side of a profession often preoccupied with tragedy:

▶ Experienced mood swings because she suffered from PBS.

▶ The patient is a 32-year-old male who was involved in an altercation with his ex-wife. He suffered a concussion, black eye, and laceration of the arm. She complained of a stress headache from the incident.

▶ Patient is separated from his wife, and he is also allergic to penicillin.

▶ The patient was bitten by a bat as he walked down the street on his thumb.

▶ The young man was seen in my office complaining of involuntary seminal fluids emission during foreplay of several weeks' duration.

▶ The sound of snoring is due to vibrations of the soft palate and the vulva at the back of the throat.

▶ On examination here, she was having pain with intercourse.

▶ The dermatologist made a recommendation for treatment of her face which is not of a serious nature.

▶ Patient's wife hit him over the head with an ironing board, which now has six stitches in it.

▶ For his impotence we will discontinue the meds and let his wife handle him.

▶ She is quite hard of hearing. In fact, she can't hear at all in the left eye.

▶ Her first and only child was born at age 44.

▶ Sinuses run in the family.

▶ She had one fall in April; she attributed this to luck, not circumstance.

▶ He was eating his tray so I didn't examine him.

▶ The patient is a 65-year-old woman who fell, and this fall was complicated by a truck rolling over her.

▶ The patient was lying flat on a guernsey.

▶ Suppositories to be inserted in the rectum at bedtime, after a sitz bath for 12 days.

▶ This 54-year-old female is complaining of abdominal cramps with BMs on the one hand and constipation on the other.

▶ She fell this morning while she was trying to get out of the commode.

▶ The patient was side-swiped by a car riding a motor-cycle.

▶ Healthy-appearing, decrepit 69-year-old white fe-male, mentally alert but forgetful.

▶ When she fainted, her eyes rolled around the room.

▶ The patient is a 46-year-old, single, unemployed, re-tired Hell's Angel.

▶ Further suggested that she avoid using toilet paper and use cotton underwear.

▶ He was advised to force fluids through his inter-preter.

▶ He states he hit his head on his forehead.

▶ Her boyfriend also apparently has vaginal warts.

▶ She is to refrain from sexual intercourse until I see her in the office.

▶ The genitalia are normal in experience . . . I'm sorry . . . appearance.

▶ Chief complaint: Auto/pederast accident. History: The patient was a pederast and was struck by an automobile of unknown history.

▶ The patient says he feels so wonderful he wonders what to do with it.

▶ He sleeps on a firm mattress with his legs straight up on his back.

▶ Since the patient stopped smoking, his smell is beginning to return.

▶ The patient is a Catholic nun currently in between missionaries.

▶ He was the first of eight children. His father died at seven.

▶ She has striking red hair and matching brown eyes.

▶ Patient stated that if she would lie down, within two or three minutes something would come across her abdomen and knock her up.

▶ He has an allergy to asthma.

▶ The rest of the physical examination is normal, including the right hands.

▶ Patient has chest pains if she lies on her left side for over a year.

▶ Patient walks six blocks now. The doctor told him it may take a year to come back.

▶ The patient and her husband are both trying to get pregnant.

▶ She has no rigors or shaking chills, but her husband states that she was very hot in bed last night.

Laugh Insurance

EMERGENCY ROOM

"I had to have my armpits removed."
"I was breakdancing, and I think the break broke me."

At the start of World War II, a young man wrote this letter to his draft board:

Dear Sirs:

This is to notify you of the symptoms I have. Swelling of ankles and feet. Right eye and ear affected by Bell's palsy. Right eye discharges white matter. Both eyes water on contact with wind.

Left great toe not active because of operation from secondary infraction from bad case of athletic foot. Left great toe develops fever on too much pressure on it, as well as left leg to knee. Left chin bone pains from sunburn two years ago.

Left leg and arm cramps or rheumatism, asthma, and sinus. Believe have touch of TB in lungs—frequent coughing and spitting of matter and substance very gluey and color brownish black. Vomitory in morning. Sometimes blood.

Stomach tender and pains. Burns like fire if drinking orange juice for breakfast. I believe I have ulcers or cancer. Right large intestines have frequent pains. Have had doctor's treatment for it. Piles sometimes bleed.

Continuous colds and head pains, fevers. High or low pressure, probably heart. Spine in my back pains and itches. All teeth ache very bad at times. Perspiration on forehead. Painful bunions on right foot and left bottom foot.

Have inferior complex and nervous conditions, 95% of my acquaintances claim that I am mentally unbalanced. Was kicked in head by a horse when very young.

P.S. I am a patriotic man and I don't want you should think I am trying to get out of draft. If I was, I would exaggerate a little.

People are wondrously creative in describing their aches and pains, and nowhere do we find more creativity than on insurance forms. Claims are normally the most serious part of the insurance business, but humor creeps in every now and then. Here are some explanations for calamitous claims, as received by various insurance company divisions and underwriters. Each is a laugh insurance policy in itself:

▶ My cartridges are shot.

▶ Fractured 37 ribs.

▶ Fallen buttocks.

▶ The car came at me like a bat out of left field.

▶ An airplane hit the house and came in.

▶ I have athlete's foot on my hands.

▶ I was up a tree after a squirrel, and a guy shot at me.

▶ A broken leg with a severe case of flu.

▶ Hernia from pulling cork out of bottle.

▶ I was crossing the street when a car hit my husband, causing me to break my left foot.

▶ I was making a turn when a car hit me and broke my arm. I no longer own it.

▶ I was looking at weights on bowling balls when a six-pound ball fell on my head.

▶ Getting on a bus, the driver started before I was all in.

▶ While dancing in the navy, someone stepped on my hand.

▶ I fell, hitting my right head.

▶ Accidentally kicked in the stomach by a customary fooling around.

▶ I put tire patch on Playtex girdle and it caused infection in right thigh.

▶ I displaced my shoulder swatting a fly.

▶ I have bad eyes and swell feet.

► I suffered burns while holding shirt tail up over an open flame to warm my back.

► I keep vomiting on an empty stomach.

► I hurt my leg and ever since have been decapitated.

► I woke up unconscious.

► I am sick now from an absence in my head.

► While at work, I was lifting a 60-inch television set and I hurt my back with the help of my co-workers.

► While waving good night to a friend, I fell out a two-story window.

► Bad corns. Could not wear shoes. Had them removed by surgery.

► I broke my foot when I jumped from a 10-foot bank to get down in a ditch so I could get up a tree.

► I am an amateur fire-eater. Blowing fire out of mouth, it backfired.

► My downfall was a stairway.

► I fell from the ceiling at home. Am nervous to work now.

► It started with a cough and ended with an appendectomy.

► I had the flue with a small touch of ammonia.

► Foot broke out and began to run.

► My wooden leg was broken when a man hit me with a ranch [wrench].

► Headaches and earaches caused by my guitar [goiter].

▶ Sickness on account of garter [goiter].

▶ Broken uncle.

▶ I have romantic fever.

▶ I had to have my armpits removed.

▶ I was break-dancing, and I think the break broke me.

▶ Shortly after the onset of pain, I became pregnant.

▶ I flunked your analysis test.

Signs of Trouble

*O*n *the freight platform of a large station stood a hefty carton on which was printed:*

> TO AVOID BREAKAGE
> KEEP BOTTOM ON TOP

Underneath this, a slightly smaller sign had been pasted:

> TOP MARKED BOTTOM
> TO AVOID CONFUSION

A sign next to an elevator in the Federal Reserve Bank building in Boston reads:

> IN CASE OF FIRE, EVACUATE THE BUILDING.
> DO NOT USE STAIRWAYS.
> DO NOT USE ELEVATORS.

Above an elevator button in a Denver office building, one finds this sign:

> BRAILLE INSTRUCTIONS
> PLEASE SEE BELOW

We live in the time of the signs, and the examples above cause us to try to find signs of intelligent life on our planet. Here are more signs of the times that tell us it is time to re-sign:

At a tourist spot in Nova Scotia: CAUTION--SLIPPERY ROCKS AND SUDDEN SWELLS AND WAVES RISING ABOVE THE ROCKS EVEN ON FINE AND CALM DAYS HAVE CAUSED MANY ACCIDENTS AND DROWNINGS. ENJOY THEM AT A SAFE DISTANCE.

On bulletin boards at a San Antonio, Texas, hospital: NURSES ARE REQUIRED TO WEAR NOTHING BUT WHITE HOSE.

At the entrance of a college cafeteria: SHOES ARE REQUIRED TO EAT IN THE CAFETERIA. Penciled underneath: SOCKS CAN EAT ANYWHERE THEY WANT.

In a Chicago department store: BARGAIN BASEMENT UPSTAIRS.

At the entrance of Texas A&M–Corpus Christi: NATIONAL COLLEGIATE ALCOHOL AWARENESS WEEK—FREE DRINKS IN STUDENT CENTER LOUNGE.

In front of a Canton, Massachusetts, filling station: OUR REST ROOMS ARE CLEAN AROUND THE CLOCK. (What about the rest of the room?)

Near a London hospital:

HOSPITAL
PLEASE GO QUIETLY

Near Heathrow Airport: TWA--FLIGHTS TO THE UNITED STATES AND CALIFORNIA.

In the window of a Boston supermarket: FOR YOUR SHOPPING CONVENIENCE WE WILL BE CLOSED CHRISTMAS DAY, DEC. 25.

In a Santa Fe, New Mexico, open-air market:

FLEA MARKET
NO DOGS

Two signs, one over the other, in Seattle: PLANNED PARENTHOOD/FREE DELIVERY.

On a traffic light in Newport, New Hampshire: OFFICER AHEAD/WHEN FLASHING.

On a Newark, New Jersey, government office building: THE STATE OF NEW JERSEY HAS MOVED FOUR BLOCKS WEST.

In the window of a Woodsville, Washington, store:

OUT OF BUSINESS
THANKS TO OUR CUSTOMERS

On the door of a men's room in West Virginia:

MEN
SLIPPERY
WHEN
WET

Over cash register in a Seattle clothing store: WE DON'T CHANGE UNDERWEAR.

In a San Diego laundromat: NO TINTING OR DYING IN MACHINE.

On a Jacksonville, North Carolina, street:

ABSOLUTELY

NO

PARKING

ENFORCED

On a Hendersonville, North Carolina, restaurant: OPEN. GREAT FOOD 'TIL 11 P.M.

In the produce section of a Kitty Hawk, North Carolina, market: IF THE PACKAGE SIZE YOU WANT IS NOT ON DISPLAY, PLEASE SEE THE PERISHABLE MANAGER.

Painted on the side of a pickup truck:

SAUSAGE DELI

TUCSON'S ALTERNATIVE TO FINE DINING

On a Minneapolis motel: MARIA'S BREAKFAST CLUB: NOW OPEN EVENINGS.

Outside a Tampa restaurant:

FRIED CLAMS

PARK HERE

At the approach to a bridge in New London, Connecticut: STOP ON WHITE LINE WHEN RED.

In a fast-food eatery: IF YOUR ORDER IS NOT SATISFACTORY, PLEASE RETURN THE PRODUCT TO THE COUNTER AND WE WILL REPLACE IT WITH A SMILE.

Outside a cabinetmaker's shop in Sperryville, Virginia:

ANTIQUE TABLES

MADE DAILY

In front of a Parkville, Maryland, seafood store: PARKING FOR PARKVILLE CRABS ONLY.

On a Newton, Massachusetts, club:

LIVE LOBSTERS

DANCING NIGHTLY

Sign outside a barbecue restaurant in Atlanta: NOW ACCEPTING APPLICATIONS FOR COOKS BETWEEN 2 AND 5.

In a pet shop: LARGE BIRDS REDUCED.

In a Naples, New York, cemetery: POSITIVELY NO HOLES DUG IN THIS CEMETERY.

At a Sandwich, Massachusetts, diner: WE GUARANTEE FAST SERVICE NO MATTER HOW LONG IT TAKES.

In the bathroom of a Chinese restaurant in Detroit: EMPLOYEES MUST WASH YOUR HANDS.

On a farm near Elizabethtown, Kentucky: USED COWS FOR SALE.

In auto-repair garage in Seattle: WE ARE SORRY BUT WE CANNOT ACCEPT ANY CUSTOMER PARTS OR FLUIDS.

At some Kentucky Fried Chicken restaurants: PARKING FOR KENTUCKY FRIED CUSTOMERS ONLY.

At a truck stop in Tulsa, Oklahoma: KIDS WITH GAS EAT FREE.

In the Glasgow, Scotland, airport: HUMPED PEDESTRIAN CROSSING.

By the road near Cape May, New Jersey:

BLUEPOINT OYSTERS

OPENED

WHILE YOU WAIT

IN THEIR OWN JUICE

On a back road in Washington State:

NEW AND USED ANTIQUES

COME IN

WE ARE CLOSED

In a Bridgewater, New Jersey, bookstore, advertising a cookbook writer: AUTHOR SIGNING AND TASTING.

In the Mammoth Caves in Virginia: BOTTOMLESS PIT—175 FEET DEEP.

At the entrance of a one-way bridge in Sonoma, California: WHEN THIS SIGN IS UNDERWATER, THIS ROAD IS IMPASSABLE.

In a Kalamazoo, Michigan, department store:

> WE HAVE BUTTON-FLY LEVIS
> OPEN TILL 10 TONITE.

At a diet center in Poughkeepsie, New York: LOSE ALL YOUR WEIGHT: $198.

In a Los Angeles dance studio: DUE TO CIRCUMSTANCES BEYOND OUR CONTROL DANCE LESSONS WILL RESUME NEXT WEEK.

At the entrance to a bridge in Philadelphia:

> IN CASE OF ENEMY ATTACK
> DO NOT STOP
> DRIVE RIGHT OFF BRIDGE

In a Portland, Maine, parking garage: TENANTS NOT PAID BY THE 15TH OF THE MONTH WILL BE TERMINATED.

In a Brooklyn barbershop window: DURING CONSTRUCTION WE WILL SHAVE YOU IN THE REAR.

In a Baltimore restaurant: ALL FOOD MUST PASS THROUGH THE CASHIER BEFORE ENTERING THE DINING ROOM.

III

COLD OFF
THE PRESS

Headline Headaches

*INCLUDE YOUR CHILDREN
WHEN BAKING COOKIES.*

In late summer, *The Dallas Morning News* published a special back-to-school section that covered new trends in education and new personnel, curriculum, and physical changes in the Dallas school system. Such a special section is often called an "extra," so the bright-red headline that lit up the top of the *Morning News* front page was:

TEXAS COLLEGES STILL A BARGAIN, EDUCATION EXTRA

Readers may have thought that Texas colleges were a good deal—as long as you weren't seeking to learn anything. Hey, we've got great cheerleaders, but we charge extra for courses in calculus.

Sometimes you need to know the context of a headline in order to guess what it's trying to announce:

MONTANA TRADED TO KANSAS CITY

Explanation: San Francisco 49ers quarterback Joe Montana was traded to the Kansas City Chiefs.

DEAD GUITARIST NOW SLIMMER AND TRIMMER

Explanation: Grateful Dead guitarist Jerry Garcia was on a diet.

HARRIS AHEAD BUT DANG LIKELY TO FORCE RUNOFF

Explanation: Oakland, California, Mayor Elihu Harris faced an election runoff against businessman Ted Dang.

SENTINEL NAMES SOBER FEMALE ATHLETE OF YEAR

Explanation: An athlete named Erin Sober was being honored.

LITTLE PEOPLE STRIKE VICTIMS

Explanation: It's the people with small businesses, not the players, who suffered most from the 1994 baseball strike.

JUST HOW LONG DOES IT TAKE
FACIAL HAIR TO GROW A FOOT?

Explanation: A man can figure he'll add another inch to his beard every eight weeks.

Now we can turn to the "How's That Again?" Department. Some call these examples blinkers because, quite simply, they make the reader blink:

FRIED CHICKEN COOKED
IN MICROWAVE WINS TRIP

AFTER DETOUR TO CALIFORNIA
SHUTTLE RETURNS TO EARTH

MAN JUMPS OFF 2ND STREET BRIDGE
NEITHER JUMPER NOR BODY FOUND

LEGISLATOR WANTS TOUGHER DEATH PENALTY

INCLUDE YOUR CHILDREN WHEN BAKING COOKIES

LEARNING TO SKI AN UPHILL BATTLE, EXPERTS SAY

WOMAN IMPROVING AFTER FATAL CRASH

MANY WHO MOVE TO FLORIDA
LEAVE AFTER DEATH

PROPERLY DRAFTED WILL
REDUCES ANXIETY AFTER DEATH

FLIER TO DUPLICATE
MISS EARHART'S FATAL FLIGHT

BOY DECLARED DEAD, REVIVES
AS FAMILY PROTESTS

MOTHER OF 18 CHILDREN IN TROUBLE AGAIN

SUICIDE BOMBERS STRIKE AGAIN

DEAD COYOTE FOUND IN BRONX
LAUNCHES SEARCH FOR ITS MATE

STUDY: THOSE WITHOUT
INSURANCE DIE MORE OFTEN

42 PERCENT OF ALL MURDERED WOMEN
ARE KILLED BY THE SAME MAN

EXPERTS INCREASE PROBABILITY
OF BIG QUAKE IN CALIFORNIA

PREVENT INJURIES TO BABY
MICROWAVE SAFELY

WOMAN FATALLY MAULED
ASSIGNED INDOOR JOB

Close kin to the blinker is the penetrating glimpse into the obvious. These self-evident headlines make us say, "Quite so. What's the big deal?"

JAIL MAY HAVE TO CLOSE DOORS

MAN FOUND DEAD IN CEMETERY

GUNFIRE IN SARAJEVO THREATENS CEASEFIRE

ACTOR'S DEATH DURING FILMING
USUALLY CAREER-LIMITING MOVE

RELIGION PLAYS MAJOR PART
IN MESSAGE OF EASTER

CITY HALL SAYS FLOODING IN LOWLANDS
WAS THE RESULT OF TOO MUCH WATER

DROWNING OFTEN CAUSE OF DEATH IN OKLAHOMA

STUDY: DEAD PATIENTS USUALLY NOT SAVED

EXTINCT ANIMALS MAY LOSE PROTECTION

STUDENTS AT COLLEGES GROW OLDER

WARRING FACTIONS DON'T AGREE

CHILDBIRTH IS BIG STEP TO PARENTHOOD

MEMORIZATION ABILITY
ATTRIBUTED TO BRAIN USE

LOW WAGES SAID KEY TO POVERTY

STUDY FINDS SEX, PREGNANCY LINK

ONLY RAIN WILL CURE DROUGHT

ECONOMIST USES THEORY TO EXPLAIN ECONOMY

BIBLE CHURCH'S FOCUS IS THE BIBLE

WHATEVER THEIR MOTIVES,
MOMS WHO KILL KIDS STILL SHOCK US

ALCOHOL ADS PROMOTE DRINKING

FREE ADVICE: BUNDLE UP WHEN OUT IN COLD

Banner Boners

SHOP SELLS SOUP TO NUTS

Headlines are literally the head lines, the most prominent part of a newspaper. Thus, when a headline runs amock and becomes a mockery, the error is there for all to see. It has been said that the pun is the lowest form of wit. When an editor inadvertently trips over a double meaning, the result can be the lowest form of headline:

NATIONAL HUNTING GROUP TARGETING WOMEN

HIGH COURT TO HEAR MARIJUANA CASE

TEEN ATTEMPTS TO QUIT SMOKING COLD TURKEY

LEGISLATORS TAX BRAINS TO CUT DEFICIT

CELEBRITIES RUB SHOULDERS ON SLOPES

PARTIAL JURY CHOSEN FOR TYSON CASE

SCHOOL TAXPAYERS REVOLTING

"WOMEN IN POLITICS" WORKSHOP
POSTPONED; MAKE-UP NOT SET

STARVING ANGOLANS EATING DOGS, BARK

PRINCE CHARLES BACKS BICYCLES
OVER CARS AS HE OPENS WORLD TALKS

CRACK FOUND IN AUSTRALIA

IOWA MAN'S SOON-TO-BE AMPUTATED
HAND COULD HOLD KEY TO MURDER

ARMLESS MUSICIAN TOUCHES AUDIENCE

ONE-LEGGED ESCAPEE STILL ON RUN

MAN MINUS EAR WAIVES HEARING

CELLULAR PHONES GROWING ON FARM

BEACHES ALL WASHED UP

ADMIRAL LIKES TO MAKE WAVES

MAN, 68, GETS 5 YEARS IN CRACK VIAL CASE

FIRST BLACK MAYOR, 5 RACES STILL UNDECIDED

BAR TRYING TO HELP ALCOHOLIC LAWYERS

NY MAYORAL CANDIDATES
DEBATE CRIME FIGURES

DON'T TIE MY HANDS ON ARMS,
REAGAN ASKS RADIO AUDIENCE

CRASH VICTIM LEAVES
A HOLE IN HER COMMUNITY

BOND ISSUE IS HELD OVER CITY INCINERATOR

SHOP SELLS SOUP TO NUTS

BUXOM STARLET KNOCKED FLAT BY FANS

FIRE OFFICIALS GRILLED
OVER KEROSENE HEATERS

POLICE SEEK AID FROM PUBLIC
IN SLAYING OF MAN

Sometimes the accidental pun turns on a quirk of grammar. Many headlines turn out to be grammatical minefields. Especially within the tight boundaries of a few picas, grammatical bombs can explode in an editor's face:

CLINTON VISITS HURT SOLDIERS

PREVENTIVE HEALTH SERVICE
FOR WOMEN BEING CUT IN HALF

TWO CARS COLLIDE,
ONE SENT TO HOSPITAL

SMITHSONIAN MAY CANCEL
BOMBING OF JAPAN EXHIBIT

U.S. SHIPS HEAD TO SOMALIA

HIGH SCHOOL HONORS STUDENTS
ARRESTED FOR HATE CRIMES

DOCTORS HELP TORCH VICTIM

VOTER FEARS ALERT POLITICIANS

FBI AGENT IN SUBWAY
SHOOTS MAN WITH KNIFE

2 SHIPS COLLIDE IN MANILA BAY;
FERRY CARRYING 500 SINKS

10% OF STUDENTS FAIL CLASSES FOR TRUANCY

YOUTH HIT BY CAR RIDING BICYCLE

FONDA GIVES POOR
EXERCISE, ACTING TIPS

ASTRONAUTS PRACTICE
LANDING ON LAPTOPS

POLICE CAN'T STOP GAMBLING

POLICE NAB STUDENTS WITH PAIR OF PLIERS

$1 MILLION GIVEN TO BETTER SLUMS

HOW TO COMBAT THAT FEELING
OF HELPLESSNESS WITH ILLEGAL DRUGS

Galley Oops!

Smoke bellowed from the windows.

The late Denys Parsons, British master collector of newspaper and magazine bloopers, created a specter named Gobfrey Shrdlu. Parsons decribed Shrdlu as "a malicious spirit with an irresistible sense of humour who lurks at the elbow of tired reporters, editors, and printers, with disastrous consequences."

My research indicates that Shrdlu was born during the reign of Charles I, when a court printer produced a handsome edition of the Bible. In it, some overworked typesetter or editor omitted the little word *not* from the seventh commandment so that it read: "Thou shalt commit adultery." As a result, that edition became known as The Adulterous Bible.

"Thou shalt commit adultery" was one of the very first printed bloopers, and the tradition of falling pratfully in public print has continued undimmed. Surely the irrepressible Shrdlu had a wispy hand in the creation of the following all-American galley gaffes:

▶ This afternoon, firemen battled a skyscraper fire in New York. It was confined to the upper floor, where smoke bellowed from the windows.

▶ The crime bill passed by the Senate would reinstate the federal death penalty for certain violent crimes: assassinating the president, hijacking an airline, and murdering a government poultry inspector.

▶ He came back to Sanford during the Depression to practice law with his father, Hiram, whose brother and law partner had just died and who needed help.

▶ The ordinance approved Tuesday night would impose a moratorium on all breeding by dog and cat owners for six months beginning in July.

▶ Political insiders call them wedge issues—raw, emotional issues like social security for Democrats and capital punishment for Republicans.

▶ The race also includes two of the five openly gay candidates running around the city.

▶ The pro–seat belt camp maintains that seat belts would keep students, particularly smaller children like Marvin, from being thrown from their seats and escaping serious injury.

▶ The department has implemented a computerized system for tracking down dead beat parents.

▶ Vincent Charles, a 14-year Secret Service veteran, said the string of incidents had heightened security around the White House. "The White House has always attracted the mentally ill," he said.

▶ Coach Mike Kyzyzewski asked some of his players over to the house for dinner one day last spring, then barbecued himself.

▶ "One in 20 women will be stalking victims at some time in their lives," said Rep. Carlin Cody, R-Hatfield, Texas.

▶ This is the third marriage of the groom. He has also been through World War II.

▶ After a Rastafarian had run amok and amputated one of his mother's and both of his father's hands, a police source described their conditions as serious. "They will just have to keep their fingers crossed," he said.

▶ Why would a young mother wait nine hours in line to get front-row tickets to a show? The Mighty Morphine Power Rangers, friends.

▶ The dead man was described as white, aged between 30 and 40, with an Irish accent.

▶ From now on, police will pick up road-killed animals, not Public Works employees.

▶ *I Spy* returns. Secret agents (Robert Culp, Bill Cosby) from the 1960s TV series reunite on a case, joined by their son and daughter.

▶ Spike Lee says his new movie *Malcolm X* ends in the townships of South Africa, not the Harlem ballroom where the black nationalist leader was assassinated for artistic reasons.

▶ Smith was one of 10 Dallas businessmen robbed and brutally beaten with aluminum baseball bats from October to January.

▶ How we feel about ourselves is the core of self-esteem, says author Mary Anne Hunter.

▶ Q. Why don't women's blouses come in sleeve lengths, like men's shirts?

A. Because there is no standard sleeve length for women's blouses. Men's long-sleeve shirts are designed to be worn with a jacket so that the sleeve will hang just below the wrist line when the wearer is standing. But women wear long-sleeve blouses with other garments or no covering at all.

▶ During the scrimmage, [Fresno State University basketball coach Jerry] Tarkanian paced the sideline with his hands in his pockets while biting his nails.

▶ Garden club members heard a talk on bugs and roaches. A large number were present.

▶ In women twice as often as in men, death was the first sign that HIV was progressing, the researchers found.

▶ The fiftieth anniversary of the bombing of Dresden by the Royal Air Force and the U.S. Army Air Forces is being observed today in Britain as an act of retaliation for the bombing of Coventry by the Luftwäffe on Nov. 14, 1940.

▶ HELP WITH KIDS. Colorado families with more than 5,000 children have sought help finding child care from the new, free Colorado Office of Resource and Referral Agencies.

▶ Jazz tunes, including "Modern Leaves," "Scrapple

from the Apple," and "The Girl with Emphysema," stopped at 8:30, when the volunteer trip packed up.

▶ An American teenager gives birth every 20 minutes.

▶ Seven pages of the biography are devoted to revelations about Coco Chanel's habit of cooling champagne by pouring it over a block of ice, her rock crystal collection, her brown pillows, and her paneled closets.

▶ Japanese tabloids are all atwitter that the wife of Crown Prince Naruhito, whose years-long search for a bride was exhaustively chronicled, might soon be a father.

▶ NOTICE: I wish to thank anyone who so kindly assisted in my husband's death.

▶ Arthritis support groups: For family and friends and all types of arthritis, including lupus and fibromyalgia.

▶ There are no national temperatures today due to transmission difficulties.

▶ The Southeast Georgia Alzheimer's Chapter will present a cabaret, "A Night to Remember."

▶ If you ask the average American for a detailed description of the bed he sleeps in, he will probably be unable to oblige you. He can precisely visualize his overcoats, his golf clubs, or his automobile, but his bed and furniture in general are merely nebulous conveniences in his mind. And the same thing is true of his wife.

All the Nudes Fit to Print

19 ☉CTOBER 96

SUN	MON	TUE	WED	THU	FRI	SAT
		1	2	3	4	5
6	7	8	9	10	11	12
13	14	15	16	17	18	19
20	21	22	23	24	25	26
27	28	29	30	31		

OCTOBER IS BREAST AWARENESS MONTH.

Possibly the most embarrassing modern-day typographical error—due to the slip of an unknown typo writer—appeared in *The Washington Post* in 1915. In a news story, it was noted that President Woodrow Wilson had taken his fiancée Edith Galt to the theater the previous night and, rather than watching the play, "spent most of his time entering Mrs. Galt." The writer meant "entertaining."

Another story included a photograph of a famous president and popular funny man. The below-par caption read: "President Richard Nixon watches comedian

Jackie Gleason tee off on the first hole as they started a golf match in Miami Sunday. The president's first shot went high and off to the left about 100 yards. But he didn't look bad compared with Gleason, who sliced his first shot to the right and teed off again, sending a grass-cutter fart to the left."

More recently, a news story reported, "Ivan Gorlen drove his motorcycle into a lamppost 12 years ago and in an instant severed not only the cartilage in his knee but his grip on the gleaming balls that were his life."

Turns out that Gorlen was a bowler.

"Sextra! Sextra! Read all about it!" newspapers seem to blare. It's amazing how lewd, lascivious, licentious, and lecherous are so many of the errors in newspapers and magazines:

▶ Katherine Innes, as the virgin in this year's production of the Passion Play, has already started her rehearsal. She is the first blond virgin for a century.

▶ The Oregon Republican admits he harassed women but vows not to quit.

▶ Matson, of Phelps County, is recuperating from wounds inflicted two weeks ago when an unknown assailant fired a shotgun at his backside. About 800 marijuana plants have been discovered in the same area.

▶ Barton, it is claimed, was driving at a high rate of speed and swerving from side to side. As he approached the crossing, he started directly towards it and crashed into Miss Palmer's rear end, which was sticking out into the road about a foot. Luckily she escaped injury and the damage can easily be remedied with a new coat of paint.

▶ Jerry Lee Lewis played the piano with his elbow, feet, and any other part of his body available.

▶ The Misses Doris, Agnes, and Vivian Jameson are spending several days at the home of their mother. This is the first time in years that the community has had the pleasure of seeing the Jameson girls in the altogether.

▶ Bronstein, a UNH entymologist, is an expert on insects that bite people in recreation areas.

▶ Policeman Bart Grayson was shot through the stomach and Bill Maybury, Indiana Harbor taxi driver, through the hip, while a guard at the jail was shot in the excitement.

▶ The bits about masturbation are especially well handled.

▶ In a wanton display of chastity, more than 100,000 Southern Baptist youngsters are pledging to abstain from sex until marriage.

It is in the art of headline writing that journalists show themselves to be so wanton that they sometimes land in the soup. *The Washington Post* printed this headline on the front page of its first edition: FDR IN BED WITH COED. Actually President Roosevelt was in bed with a cold, as the story made clear.

The New Orleans *Morning Tribune* ran a story covering King Edward's courtship of Mrs. Wallace Simpson. The headline: GIVES KING TWO DAYS ON WALLY.

Many a suggestive headline is explained with a little background information:

MANLY MAN MARRIES FERTILE WOMAN

Explanation: A man from Manly, Minnesota, married a woman from Fertile, in the same state.

LAY TEACHERS FOR FIRST TIME IN SCHOOLS

Explanation: A local Catholic school can no longer fill its staff with nuns.

CHICK ACCUSES SOME OF HER
MALE COLLEAGUES OF SEXISM

Explanation: Los Angeles councilwoman Laura Chick lashed out at City Hall as the "most sexist good-old-boys environment that I've ever been in."

IDAHO BRIDES CAN'T TAKE HEAVY G.I. TRAFFIC

Explanation: The story is about Idaho *bridges*, but the printer carelessly dropped a *g*.

VIRGIN TO PROVIDE WEEKEND EXCITEMENT

Explanation: Famous runner Craig Virgin will enter the local race.

SURGERY FOR BUTTS

Explanation: New England Patriots running back Marion Butts needs an operation.

HELEN WILLS MOODY ON 3-WEEK HONEYMOON

Explanation: Tennis champion Helen Wills Moody is on her honeymoon.

BRANDEIS PLAYERS MASTER BATES

Explanation: Brandeis University defeated Bates College in football.

RECORD SOVIET CROP: TURD

Explanation: Crop production was announced by the communist news outlet Trud—creating an accident waiting to happen.

ALLIES PUSH BOTTLES UP 10,000 GERMANS
Translation: Advances by the Allied forces in World War II contained the German forces.

Here are some more headlines that would keep Sigmund Freud busy for many sessions:

FREE VACCINATIONS SOUGHT
FOR EVERY CHILD BY CLINTON

SEMINAL ISSUE RESURFACES
IN PRISONERS' SUITS

PRIVATES HELD IN SEXUAL ASSAULT

ADULTS THINK TEENS HAVING
MORE SEX THAN THEY ARE

AWALT READY TO PLUG
BILL'S HOLE AT TIGHT END

LAY POSITION PROPOSED
BY BISHOP FOR WOMEN

BARBARA BUSH TALKS ABOUT HER LIFE,
ABORTION, HOMOSEXUALITY

TEEN SEX DELAYED WHEN DAD'S AROUND

FUMES FORCE HUGE NOGALES EVACUATION

WIFE LOSES 86 POUNDS BEFORE HUSBAND COMES

PECK RECALLS MOBY DICK AS HIS HARDEST

OCTOBER IS BREAST AWARENESS MONTH

BOY WANTS TO MOUNT AUTOGRAPHED GUITAR

AFTER SPILL, JOCKEY'S BUSINESS FALLS OFF

FRENCH DAM SITE BETTER OFF WITH U.S. AID FUNDS

ADMIRALS AXED FOR ROLL IN TAILHOOK

BRISBANE BROKEN DOWN BY AGE AND SEX

POWER POLE ERECTION CUTS
POWER IN CHALAN PAGO

POLICE WANT TO SEE MORE
OF MAN WHO EXPOSED SELF

MARY SMITH TO PRESENT RECTAL

PROBE UNDERWAY ON STRIPPER

EX-FIREMAN STARTS PRISON FOR SEX CRIMES

TAXIS TRY FLASHERS

We Stand Korrected

Mr. Hoffnagle is, of course, a detective on the police farce.

"Our paper carried the notice last week that Mr. Oscar Hoffnagle is a defective on the police force. This was a typographical error. Mr. Hoffnagle is, of course, a detective on the police farce."

It has been said that journalism is the first rough draft of history. Reporting can also be the first rough draft of more accurate reporting in the form of "corrections" that appear a day or two after the original stories. The problem is that sometimes corrections turn out to be defectives on the paper's policing farce. At other times, the corrections that turn out to be incorrections make you wonder what the newspaper is trying to correct:

▶ The marriage of Miss Frieda van Amburg and Willie Branton, which was announced in this paper a few weeks ago, was a mistake which we wish to correct.

▶ A news analysis article on Saturday about the politics behind Gov. Pete Wilson's role in eliminating affirmative-action programs at University of California campuses rendered a word incorrectly in a question from Sherry Bebitch Jeffe, a former legislative aide in Sacramento.

    Ms. Jeffe said of Mr. Wilson: "He's biding his time on this, knowing all along what he was going to do when the time was ripe. It's ripe. He's picked." She did not say, "He's pickled."

▶ An interview with Mary Matalin, the former deputy manager of the Bush campaign, quoted her incorrectly on the talk show host Rush Limbaugh. She said he was "sui generis," not "sweet, generous."

▶ The Pacific Rim column in yesterday's Business/Extra section should have read that "*Fine Boys* is a leading Japanese fashion magazine for guys," not gays. The *Chronicle* regrets the editing error.

▶ Rape suspect Fred A. Zaroff told state police September 16 that he had sex with a 25-year-old woman, but it was "not a rape," according to testimony in the Crown County Court. A story in Monday's *Times* incorrectly said that Zaroff told troopers sex with the woman was "not that great."

▶ Because of a telephone transcription error, an article yesterday about Mary Allison Graves, a lawyer, included an erroneous description. The first sentence should have begun, "Attorney Mary Allison Graves," not "A tiny Mary Allison graves." Ms. Graves is 5 foot 7.

▶ An item in our newspaper erred in reporting that a cash bar will be part of the First United Church's Back-to-School Bash on Friday. A "car bash" will be part of the event.

▶ Our report on Monday said that up to 6 million had died in a gun battle in Sri Lanka. It should have read up to 6 militants died in a gun battle.

▶ We would like to point out that the previous writer on the subject, who was referred to as Miss Turner, was in fact Ms. Turner, not Mrs. Davis as we stated last week.

▶ Due to an error, the October 22 story on the ABC bond read that John Gorham said "diddly squat" when asked to explain consultant recommendations in the bond. The story should have read that we were unable to reach Gorham for comment. We apologize for the error.

▶ The article about the Ladies' Craft Club should have stated that Mrs. Brown and Mrs. Smith have talks on "smocking and rugs," not "smoking and drugs," as previously reported.

▶ There was a typo in lawyer Griswold's ad. His logo name is: "Your case is no stronger than your attorney," not "stranger."

▶ For the old-style corn chowder recipe from the Wooden Spoon column: Add one big onion, not one bag of onions.

▶ An article in Saturday's local edition incorrectly reported that a suspect who had been indicted by a federal grand jury had been identified as "Fnu Lnu." "Fnu Lnu" is not a name. "Fnu" is a law-enforcement abbreviation for "first name unknown," "Lnu" for "last name unknown."

► Burlington County Commissioner Bert Greenough has 100 percent support from his family, not 10 percent, as was stated in last week's article on Greenough's announcement to seek re-election.

► The "Candidates on Television" listing yesterday misspelled the name of the vice president in some editions. It is Quayle, not Quale. The *Tmise* regrets the error.

► The Auctions column in Weekend yesterday misidentified a brand of watch. It is a World Time, not a Waldheim. [Oh well, that's what happens when you forget to Adenhauer.]

And especially loopy is this incorrection:

► Erroneous information was inadvertently inserted into the biographical summary accompanying a story on Joseph Argyle. Mr. Argyle cannot simultaneously whistle, stand on his head, and drink beer.

Classified Classics

Conscious Attorney

A company ran an advertisement for a portable camp shower, emphasizing the ease with which it could be assembled. In a full-page ad, showing a bikini-clad woman screwing the shower to the wall, the big, black headline read: TWO SCREWS AND YOU'RE READY FOR A SHOWER.

Encyclopaedia Brittanica's boxed ad in the Yellow Pages prominently featured the following slogan in both boldface and quotation marks: **"Crib Through College."**

A Manitoba reader winged me this advertisement for a Kentucky Fried Chicken "event:"

KFC Express!
Grand Opening Special
"Super Value Meal Deal"
10 pieces of children, 5 hot wings,
large taters, large salad,
and one liter ice cream for only $19.99.

"It makes you wonder what KFC stands for, doesn't it?" quipped the reader.

Sure does, and it makes you wonder if anybody is out there proofreading all those advertisements that bombard us every day in an ad, ad, ad, ad world. As a seniors center's flier advises, "Please Patronize Our Advertisers." The following ads deserve our most fervent patronization:

▶ Giant Stuff-A-Pumpkin Bag. Have fun stuffing this giant pumpkin with friends & family. Great Halloween parties!

▶ Beautiful rocking baby cradle, solid cherry, 110 years old, original owner.

▶ Use our medicine and you can kiss your hemorrhoids goodbye!

▶ Kinney shoe stores: We only sell the right shoe.

▶ Our goal is to have you drive away a satisfied customer.

▶ Van—'94 Dodge Grand Caravan. One owner, lady driver, loaded.

▶ Feline Ultramilk is a low-lactose milk replacement for cats packaged in a disposable carton.

▶ The Best Collection of Enticing Lingerie! The dazzling

lingerie that California women are wearing is now available to you.

▶ Listing in Tucson, Arizona, Yellow Pages: Antidefecation League of B'Nai B'Rith.

▶ Turkey Carpet for Sale good condition the property of a lady too large for her rooms.

▶ In a flier for a child-abuse charity golf tournament: To stop child abuse, shoot a hole in one.

▶ ATTENTION CUSTOMERS. Due to flooding at a Proctor & Gamble plant in Albany, Georgia, we are experiencing some temporary out of stocks on Bounty Towels.

▶ On Red Cross cards asking recipients to donate their blood: Give blood again. It will be felt for a lifetime.

▶ MEDICAL MALPRACTICE. Former military attorneys specializing in claims arising out of military and VA hospitals. Free Consultation—No Fee Unless You Recover.

▶ Narcolepsy Support Group, a new group for individuals who suffer from this sleep disorder and their families, will begin at 2 P.M.

▶ Man with power, two sweet to be sour. Successful real estate typhoon, 40, 6'3", handsome, muscular, gentle, fun-loving, adventurous.

▶ Law-firm ad: If you have experienced accident, injury, or even death, please call us.

▶ Conscious Attorney. 11 years' experience. Brooklyn, Manhattan locations.

▶ In a brochure advertising a seminar on sexual harassment in the workplace: Experts will define issues, clarify laws, and conduct hands-on training.

▶ *On a menu in Healdsburg, California:* Two fried eggs, any style.

▶ Bras—$1/2$ Off!

▶ WANTED. Looking for hanging cage for my daughter. Must have exercise wheel.

▶ WANTED. Help for parents of children with attention deficit and lystexia.

▶ WANTED. 100-year-old bridge repairers.

▶ WANTED. A steady young woman to wash, iron, and milk two cows.

▶ WANTED. Boring Mill Operator.

▶ WANTED. Waitresses. Male or female may apply.

▶ WANTED. Emotionally Handicapped Teacher.

▶ WANTED. A boy to open oysters 15 years old.

▶ FOR SALE. Pointsetters, from 4 inches to 4 feet high.

▶ FOR SALE. Stimulated pearls.

▶ All Satin Shoes $9.99. Dying $4.99 extra.

▶ XYZ Motors is the oldest Saab dealer in the Upper Valley since 1968.

▶ Sensual Aides: How to order them without embarrassment. How to use them without disappointment.

▶ Osculating fan. Great Value. Only $8.93.

▶ Cupid's Restaurant. Beautiful ladies to serve you. We've Upped Our Standards. Up Yours.

▶ Equestrian Mom seeks pony or horse to rent to teach English to kids 5 & 7.

▶ There will be plenty to eat: hot dogs, hamburgers, children under 12, only a dollar.

▶ Laser Surgery Available for the Prostrate.

▶ Waterproof pigskin suede protects your ankles and feet in cool and incontinent weather.

▶ Widow, 73, would like to meet gent with a car of similar age.

▶ Consummate your marriage in one of our beautiful gowns.

▶ New and used hay and firewood for sale.

▶ Sale: Tires Slashed!

▶ Epoxy Rock, a durable, high-quality surface, is guaranteed for life. Never resurface again with Epoxy Rock.

▶ At the Cleveland Clinic, some of our surgeons can add years to your life. Others are equally expert at reversing the process.

▶ Mattie's. Yogurt and Ice Cream Parlor
    "An Alternative to Good Eating"

▶ Wow! Ferrari, red, with buckskin leather: 1984 308 GTSi QV, 1 owner with removable top.

▶ Treadmill $100, stair-stepper $75, mini trampoline $10, Thigh master $10, crutches $10.

▶ Dentistry for Adults and Children: Emergency Services Available, Quality Dentistry for All Ages, Strict Sterilization Between Patients.

▶ Grand piano for sale by young lady with mahogany legs.

▶ Our Brake and Tire Service Will Keep You Coming Back.

▶ Mattress company slogan: Why Not Sleep With the Best?

▶ Men and Women Heels: $1/2$ Price.

▶ Apple Brown Betty—$4.00. Heated with vanilla ice cream.

▶ Picked Fence, white 4×8, $7

▶ GLASS. 24 hours. Day or night.

▶ Special This Week in the Service Dept. at Jim Jakes Chevrolet: Front Brake Job, Inspect Rears.

▶ ATTENTION: If you're looking for a quiet lot with a large pond for your mobile home, we have the place for you.

▶ Will swap new handmade pairs of shorts for your child, sizes 2–6, for a weekend stay at your bed-and-breakfast.

▶ On a Mexican take-out menu: Melted Cheese on a flour tortilla, topped with chili, sour cream, and glaucoma.

▶ On a grocery bag: Save-Rite Proudly Supports Muscular Dystrophy.

▶ Allow me to recycle your unwanted children and infant clothing. Free pickup.

▶ Ace termite and pest control. Complete satisfaction or your money back. Ideal for children and pets.

▶ Sale: All Furniture Slashed!

Finally, this most classic of classified gems:

LOST DOG—Mixed breed, shaggy, left front leg amputated, missing top of right ear, partially blind, bad case of mange, tail was broken and healed crooked, some teeth gone, scars on head and back, has been castrated. Answers to name of Lucky.

IV

CLEAR AS MUDDLE

Fractured English Abroad

Go soothingly on the grease mind as there lurk the skid demon.

In 1962, during the Cuban missile crisis, Secretary of State Dean Rusk announced, "We're eyeball to eyeball and I think the other fellow just blinked." Soviet Foreign Minister Andrei Gromyko responded to the comment by announcing, "I am looking forward to talking with you balls to balls."

When a French-Canadian politician was applauded by an American audience, he beamed, saying, "I thank you for giving my wife and me the clap! I thank you from the heart of my bottom and my wife thanks you from her bottom too!"

These charming efforts remind us that few idioms and expressions can be literally translated word for word from one language to another. Every traveler and tourist in a foreign land has a tale to tell about the fractured English of signs, menus, and advertisements.

A classic of global gabble is this list of Japanese rules for the road:

1. At the rise of the hand of the policeman, stop rapidly. Do not pass him, otherwise disrespect him.
2. When passenger of the foot heave in sight, tootle the horn trumpet melodiously at first, If he still obstacles your passage, tootle with vigor and express by word of mouth the warning "Hai. Hai."
3. Beware of the wandering horse that he shall not take fright as you pass him. Do not explosion the exhaust pipe. Go soothingly by him or stop by the roadside till he pass away.
4. Give big space to the festive dog that make sport in the roadway. Avoid entanglement with your wheel spoke.
5. Go soothingly on the grease mud as there lurk the skid demon.
6. Press the brake of the foot as you roll around the corner to save the collapse and tires up.

Here is a string of additional Japanese pearls:

▶ Be considerate—think for others.

▶ Artistic barber for cutting off of head.

▶ No horse back riding except in carriages.

▶ Outside a bar: Yo Come In. Yo Love Our Girls/And No Sheet-Keecking Music!

▶ Notice pasted on a door: Shut Up.

A notice in a Madras, India, newspaper proclaimed, "Our editors are colleged and write like the Kipling and the Dickens." *The Moscow Times* ran an ad under the heading INTERPRETING that advised, "Let us your letter of business translation do. Every people in our staffing know English like the hand of their back. Up to the minuet wise-street phrases, don't you know, old boy." With instruction like this, it's no surprise that globe-trotting blooper snoopers uncover exotic jewels like the following:

▶ *In a Sarajevo hotel:* Guests should announce abandonment of their rooms before 12 o'clock, emptying the room at the latest until 14 o'clock for the use of the room before 5 at the arrival or after the 16 o'clock at the departure will be billed as one more night.

▶ *In a hotel in Weifang, China:* Invisible service is available for your rest being not disturbed.

▶ *In a Polish hotel:* The lock of our hotel room is efficient and warranting the safety. Pressing the handle in the room means that the door are open but nobody outside can not open your room. We wish you pleasant stay and secure against attack.

▶ *From a hotel brochure in Qingdao, China:* Hua Tian Hotel is among the few best foreign affairs hotels.

▶ *In the brochure of an Italian hotel in the Dolomites area:* Standing among savage scenery, the hotel offers stupendous revelations. There is a French widow in every room. We can offer you a commodious chamber, with balcony imminent to a romantic gorge. We hope you want to drop in. In the close village you can buy jolly memorials for when you pass away.

► *In a brochure promoting a Sorrento, Italy, hotel:* Syrene Bellevue Hotel joins a modern functional equipment with a distinguished and smart style of the 18th century. It is located on the sea, far off the centre a few minutes afoot and owing to a number of gardens and sunny terraces, guarantee is given for an ideal stay in stillness and absolute rest. The restaurant salon with a large view of the Gulf of Naples, a restaurant service with a big choice, the private beach to be reached by a lift from inside directly, complete the undiscussable peculiarities of this unit.

► *In the English translation of a Spanish menu:* This joyful union of comestibles, chefs, and grateful appetites, holds as a stage this grand restaurant Don José, which dedicates itself to be the temple of the new racionalist religion called gastronomy. Intending to convert itself as the required pilgrimage for the great lovers of excellent cuisine.

► *At the front desk of a fancy Acapulco hotel:* If you presume to be in a hurry the day of your departure, ask our Front Desk personnel information about our Express Check Out.

► *From a Venezuelan travel brochure:* In this Expedition you will know the highets waterfall in the world. From Canaima, through the Sabana, the Jungle and the rivers Carrao & Churun, you'll enjoy one of the biggets emotions of this life. All the facilities Camp. Guides as natives, all experts, will bring you trough troubles waters, just where a few have made it. Be you one of them. Meals in open fire never taste so goo.

► *From a China Southwest Airlines in-flight magazine:* Not drink tea just after dieting. Otherwise, the tea will dilute gastric juice and play down digestion. While, the tannate of the tea will turn protein to a coagulum that uneasy to digest. This will heavy the bear of stomach. So, you would better drink tea one hour after dieting.

▶ *On a "Family Style" restaurant in Hong Kong:* Come Broil Yourself at Your Own Table.

▶ *On a Chinese menu:* Mr. Zheng and his fellowworkers like to meet you and entertain you with their hostility and unique cooking techniques.

▶ *On another Chinese menu:* Special cocktails for women with nuts.

▶ *On a Greek menu:* Spleen omelet, fisherman's crap soup, calf pluck, bowels.

▶ *On a Budapest menu:* Special today—no ice cream.

▶ *Outside a Mexico City disco:* Members and Non-Members Only

▶ *Sign on a ferry in San Juan harbor:* In case of emergency, the lifeguards are under the seat in the center of the vessel.

▶ *In a German pamphlet:* Our ETERNA Fountain-Pen is a revolting invention.

▶ *In a jeweler's window in India:* We shoot earholes.

▶ *In a Chinese in-flight magazine:* The stewardesses of Southwest Airlines must go through four steps, such as hardship, tiredment, dirt feeling. Beside the quality of general stewardess.

Like you, I chuckle at these skewed idioms and absurdly literal translations and wonder if foreign speakers of English are erecting a veritable Tower of Babble. On the other hand, I know that their English is a lot better than my Japanese, Chinese, Italian, Spanish, Polish, and German.

What do you call a person who speaks three languages? Trilingual. What do you call a person who speaks two languages? Bilingual. And what do you call a person who speaks one language? American.

I commend our foreign friends for making the effort at elegant expression in English and thank them from the heart of my bottom.

Brand New Bloopers

Come out of the grave with Pepsi.

A gourmet coffee was sold in Tokyo as an antidote to stress. Its name in English was intended to indicate that the product would soothe the troubled breast. Thus, the manufacturer chose Ease Your Bosoms.

The Japanese possess a special talent for concocting goofy brand names:

- A Gatorade-style sports drink called Pocari Sweat

- A line of stylish trousers called Trim Pecker

- A lawn fertilizer called Green Piles

- ► A nondairy creamer called Creap

- ► A candy called Carap

- ► A soft drink called Calpis

- ► Chocolates in a Band-Aid–style box called Hand-Maid Queer Aids

- ► A fingernail cleaner called Nail Remover

Other brand names that don't sell well in English-speaking markets include a canned spicy pepper sauce from Ghana named Shitto, a French soft drink called Pschitt, and a Finnish product used to unfreeze car locks called Super Piss.

The Germans named one of their products Merdol. They found they couldn't sell it in France.

The original ad slogan that the Swedes used for their Electrolux vacuum cleaner was "Nothing Sucks Like Electrolux!"

In Seoul, South Korea, the government received so many complaints about taxi drivers that it had to set up a telephone hotline for passengers who encountered rudeness or dangerous driving. To advise customers of this service, a sign was posted on the inside rear door of cabs, notifying English-speaking passengers of the availability of an "Intercourse Discomfort Report Center."

We laugh at such clumsy translations, yet we don't realize how equally susceptible we English speakers and writers are. Despite endless boardroom cogitation, many a multinational corporation has ended up with its brand name or slogan on its face. Global slip-ups remind us that few words and idioms can be literally translated. *Caveat vendor*—seller beware: it's best to hire the best for translation.

More than others, the automobile industry seems to be prone to linguistic accidents. The classic story of vehicular misnaming is associated with General Motors. As the literal translation of the brand name Nova to Spanish means "star," why then, GM wanted to know, were Hispanic Chevrolet dealerships so unaccommodating to this model? That's because, when spoken aloud, Nova sounds like *no va*—which means, "it doesn't go." GM changed the name to Caribe.

Ford Motor Company's Caliente turned out to mean "streetwalker" in Mexico. Ford came up with a second flat tire in Japan, where Cortina translated as "jalopy." The company discovered that a truck model it called Fiera means "ugly old woman" in Spanish. As if this was not enough, it turns out that Pinto is a slang term meaning "small male appendage."

Even the luxurious Rolls-Royce Company found out the hard way that in German, Silver Mist means "human waste."

Here are more classic cross-border marketing misfortunes that got lost in translation:

▶ The colas of the world have been shaken up explosively by mistranslation. When Pepsi-Cola invaded the huge Chinese and German markets, the effort initially fizzled. The product's slogan, "Come alive with the Pepsi generation," was rendered (or should I say rent?) into Chinese as "Pepsi brings back your dead ancestors" and into German as "Come out of the grave with Pepsi."

▶ Coca-Cola also discovered in Taiwan that the Chinese characters chosen to sound like its name mean "Bite the wax tadpole." Coke then changed to a set of characters that mean "Happiness in the mouth."

▶ Fresca's brand name fizzled in Mexico, where its name turned out to be slang for "lesbian."

▶ When Coors Beer cast its slogan, "Turn It Loose," in Spanish the statement read as "Suffer from diarrhea."

▶ Perdue chicken's slogan "It takes a tough man to make a tender chicken" read, in Spanish, "It takes a sexually stimulated man to make a chicken affectionate."

▶ Braniff Air Lines, promoting its comfortable leather seats, used the headline *"Sentado en cuero,"* which was interpreted as "Sit naked."

▶ Clairol hair products introduced its Mist Stick curling iron in Germany only to find that *mist* is German slang for "manure." Germans did not stand in long lines waiting to buy Manure Sticks.

▶ 3M translated its Scotch tape slogan, "Sticks like crazy," into Japanese and came up with a sticky problem. The slogan translated literally into Japanese as "It sticks foolishly."

▶ Kellogg encountered a problem when it introduced its Bran Buds to Sweden. The name translates loosely into Swedish as Burnt Farmer.

▶ Vicks had to change its product name to Wicks before entering the German market when it was discovered that Vicks sounded like a vulgar verb in German.

▶ Not to be outdone, Puffs tissues found that *Puff* in German is a colloquial term for a whorehouse.

▶ Parker Pen's Jotter ballpoint pen could not be marketed with that name in some Latin countries because *jotter* happens to be slang for "jockstrap."

▶ Colgate Palmolive had to discard Cue as the name for its toothpaste in France. *Cue* is the name of a widely circulated French pornographic magazine.

Even the wrong nonverbal cue can play hob with a product's reception in a far-off land:

▶ Gerber baby food initially packaged their African product just the same as in the United States—with a cute baby picture on the jar. They didn't realize that because so many Africans cannot read, nearly all packaged products sold in Africa carry pictures of what is inside. Puréed baby—horrors!

▶ Muslims in Bangladesh rioted and ransacked Thom McAn stores when they mistook the company's logo on some sandals for the Arabic letters for Allah. One person was killed and 50 people were injured before the melee ended.

Misdirected Directions

When the Basic Time corresponds to the preset Alarm Time, the alarm is generated. If you have a depress on 'snooze' while it is alarmed, the loud will stop immediately and loud for another 8 minutes after having this 'snooze' 8 minutes and so on. However, alarm will not effect if it has lasted for fully 8 minutes unless the second correspondence that is to say after 24 hours.

Watch out for a new crisis: imported English. Many foreign products are worth the price, if only for the instructions. My fellow Americans, we need protection, if not protectionism, against these assaults from abroad on our English language.

A portable fan made in Hong Kong "has been realised in a way to solve the problem of an exceptional practicality." On the box is written the injunction to "unscrew the lamp and screw your small fan."

The instructions accompanying a humidifier made in Japan warn, "Avoiding wind blowing directly to human body at a long period of time. Especial for patient, childern, drunken, and people with heart disease."

Here is a catalog of misdirected directions that get lost in translation. All spelling and syntax are reproduced exactly as printed:

▶ Washing instructions for a track suit manufactured in Bangladesh: Impregnation after wash is recommended.

▶ Selected instructions for the use of the washer/dryer in a Spanish youth hostel:

AUTOMATIC SELF-SERVICE
CLOTHES WASHING AND DRYING

The direction of this establishment, with the purpose to make your stay more comfortable, offers you a clothes washing and drying self-service. We wish this service make your stay here more pleasant.—The Direction

Put the detergent in the bottom of the machine and don't get your clothes in bend and tight.

Don't put in metallic objects neither shoes. Your clothes can be spoilt.

Shut the cover, introduce the chip, and move the purse down to the bottom, and get it back to the inicial position.

If the red light of unstable starts to shine, get up the cover and distribute uniformently the clothes.

Consult in reception the machines situation.

▶ On the back of a Korean "New Adhesion Fuzz Roller," one of those permanently sticky lint and hair removers:

How to Use It
1. Pulling to the arrow direction, the cover will be open.

2. Stripe off the transparent vinyl cover the adhe-sion-roll.
3. With the rolling action back and forth, the dust is absorbed.
4. Deserve it inside its cover after use it.

Warning

As it is used by washing repeatedly roll without exchange: Suit, Sweater, Carpet, Sofa, Cushion, Car seat, and cover, Dust or thread of handcrafts, The fur of pet, etc.

Don't use it on the plastic file or glass, because the roll is sticked to and separated from the body.

Don't use it to cleanse of the glass splinters or ce-ramics.

Keep it from the direct sunrays.

▶ From Taiwan swoops in the Waden Spring Magic Air Plane (Hand-Play is Available):

The method to fly the magic Airplane is different from the other conventional toy Airplanes flying hori-zontally.

1. Spring-Play Flying. Spring this Airplane to left (or right) hand and it can fly back circularly from reverse direction.
2. Spring it 45 degrees downward and it can fly back circularly from upward direction.
3. Spring is upward and it can roll and go back from rest direction.

HAND-PLAY FLYING: The best fly is to extend our arm holding the metal clamp on the Airplane head diago-nally with the Airplane wing vertically against the ground then throw it right or left hand direction.

▶ For a paper-and-plastic model glider kit manufac-tured in Romania:

1. Matching weight balance, and toss 5 or 7 angle down direction.
2. Right flying as the picture 1 shown.
3. Remove back fore wing when bouncing fore-head up, and then get it down as the picture 2 shown.
4. Remove forward fore wing when fore-head going downward on a sudden as the picture 3 shown.

► Writes a Damariscotta, Maine, reader, "A friend received this 'Stove Top Grill' three years ago at Christmas but has been unable to figure out the Korean directions and has, therefore, never used it":

Please use the holding dish after pouring water in.

In case of use for the first time it is necessary to be adopted with the edible on the surface of the plate upon a little warmed up.

Please avoid heating with empty or excessive heating.

Taking cares after use should use water or detergent of table wares and wash with soft sponge. Please avoide use of cleanser or metal scrubbing brush.

► From a Chinese manufacturer of alarm clocks:

When the Basic Time corresponds to the preset Alarm Time, the alarm is generated. The Alarm tune will automatically cease after 1 minute working. If you have a depress on 'SNOOZE' while it is alarmed, the loud will stop immediately and loud for another 8 minutes after having this 'SNOOZE' 8 minutes and so on. However, alarm will not effect if it has lasted for fully 8 minutes unless the second correspondence that is to say after 24 hours.

► Clients of a Hong Kong manufacturer some years ago

took delivery of an electric compressor, to which was attached the following "Instruction and Guarantee Card":

1. This is an excellent equipment with very few noise and excessive reliability. Though unfragile, it is also robust, and should not be belted.
2. Circuit arrangements ensure environments, and imput current is best at both temperatures, including snow and hot.
3. Stability is too good on full battery and this should be lowered, but the imput may be reduced to danger level if preferred.
4. The negative will be and the positive is not if supply polarity is incorrect; also a humming noise will be introduced together with smoke. When setting up, the best angle has no smoke and slight smell.
5. When aligning, twiddle for strong current and prevent sparks.
6. The motor should be good for ever, but pregnant wear-out may occur after a few summers if heat is applied.

DO NOT DOUBT THE GUARANTEE. IT IS BACKED BY MANY YEARS IN HONG KONG WITHOUT ODOUR, PATIENCE, OR THREAT.

Loopy instructions are also manufactured right here in America. Here are a few examples of homemade gibberish:

▶ Take 1 Teaspoonful 4 times a day. Swish and spit. Do not swallow for 10 days.

▶ We Make It! You Bake It! Pizza. Why call & wait 30 minutes for a pizza to be delivered when you can

Take-N-Bake from Buscemis. Take home & cook yourself in 10 minutes fresh out of your own oven.

▶ Instructions for a golf tournament: Closest-to-the-pin
competition. Measure your distance quickly and record on the clipboard at the green. While you are
doing this, the rest of your group can be putting out.

Mrs. Malaprop Lives!

"I'm calling on my cellulite phone."

More than 200 years ago, Mrs. Malaprop first bustled onto the stage, her nouns whirling, her verbs twirling, her adjectives swirling. Mrs. Malaprop, you may recall from high-school English, was the "old weather-beaten she-dragon" in Richard Brinsley Sheridan's *The Rivals*. Malaprop took special pride in her use of the king's English: "Sir, if I reprehend anything in this world, it is the use of my oracular tongue and a nice derangement of epitaphs!" What a shame, she lamented, that so few gentlemen "know how to value the ineffectual qualities in a woman!"

The delightful dowager was such "a pineapple of perfection" of her type that her name has come to stand for the confused and befuddling misapplication of words. Nowadays a malapropism means the replacement of a big word with another that often has a parallel but unintended sense.

Some people will insist that Mrs. Malaprop was merely a creature of the dramatic imagination. But I am here to tell you that people like her actually exist. You may be one of them, or married to one of them, or friends with one of them, or work with one of them.

"I stand before this court chaste," an O. J. Simpson defense lawyer told Judge Lance Ito. He meant *chastened*, of course.

A letter describing the "new navy" included this incentive: "Then there are the free medical benefits and low-cost insurance. And travel to foreign ports—with 30 days' paid vacation to see and enjoy these erotic places."

The West Virginia legislature passed a law forbidding "the picking of flora or fauna within 100 yards of a highway."

A news photo pictured a woman walking around an old cemetery in San Antonio, Texas. The caption read: "Judy Fisher reviews these hollowed grounds."

Because they are the very pineapple of verbal foe paws, I receive more malapropisms from my contributors than any other kind of gaffe:

▶ In Venice, the people travel around the canals on gargonzolas.

▶ In the United States, people are put to death by elocution.

▶ The two sides in a court trial are the defense and the prostitution.

▶ I haven't seen him in over a year. I hear he went to one of those ivory league colleges.

▶ Okay, ma'am, I'm going to give you a ballpoint figure.

▶ Isn't Rogaine the stuff that if you apply it tropically, you can grow hair?

▶ I didn't like the writer because he was sarcastic with a pestamistic view of life.

▶ The church service was so beautiful it was positively urethral.

▶ She's led a sedimentary life.

▶ The sponge was very exorbitant.

▶ He's always hurling epitaphs at people.

▶ I can't advise you on this, so use your own discrepancy.

▶ My check bounced because of insignificant funds.

▶ Remember that the participation of all CCHS members is detrimental to our success!

▶ When the Martians' spaceship landed, they got out and had testicles all over their heads.

▶ The food in our cafeteria is so bad it's not fit for human constipation.

▶ The Alberta Pipeline was largely financed through private investigators.

▶ Freud constructed the Edifice complex, Vienna's first shopping mall.

▶ In families with incest, there seems to be a marked

dispurity in the amount of power held by the man and the wife.

▶ He was arrested for parking tickets and other mister meaners.

▶ In a university commencement program: The audience is asked to remain seated until the end of the recession.

▶ In America the elderly are often whorehoused.

▶ I've got Elvis records up the kazoo.

▶ I was so hungry I was absolutely ravished.

▶ A Spanish Armada ship sank years ago off the coast of Florida. When I lived there, divers would search the wreckage for gold bunions.

▶ Many college students are abscessed with TV.

▶ In the afternoon, I like to lay on my bed, rest, and watch the so-poppers.

▶ President Clinton was a Road Scholar.

▶ Adultery is what adolescents are practicing for.

▶ I want that list arranged in condescending order.

▶ Children tend to put their parents on a petal stool.

▶ The pirate leaped upon the deck with a cut glass at his side.

▶ The British Museum was a millstone in the development of civilization.

▶ I plead the fifth commandment.

▶ I drank myself into Bolivia.

▶ I'm calling on my cellulite phone.

▶ I'm blessed with a photogenic memory.

▶ Game canceled due to inclimate weather.

▶ I offer this solution to the problem that plagiarizes all of us.

▶ This looks just like the American deadly lampshade.

▶ He suffered from low self of steam.

▶ You're hand stringing my creativity.

▶ I am utterly dumbfolded.

▶ Our daughter got an A in suppository writing.

▶ Children so smart they are in exhilarated classes.

▶ Several workers were laid off, but they all received sufferance pay.

▶ I can give you the recipe for my fruit compost.

▶ Now it might get a little cool tonight, so just pull that African at the foot of the bed over you.

▶ Her ex-husband received a decease-and-desist order.

▶ A few members argue that it would be a mute point if the majority doesn't speak out.

▶ She digressed back to her childhood.

▶ I refuse to answer on the grounds that it may incinerate me.

▶ There's no astigmatism attached to that.

▶ My contact lenses adhere to the contortions of my eye.

▶ The decimal level was too high to measure.

▶ She was dressed in full regatta.

▶ I have a good rappaport with just about everyone.

▶ This letter is to memorialize our telephone conversation of October 22nd.

▶ This list is impartial. I need a complete list.

▶ This will only exasperate the problem.

▶ We hired a new salesman because we were so underhanded.

▶ It was a real cliff-dweller.

▶ His attendance has been very erotic.

▶ The museum contains many artifacts and pimentos of the past.

▶ Make your homecoming a memorial one.

▶ They attend the Conjugal Church.

▶ Meanwhile, the state has already spent the money collected from the exuberant fee.

▶ My son's grades have taken a real nosedrop.

▶ I'm taking desecrated liver tablets.

▶ After the service, entertainment will follow at the local cemetery.

▶ The world today is full of crime and phonography.

▶ I don't believe in heaven or hell, but I do believe in puberty.

When Metaphors Collide

You can't change the spots on an old dog.

"The Communist menace is a snake in the grass that is gnawing away at the foundation of our ship of state" is a classic mixed metaphor from a University of Chicago student's essay.

"You're biting the hand of the goose that laid the golden egg," Hollywood mogul Sam Goldwyn once Goldwynized.

Chicago mayor Harold Washington carved out a niche of his own in the Mixed Metaphor Hall of Shame when he explained to the local press the objective of his planned news conferences: "It has been our purpose all along to have a sort of a periodical potpourri to cover all of this flotsam and jetsam that flies through the media that can get nailed down on a regular, periodic track. So, in a sense, that can be interpreted as open sesame, but don't throw darts."

I never metaphor I didn't like, and I never met a mixed metaphor I didn't collect. I now grab the bull by the tail and present the cream of the dregs of figures of speech that just don't add up:

► Hillary Clinton's ratings are dropping through the roof.

► Senator Dole is off on the wrong foot in a head-to-head comparison with President Clinton.

► Detroit Pistons star Grant Hill praised his new coach, Doug Collins, for his drive: "It's a fire that starts at the top and trickles its way back down."

► The inimitable Robert J. Lurtsema, music host on Boston public radio, introduced a collection of new phonograph records just received, by saying, "We've just barely begun to scratch the surface of this new set of records."

► Answering a reporter's question, an interviewee opined that not paying federal workers for time missed in a government shutdown was "the only way to get President Clinton to hold his seat to the fire."

► What with all this new technology, Newtown is standing on the verge of a minefield of opportunity.

► Let's jump right in and get our teeth wet.

► That's water under the dam.

► Let's not stir up sleeping dogs.

▸ We've just scratched the tip of the iceberg.

▸ Let's be sure that the contract covers all the asses.

▸ My new Saab is unbelievable. It's the Cadillac of cars.

▸ For too long the Prime Minister has been sitting on the fence with both ears to the ground as part of his play-safe political style.

▸ The light at the end of the tunnel is just the tip of the iceberg.

▸ This is the story of a boy who wore his buck teeth like a chip on his shoulder.

▸ I've got an ace up my hole.

▸ He was bleeding like a stuffed pig.

▸ That was the last straw on the camel's back.

▸ I'm drinking enough soup to float a battle-ax.

▸ You can't change the spots on an old dog.

▸ She put her head between her tail and apologized.

▸ We had some disagreements early in her career but she's turned her attitude around 360 degrees since then.

▸ Raines spearheads Whales Alive, one of several non-profit organizations dedicated to saving the world's whale population.

▸ There's so much going on at work, I can barely keep my feet above water.

▸ It was like pulling hens' teeth.

▸ You're dead meat in the water.

▸ Separate the wheat from the shaft.

- The pianist has the fastest fingers ever to set foot on stage.

- The underground parking garage will never see the light of day.

- The worm is on the other foot.

- It's time to fish or get off the pot.

- John Brown fired the shot that set the ball rolling right up to the gates of the Civil War.

- I wouldn't eat it with a 10-foot pole.

- If you jump the gun in the realty business, you can end up with egg on your face.

- He smokes like a fish.

- If the hand were on the other foot . . .

- I let my hair down and got it off my chest.

- Remember, she's no fried chicken.

- Bob Dole praised President Clinton for fielding a flood of questions about Whitewater.

- I hope in my next life I can be a government official so that I can feather my own pockets for a change.

- This is a clear case of the cart wagging the donkey.

- What can I do? I'm only a big wheel in a small pond.

- This field of research is so virginal that no human eyeball has ever set foot on it.

- I don't mind having my feet to the fire. My problem is that I've got so many balls in the air.

- Her leg was amputated after a long-standing illness.

► In our family we bend over backward to be upright and honest.

► Oral sex is distasteful.

► I made out like a banshee.

► Let's get down to brass tactics.

► It's a Pandora's box hanging over our heads.

► We are on parallel tracks that are unlikely to cross over since they are divergent.

► The future is an uncharted sea full of potholes.

► The matrimonial agency was barely making ends meet.

► The diving school was barely keeping its head above water.

► Let's try, by a process of elimination, to discover what caused your diarrhea.

► We're back to square zero.

► A wedding aboard a luxurious cruise boat can run from $3,000 to $20,000, if someone wants to go overboard.

► The chasms in my general knowledge are abysmal.

► I was way out on third base.

► He was three shades in the wind.

► She was born with a silver slipper in her mouth.

► She has more jewelry than you can shake a cat at.

► You've got to put your foot down with a firm hand.

▶ What can you do when you're at the bottom of the rung?

▶ You've hit the iceberg on the head.

▶ They're trying to pull the wool over my face.

▶ I'm not mending bridges we've already sold down the river.

▶ With our new fall line, we're going to plummet right to the top.

▶ They're coming out of the wormwood.

▶ I only have two pair of hands.

▶ Let's bite the bull by the horns.

▶ He's foaming at the bit.

▶ Treat him with golden gloves.

▶ This is where the rubber hits the road. This is the kickoff, not the end product. We're throwing down the gauntlet.

And from *The Acting President*, by Bob Schieffer and Gary Paul Gates: "He could not shake the feeling that he and all the others who had been involved in those projects were sitting on a bomb that, sooner or later, would explode in their faces."

How's That Again?

I don't think people realize how difficult it is to be a pawn of labor.

Dear Son:

I am writing this letter slowly because I know you can't read fast. We no longer live where we did when you left. Your dad read in the paper that most accidents happen within 20 miles of home, so we moved. I won't be able to send you the address because the last family that lived here took the house numbers with them so they wouldn't have to change their address.

This place has a washing machine. The first day,

I put four shirts in it, pulled down the handle, and haven't seen them since.

The coat you wanted me to send you—Aunt Sue said it would be too heavy to send in the mail with all those big buttons on it. So I cut them off and put them in the pocket.

It rained twice this week, three days the first time and four days the second time.

Your sister had a baby this morning. I don't know if it was a boy or a girl, so I don't know if you are an uncle or an aunt.

I was going to send you some money, but the envelope was already sealed.

Love,
Your mother

P.S. Hope you get this letter. If you don't, let me know.

As much as this folk-letter tears logic to tatters, there are plenty of real-life examples that match it, non sequitur for non sequitur.

The Illinois Department of Public Aid sent the following letter to a dead person: "Beginning in February 1976 your assistance benefits will be discontinued. Reason: it has been reported to our office that you expired on January 1, 1976. May God bless you. You may reapply if there is a change in your circumstances."

An obituary in a Peoria, Illinois, newspaper read: "Mr. Martin Shore was born in Madison, Wisconsin, where he died and later moved to Peoria."

During the Vietnam War, a U.S. military officer explained, "We had to destroy that town in order to save it."

On a widely used jury qualification questionnaire is

printed this question: "Do you read, speak, and understand English?   Yes ☐   No ☐."

Near Warrenton, Virginia, stand two signs that redefine the meaning of *trespassing*. At a construction site is placed a warning that reads: NO UNAUTHORIZED TRESPASSING ALLOWED. I didn't know that there was such a thing as authorized trespassing. A sign on a country store in the same area advises: NO TRESPASSING AFTER 10 P.M. Apparently trespassing before 10 P.M. is perfectly all right.

Actor Dennis Hopper sagely observed, "After the eighties, the nineties will make the fifties look like the sixties." Quite so.

A husband and wife were watching a television show she had taped. The wife kept getting up during the commercial breaks to do chores and hurrying back each time the program resumed.

The husband asked, "Have you forgotten that this show is on tape? You can fast-forward through the commercials."

Her reply: "If I don't work during the commercials, I'll never get anything done."

A woman explained how she continued to get involved with men who abused her. She would break free from one and promptly get involved with another who would beat her. "I swear, I wouldn't know a good man if he came up and hit me on the head," she lamented.

The sagacious Hobbes, of the late comic strip *Calvin and Hobbes,* once predicted that "we can eventually make language a complete impediment to understanding." Hobbes had it just about right when it comes to statements such as the following:

▶ Perhaps the most cruel tragedy in the death yesterday of Caleb Witherspoon is that had it happened a few minutes later, he might still be alive.

► The Pharmacology Unit seeks healthy male or female volunteers, who have had a hysterectomy, tubal ligation, or are at least three years past menopause, to participate in a research study.

► The most common surgery in America today is total hysterectomy, and operations for women are more common than those for men.

► I'll tell you one thing. He always ceases to amaze me!

► Sign on the men's room door at the offices of the Detroit School Board: Please keep the door closed when coming in or going out.

► Label on a bag of dry cat food: $1/2$ Lb. More Than Other 3.5 Lb. Bags.

► Instructions on a paper-towel dispenser: Pull down. Tear up.

► Store ad: Semi-Annual Clearance Sale
                   Once-In-A-Lifetime Opportunity

► A Denver TV channel offered this sage advice: "Don't go into darkened parking lots unless they are well lighted."

► Newfoundland is a very small island, but its size is bigger on land.

► The dead live in the cemetery.

► I don't think people realize how difficult it is to be a pawn of labor.

► We're launching a new innovation for the first time.

► We can't make good grammar great. But we want to make flawed writing acceptable.

▶ If you missed seeing Desmond Morris's *The Human Animal* the first time, now you can see it again.

▶ Your subscription is about to expire, and delivery will stop. Please send payment now to avoid uninterrupted delivery.

▶ After finding no qualified candidates for the position of principal, the school department is extremely pleased to announce the appointment of Arthur Harrison to the post.

▶ A bachelor's life is no life for a single man.

▶ Closed for official opening.

▶ Wood doesn't grow on trees, you know.

▶ You have no idea what a poor opinion I have of myself, and how little I deserve it.
  —W. S. Gilbert

▶ Boys, elevate them guns a little lower.
  —Andrew Jackson at the battle of New Orleans

▶ You gotta remember—nobody's human.

▶ Annual Polish Day Picnic—Sunday September 8 & 9.

▶ Working together to solve a problem with the result not only resolving the initial problem but improving it as well.

▶ Display ad for a monster movie: Due to the horrifying nature of this film, no one will be admitted to the theater.

▶ Label found on the bottom of a wind-up kitchen timer: Do not place on or near heat-producing appliances.

▶ Inscription on a bathroom scale: Permanently Adjusted.

▶ WEATHER FORECAST—Thunder showers Friday probably followed by Saturday.

▶ Law office advertisement: Permanent Injuries Last a Lifetime.

▶ At a health center: Prescriptions required the following day must be handed in the day before.

▶ Mr. Garver will remain Director of the Company throughout the end of the fiscal year, except in the event of his death, in which case he will no longer be Director of the Company.

▶ Two-dimensional photographs simply don't do this car justice.

▶ Killing an animal while it is still alive is unacceptable.

▶ There is a fundamental difference between male and female homosexuality, which is that the former concerns men and the second women.

▶ Standing at the casket of her husband, who was mangled in a car wreck, a grieving widow said, "Oh, God, he'd die if he knew he looked like that!"

▶ The most important thing in acting is honesty. Once you've learned to fake it, you're in.

▶ A mother warned her son: "If you climb that tree and fall out, don't come running to me!"

▶ 21% of girls left because they had become a mother, as did 8% of the boys.

▶ Dates from Zafarraya Cave, Spain, indicate that Neanderthals lived millennia longer than once believed.

V

MECHANICAL
BREAKDOWNS

Under a Spell

ESCAPEE CAPTURED AFTER 10 DAYS ON THE LAMB.

Because of economic conditions, a famous English private school was obliged to raise its tuition. A letter informing parents of this fact stated that the increase would be 500 £ per annum, except unfortunately it was spelled *per anum.* An irate parent wrote to the headmaster, thanking him for the notification but saying, "For my part, I would prefer to continue paying through the nose, as usual."

A similar error occurred when the *Los Angeles Times* reported that 1992 was a fiery year for the royal family in England. It was a year of flame-ups, flame-outs, new flames, and just plain flamers among her family: fire in Windsor Castle and tremendous marital shake-ups. Quoting Queen Elizabeth II, the *Times* reported that "the queen said that the year had been an *anus horribilis*." Considering what had happened, one would certainly have to agree.

A friend and fellow word watcher stopped to buy some writing supplies in Kansas City and noticed that the gold-lettered sign in the window read STATIONARY STORE.

She pointed this out to the woman behind the counter and explained, "That one means immobile, unmoving, in one place."

"Well, honey," said the clerk as she counted out the change, "we've been at this location for 17 years."

A geography quiz question asked: What's the oldest desert in the world? Wrote one student: apple pie.

A transplant from northern California got a taste of Utah culture when he ordered a cake from a Salt Lake City grocery store for his wife's fiftieth birthday. He requested this inscription: IT'S BETTER TO BE 50 THAN PREGNANT. When he picked up the cake, the inscription read: IT'S BETTER TO BE 50 THEN PREGNANT.

A New Jersey woman hired a desktop publisher to make invitations for her birthday celebration. It wasn't until after they were mailed that she noticed the error:

Grace Mortonson
Requests Your Presents
For Her
40th Birthday Party

Mark Twain once wrote, "I don't see any use in having a uniform and arbitrary way of spelling words. We might as well make all clothing alike and cook all dishes alike.

Sameness is tiresome, variety is pleasure. *Kow* spelled with a large *K* is just as good as with a small *c*. It is better. It gives the imagination a broader field, a wider scope."

Andrew Jackson, who may have been our only illiterate president, once thundered, "It's a damn small mind that can think of only one way to spell a word!"

Twain and Jackson would be delighted with the creativity and broad-mindedness shown in the misspellings that follow. They certainly fill the imagination with all sorts of original images. As a famous bumper sticker proclaims, BAD SPELLERS OF THE WORLD, UNTIE!

▶ Meanwhile, Richard Parker Bowles, brother of Camilla's ex-husband, Andrew, said that from the beginning Camilla approved of Charles's marrying Diana while she remained his power mower.

▶   Only Worn Once
                   Wedding Dress for Sale
          Victorian style, ecru lace, long sleeves,
          high neck, drop-waste tea-length, size 10

▶ Volunteers needed for the Grater Indianapolis Literacy League.

▶ Nationally reknown literary consultant. There is no substitute for excellence.

▶ The Production Department is looking for a part-time proofreader. This person must be proficient in spelling grammer and punctuation, able to work on their own, as well as with a team of salespeople and production staff.

▶ The Home Education Association invites your organization to be a part of the Annual Cirriculum Fair.

▶ Microsoft Word advertisement: You'll get a grammer checker and a spelling checker.

▶ Need to be a better reader? John Atkinson is available as a reading tudor.

▶ Congratulations to all 1st graders who participated in the annual Spelling Be.

▶ Congradulations to our school's champion spelers.

▶ Say "yes" to eduction.

▶ FOR SALE. Two-story 1500 sq. ft. on 2 acres with privacy fencing along road frontage. On hill with beautiful view of damned creek below property.

▶ ATTENTION MEMBERS: During the week of December 14th, the pool will be painted with an epoxy paint. There will be fumes in the club. Please bare with us.

▶ No smoking aloud.

▶ The prisoner was sent to solitaire confinement.

▶ An inspired Illinois team yesterday reached the pinochle of success.

▶ Children waded in the clear blue-green waters yesterday while fishermen stood waste-high in the calm current, casting and reeling.

▶ Taped to a cash register in a convenience store:
No Checks Excepted!
No Acceptions!

▶ FOR SALE: String of perils, 30 years old, with box.

▶ She arrived at the castle and spent the knight.

▶ He was a short, fat, semi-balled man.

▶ I believe in family values too, but I'm really annoyed by the oblique view of abortion. I don't think it's an issue that belongs in government. We're back to arguing morals and morays that belong in church discussions.

▶ Mrs. Travis unveiled a plague in memory of her late husband.

▶ Escapee captured after 10 days on the lamb

▶ Wedding gown: Satin with sequence & beading.

▶ He killed the men with his bear hands.

▶ Six years ago Vinny Testaverde played catch with a toe-headed high school kid.

▶ You'll have the special facts you need to analize the market.

▶ She slipped into a comma on Thursday.

▶ Church Bizarre Sale. Refreshments. Saturday, June 24. 9 A.M.

▶ On the menu of a Rockford, Illinois, restaurant: Toasted Beagal and Cream Cheese.

▶ He went to the carnival and rode on the fairest wheel.

▶ The weather was wonderful and the little boy did summer salts.

▶ Divorce has become so common that we take it with a grain assault.

▶ A story in a Florida newspaper quoted a minister as saying, "God told me to hold my piece."

▶ I stood on the beach as the serf blew in my face.

▶ He was arrested for evading an officer and for wreckless driving.

► When his Gravol injection was due, he was found coward in the corner wretching.

► In order to ensure safety, all our cars are fitted with duel controls.

► He was best known for his pukish humor.

► Insanity is a problem of considerable dementions.

► Choice of dressing: Italian, Ranch, Blew Cheese.

► They unleashed the attack dogs that go for the juggler.

► Give Your Sweatheart a Dozen Roses for Valentine's Day.

► Bracelets $8.00
Neckless $10.00

► While the car is a wreck, its occupants can be truly grateful that they escaped with their lives. The tree is badly scared.

► The woman's basketball team earned a birth in the finals.

► A girl bought a boot and ear for her boyfriend when they went to the prom.

► Platonic love is where you first love a single woman. Then you come to love women as a hole.

► It's better to slow down then get a ticket.

► A flaming desert complimented the dinner.

► No dumping aloud.

It's best to heed the advice of the *United Press International Stylebook:* "A burro is an ass. A burrow is a hole in the ground. As a writer, you are expected to know the difference."

Back to Grammar School

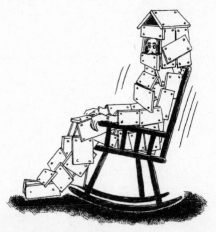

The house belongs to Martha Bender who is in a nursing home and has been boarded up for several years.

Many of us find that grammar gaffes are like chewing tinfoil, or like chalk squeaking over the blackboard of our sensibilities. The tinfoil is especially metallic and the chalk especially squeaky when the mistake is perpetrated by people who obviously should know better.

"Students don't have to fail. Exhilarated classes day or evening," claims one newspaper ad. "Develop interpersonal conversational skills by learning to talk good," boasts a second ad. "Can't tell *who* from *whom?* Help is available from the Lowe University grammar hotline. We get a lot of business-writing calls and how to deal with a salutation when you don't know who you're writing to,'' a third points out.

No wonder teachers receive student evaluations like these:

► While in the writing program, I learned a lot about sentence structure, punctuation, and capitalism.

► I past all my testes. My grade should be hirer.

► I have learned a lot about life here at college. For instance, I have learned to do minor household repairs such as painting, fixing old windows, and replacing old broads.

► Another thing I learned was way's to use apostrofe's and where it goe's and sometime's not to use them.

► Your a fine teacher. I would recommend you at any time.

Makes teaching all worthwhile, doesn't it?

Squeak! Squeak! Yikes! Yikes! Here are some more grammar gaffes gouged into the blackboards of our minds:

► Old Sedberghians are invited to a weekend reunion at the school. We would like to extend a particularly warm invitation to all of you who left Sedbergh and your wives.

► The easiest hole on the course, Deb Richard found the fairway bunker both times she played it.

► Two new booklets are available for South Carolinians who are survivors of head injuries and their families.

► He was arrested Saturday, hours after the most recent

victim's body was discovered and questioned for 12 hours.

▶ Ms. Duncan distributed several door prizes at the conclusion of her talk, including a sample of jewelry made by craftspeople, meticulously lacquered to preserve them and make them safe.

▶ Many people have no respect for the American flag. I have seen them hanging from windows, dirty and sometimes torn.

▶ Gabriel Pincus is the proud possessor of a brand new Chevrolet sedan and also a new wife, having traded in the old one, for which he received a liberal allowance.

▶ I had an infection after the operation and was on antibiotics for two weeks before going home. There were still some minor pains in my testicles, but they disappeared.

▶ Mr. and Mrs. Crane Lauder, of Tennessee, are seeing their loved ones here. Dr. C. H. Karston removed Mr. Lauder's tonsils and they are now with his sister, Mrs. Peyton.

▶ If Ms. Hunter and Ms. Brown agree to relinquish ownership of the dogs, they will be euthanized.

▶ Joe Harrigan's father passed away yesterday from a massive heart attack. He won't be back in the office until Tuesday.

▶ It was called into the Burbury P.D. that a deer had been hit north of Gendry Bros. The deer is dead and he has locked himself out of the car and is waiting for a locksmith.

▶ And now for a look at the weather, made possible by Foam Shampoo.

▶ The house belongs to Martha Bender who is in a nursing home and has been boarded up for several years.

▶ A Groveton officer described the driver as a white male with blond hair, wearing shorts, a gray tank top and bare feet.

▶ All proceeds from the sale of carved ducks will go to handicap children.

▶ The bride carried a bouquet of spring blossoms as well as the three bridesmaids.

▶ Air piracy charges were filed Sunday against a man who used grenades to hijack a Russian airliner and his wife.

▶ Females should have the same athletic opportunities as males: it is an almost universal medical opinion that there is no sport more dangerous to a girl than a boy.

▶ Asphalt tennis courts are hard on the soles of the feet and balls.

Some of the most subtle errors are generated by poor punctuation. Note the havoc wreaked—and reeked—by a missing comma in this ad: "Lady desires post: domesticated, fond of cooking children."

Now consider the effect of a misplaced or missing apostrophe in these unexemplary examples:

▶ Police report that the man took a crescent wrench and swung it at one of the victim's heads.

▶ We sell children's clothes and babies too.

▶ WANTED: Guitar for college student to learn to play, also piano to replace daughters lost in fire.

Even the absence or misplacement of a hyphen can produce bizarre results:

► Museum staffer Jill Dorman checks out 65 million year-old eggs.

► Cases of Lyme disease, which is transmitted by deer-carrying ticks, are on the rise.

► CHILD ABUSING PRIEST TO FACE NEW CHARGES

That headline seems extremely weird until you read the story that follows: "A convicted pedophile priest is due to appear in court in Belfast next month to face new charges of child sex abuse."

Those Dang(ling) Modifiers

The Collier County sheriff's office has announced that one of its dog deputies has been named number one dog deputy for capturing a kidnap suspect after holding a female hostage for several hours.

Reading the following statements from newspaper stories, we may well ask ourselves what's going on in our courts these days:

▶ The juror never was asked if he had been molested by either defense or prosecution attorneys.

▶ Bernard Constantino pleaded guilty to charges of distributing marijuana Wednesday in front of Judge Hart.

▶ A homeless man accused of breaking into a whale watching boat on Rose's Wharf was ordered to receive inpatient treatment in the Plowshare program for his drinking problem in district court Monday.

▶ The Collier County sheriff's office has announced that one of its dog deputies has been named number one dog deputy for capturing a kidnap suspect after holding a female hostage for several hours.

▶ Grodskins was arrested for illegal consumption of alcohol by the sheriff's department on Sunday.

▶ Ms. Innes testified that the defendant was told by a child abuse specialist that her daughter was more than likely being sexually abused in Belknap County Superior Court.

▶ Arlene Tollman received a suspended sentence for operating a motor vehicle with a blood-alcohol level of more than .10.

Yes, dear reader. I've got bells that jingle jangle jingle and phrases that dangle dingle dangle. In every one of the reports above, a wayward modifier gives the impression that something shocking was going on in our very halls of justice. If you think the structure of those court sentences is rickety, ask yourself what the following TV listings have in common.

The very last blooper I was able to insert in my book *Anguished English* was this one, which appeared in a major TV magazine in 1987: "Yoko Ono will talk about her husband John Lennon, who was killed in an interview with Barbara Walters."

As I was compiling *More Anguished English,* a reader sent me this cracked gem from the *Boston Globe* TV section: "Former hostage Terry Waite talks about five years of confinement in Beirut with Barbara Walters in a specially expanded segment of *20/20* at 10 on Channel 5."

Incredibly, an Associated Press (AP) story that came my way as I was preparing this book included this sentence: "The diving and amateur sports community was in shock Thursday following disclosure by diver Greg Louganis, who speaks freely of his contracting AIDS in a *20/20* interview with Barbara Walters to be broadcast by ABC tonight."

What is it about Barbara Walters, I ask myself, that causes people to dangle their participles in public?

What is it about the American understanding of grammar that causes people to misplace their modifiers so habitually?

The AP carried a feature story on sexual practices in America: "Author Shere Hite wrote that 75 percent of women married more than five years reported having affairs in response to her questionnaire." Let's have a look at that questionnaire!

Celebrating the iron man achievement of Baltimore Orioles shortstop Cal Ripken, a *Washington Times* reporter wrote, "Cal Ripken tied Lou Gehrig's record for playing 2,130 consecutive games against the California Angels." Must have been a two-team league.

The poet and professor James Dickey was guest of honor at "a surprise luncheon with a birthday cake thrown by several close friends in the English Department." With friends like that, who needs enemies?

"There will be a week-long conference for men who experienced incest with speaker Dr. Jarvis at Ranchero Capistrano." I don't recommend Dr. Jarvis.

Here are more of my favorite mangled modifiers:

▶ They gathered in his Queens Road condominium and

sat on the red velvet sofa and the upholstered rocker with carved gooseneck arms that belonged to his mother.

▶ Anna Anderson requested that she be cremated before her death.

▶ Nelson became the 1,919th actor to be honored this week with a star on the Hollywood Walk of Fame.

▶ She danced every night with the captain of the boat in high-heeled shoes.

▶ Through the use of ultrasound, a University of Washington researcher studies women who develop high blood pressure during pregnancy with the assistance of AHA-WA funds.

▶ The blaze was extinguished before any damage was done by the local fire department.

▶ Most of the nation's corporate honchos are white Protestant males, with three kids who have been married to the same stay-at-home woman for 20 years.

▶ Gregory Hartell, Dover Township, is awarded a Purple Heart Medal 41 years after he was injured in the Korean War by George Best, commissioner of the State Veterans Affairs Office.

▶ State Rep. Ira Farrar explains legislation that would restrict abortions in Pennsylvania to members of the state House of Representatives.

▶ I am a single parent with a 2-and-a-half-year-old daughter who has been unable to attend Craig University because of student loans.

▶ The meetings held on Monday and yesterday included presentations by a priest who is a psychiatrist specializing in the diagnosis and treatment of sexual disorders among other experts.

▶ Vice President Gore hobbled up to a small stage filled with Democratic candidates on crutches, having ruptured his Achilles' tendon while playing basketball.

▶ On last Saturday, while driving down East Vance Street, a tree limb fell to the ground along with live wires.

▶ One longtime resident recalled the days when Manhattan Burrough President Mary Slocumb used to stroll around the neighborhood gathering signatures in long skirts.

▶ American Catholic theologians will have to wait and see the exact wording of a French document permitting the use of condoms before engaging in theological debate.

▶ They saw a car sitting on top of a three-foot stone wall up against a tree with a lady in it.

▶ Three tenements on Spring Street were seriously damaged when a man ignited a gas tank that had been removed from a car with his cigarette lighter.

▶ Advil should not be taken if you've ever had a severe allergic reaction to aspirin or any other form of pain reliever without consulting your doctor first.

▶ He provided background information about the life of a man who gained national attention after being mutilated by his wife for the NBC news program *Now* with Tom Brokaw.

▶ After three days of lying in state in Montreal and

Quebec, the high and mighty came to Quebec for Levesque's state funeral at Notre Dame Cathedral.

► Sponsored by the Winthrop House, the Beaux Arts Trio will perform Zemlinsky's Trio in D minor, op. 3, Schubert's Trio in E-flat Minor, op. 100, and a work to be announced by Mozart at 8 P.M. in Sanders Theatre.

► The senator used the term *the titty bill* in referring to a bill that would ban nude dancing during a discussion with another lawmaker.

► Children on school buses weighing less than 10,000 pounds must be restrained.

► We will not accept a gift from anyone larger than $5,000.

► Do not sweep an area where there have been rodents with a broom.

► A Grand Rapids neighborhood is getting some help in fighting crime and protecting children from the city commission.

Typographical Terrors

Great Panty Fillers

Written by the famous Irish poet, Ann O'Nymous, "The Typochondriac" is a popular item in the folk-photocopy and e-mail circuits:

> The typographical error is a slippery thing and sly.
> You can hunt till you are dizzy, but it somehow will get by,
> Till the forms are off the presses. It is strange how still it sleeps.
> It shrinks down in a corner, and it never stirs or peeps.

That typographical error, too small for human eyes,
Till the ink is on the paper, when it grows to mountain size.
The boss just stares with horror, then he grabs his
hair and groans.
The copy reader drops his head upon his hands and
moans.
The remainder of the issue may be clean as clean
can be,
But that typographical error is the only thing you
see.

INJURED? blares the headline of a full-page ad in the
"Attorneys" section of the Albuquerque, New Mexico,
Yellow Pages. "We Can Help You—Madden, Berkes &
Doyle." The three partners go on to promise "24-Hr. Ser-
vice. Free Consultation. No Fee Until Successful. Proven
Results!" But then the Madden, Berkes & Doyle display
ends with its Freudian slip showing: "Representing the
Seriously Insured."

Ah, the difference a single letter can make.

Writer Max Hall explains, "Some words are more vul-
nerable to misprinting than others. Consider the word
public. Proofreaders should give it special attention because its skinny fourth letter has a mysterious tendency
to slip away."

Indeed, I receive at least fifty examples of *public*-gone-
pubic mistakes every year—pubic lectures, pubic beaches,
pubic everything. A sign on a city park fence reads, "This
pubic area is open to all." A huge front-page headline in
a Massachusetts daily newspaper blared, $500 MILLION
PLEDGED FOR PUBIC EDUCATION. Typos like these hit below
the belt.

A few of the *pubic* submissions marvelously unite
topic and typo. A typing error in a letter to *The Miami*

Herald about press coverage of Colorado Senator Gary Hart's amorous escapades with Donna Rice made it read, "Let us not forget that the American press spares no one in pubic life." About Puritan adulterers in the 1660s, a student wrote that they were "branded or pubically punished as an example to others." In an *Atlanta Journal* article headlined JUDGE TAGS FILM OBSCENE, this sentence stood straight out: "A civil suit was filed against the theater by the district attorney, asking the court to declare the movie a pubic nuisance."

The best *pubic* gaffe I've ever received comes from a reader in Fryburg, Maine: "Sexually addicted professionals who have successfully completed comprehensive assessment and primary treatment can usually return to practice without compromising pubic health and safety."

The parade of typos that follows is enough to make anyone a typochondriac:

▶ *An interoffice memo:* Although she is bright, I would not recommend this typo of person for the job.

▶ Representatives of the American Cancer Society will be on campus next Friday to provide instruction on self-examination for signs of cancer. A registered nurse will explain how to look for signs of breast cancer, and another representative will show you how to examine your elf for cancer of the testicles.

▶ OPERA: The Lady of the Camellias travels her tragic path in *La Triviata,* performed by the Davisville Opera Feb. 3 and 5.

▶ Mr. Alfred Dayton, of Lisbon, North Dakota, stopped here en route to Fostoria to say hell to his many friends.

▶ *At the top of a full-page grocery ad:* Great Panty Fillers.

▶ When telephone directors become obsolete, they are usually gathered and sold to waste-paper companies for conversion into pulp and the manufacture of new paper. They are torn in two lengthwise, then chopped into small bits in a powerful machine.

▶ An invitation to a testimonial dinner announces enthusiastically, "We are honored to saute Megan Casey and Brian Cafferty." (Can't we have them lightly fried instead?)

▶ She received a B.A. in International Relations (magna cum laude) at the University of Southern California in 1962 and pursued graduate students at the London School of Economics.

▶ Queens prosecutors will fight the ruling that overturned the conviction of Michael Nussbaum on charges that he helped Donald Manes solicit a bride for the awarding of cable television franchises.

▶ Downtown L.A. has its fair share of buried treasurers.

▶ Self-Realization fellowship is resolved to show you that Comic Consciousness is attainable in one lifetime.

▶ Spend an evening listening to the Boston Poops.

▶ Try Lifebuoy soap for around-the-cock protection.

▶ Suzanne Wiley's gladiola garden has been attracting considerable attention of late. She spends many hours each day in the garden with her large collection of beautiful pants.

▶ Estelle Benzinger, 37, suffered the loss of the tip of the third finger on the right hand when she fell from a moving taxicab Friday night. Police reported that Benzinger was shitting in the back seat of the cab and had been leaning forward conversing with another passenger in the front seat.

▶ According to sources, negotiations between the school board and the teachers is at an impasse. The next step is medication and this cannot be completed in time for any raises to be voted on at the March 3 school meeting.

▶ Dolores Del Rio in the romantic story of *Evangeline,* Henry Wadsworth Longfellow's immoral love epic.

▶ If prime rib is your thing, they have a dull dinner with salad, potato, and beverage.

▶ It took many rabbits many years to write the Talmud.

▶ His Republicans are a couple of dilettantes looking for six years on the public doll.

▶ The victim was taken to the hospital, where his position was undermined.

▶ George Washington's Mike Zargado goes up for an easy shit in Colonials' losing effort against Villanova at Smith Center.

▶ A turdey dinner sponsored by the West Lenoir P.T.A. will be held in the school cafeteria from 4:30 until 7 P.M. Friday.

▶ An estimated 129,000 Americans had returned to the upper Chesapeake Bay this spring to spawn, evidence that the gradual comeback of the ravaged species had resumed after an off-year in 1993.

▶ GIRL. Reliable, wants afternoon work five lays a week.

▶ Weather: Cloudy with a chance of this morning.

▶ Patient complains of pain in humerous other regions. [Like the funny bone?]

▶ Eloise Wilkins was 100 Wednesday, but she had no advice on how to love a century.

▶ "A few years ago an 83-year-old woman I met on a bus told me she was convinced good thoughts and a good disposition provided the foundation for living to a ripe 5d tO," she said.

▶ Defendant was charged with carless driving.

▶ Three bedroom brick ranch, LR with fireplace, new family room with fireplace and large dick.

▶ HELP WANTED: Two part-time Certified Nursing Assistants. P.M. Shit, every other weekend.

▶ Heartworm is an infectious, life-threatening, cardiovascular disease spread by misquotes.

Homebuyers take a look at the classy new 3 bedrm. 2400 sq. ft. home. Located in nice neighborhood with breeding space.

27 Acres. Nicely wooded. White bitch and oak.

▶ *From a Vespers liturgy:* Keep us toady, Lord, without sin.

▶ As a result of the explosion, a number of area widows were shattered.

▶ One man was electrocuted when he came in contact with a live wife.

▶ VICTORY IN DSYLEXIA BATTLE

▶ She drives a turk for a construction company.

▶ Dig the ground over thoroughly and then pant.

▶ Question: What will take the wrinkles out of a diplomat?

▶ The children had a turkey raffle in November and some children have participated in the Rend-A-Kid project.

▶ As no payment is forthcoming, we are closing our flies at this time.

▶ ETHIOPIA GETS TWO LOANS; $17.45 TOTAL

▶ CITY ABOLISHES REALITY LICENSE

▶ SWF wanted, 18–25. Attractive and physically fat.

▶ Her partner, Randy Gelo, is one of the Chief Teachers in the Body Works School of Marital Arts.

▶ Following a trip to Mexico, the couple, who met on a blind date set up by a fiend, will live in Waco.

▶ A lumber truck lost part of its load when several broads fell into the middle of Dalton Street.

▶ Replacement Insurance Company. Without it, your lice will never be the same.

▶ As your assemblyman, I will bring real-world experience to Sacramento to fight for lover taxes.

▶ California workers are overworked and underlaid.